Culture, Space and the Nation-state
—— ❄ ——

Culture, Space and the Nation-state

From Sentiment to Structure

Dipankar Gupta

Sage Publications
NEW DELHI ❊ THOUSAND OAKS ❊ LONDON

Copyright © Dipankar Gupta, 2000

All rights reserved. No part of this book may be reproduced or utilized in any form or by any means, electronic or mechanical, including photocopying, recording or by any information storage or retrieval system, without permission in writing from the publisher.

First published in 2000 by

> Sage Publications India Pvt Ltd
> M-32 Market, Greater Kailash, Part-I
> New Delhi 110 048

Sage Publications Inc
2455 Teller Road
Thousand Oaks, California 91320

Sage Publications Ltd
6 Bonhill Street
London EC2A 4PU

Published by Tejeshwar Singh for Sage Publications India Pvt Ltd, typeset by Asian Telelinks, New Delhi, in 10 pt. Palatino, and printed at Chaman Enterprises, Delhi.

Library of Congress Cataloging-in-Publication Data
Gupta, Dipankar, 1949–
  Culture, space, and the nation-state: from sentiment to structure/ Dipankar Gupta.
    p. cm.
  Includes bibliographical references and index.
  1. State, The. 2. Culture. 3. Political geography. I. Title
  JC336.G93   306—dc21   2001   00–062685

ISBN: 0–7619–9499–8 (US–HB)   81–7036–976–2 (India–HB)

Sage Production Team: **Vineetha M., Jaya Chowdhury, N.K. Negi and Santosh Rawat**

To
Dipayan

Contents

Preface   9

Part One: *From Sentiment...*

Chapter 1
    Introduction: Culture, Space and Social Membership   17

Chapter 2
    Space, Non-space and Site: Root Metaphor and *Lex*   28

Chapter 3
    Root Metaphors and Regnant Sets of Meaning   66

Chapter 4
    Space, Territory and the Nation-state   96

Chapter 5
    Sentiment and Structure: Nation and State   136

Part Two: *...To Structure*

Chapter 6
    Civil Society or the State: What Happened
       to Citizenship?   159

Chapter 7
    Fraternity, Citizenship and Affirmative Action:
       Recasting Reservation in the Language of Rights   192

Chapter 8
    Positive Discrimination and the Question of
        Fraternity: Connecting Durkheim to Rawls   210
Chapter 9
    Minoritization and the Public Sphere   236

References and Select Bibliography   266
Index   277
About the Author   283

Preface

This book is about extending the concerns of anthropology to include considerations of the nation-state. As it has been often noted, anthropology today can hardly be unmindful of the reality of sovereign states for their influence has a wide-ranging effect on social life. I have always been dissatisfied with studies, some of which are admirable in their own right, that detail either village life, rituals, or caste observances, without figuring in the reality of the Indian nation-state.

The problem with examining nation-states is that one often gets trapped in defining a 'pure' nation-state. It would be much better, instead, to see what a nation-state does when it comes into being, and the kinds of loyalty it excites. To see a nation without the component of the state is not the same thing as a nation-state. It is not as if one half is missing, but the combination of the two brings out something new. Nation is primarily *sentiment* on which the *structures* of the state aspire to organize a collective life. This collective life is not based on face-to-face relations, but is at the same time not always rationally and bureaucratically managed either. This is why the tools and concepts of anthropology are particularly appropriate for studying contemporary nation-states, even if this may appear counter-intuitive at first sight. Once the nation-state is factored in, it is difficult to desist from making academic interventions in matters of government and public policy. Consequently, this book is equally weighted towards an understanding of the sentiments and structures that bind nation-states.

The analytical aperture I employ in this book is the concept of culture. The fact that culture is dynamic and internally differentiated has been accepted by many. Yet, when it comes to theorizing about culture these factors are often left out of active consideration. Though such an approach gives prominence to other attributes of culture, such as those of bonding and communication, I believe these aspects too remain under-theorized as a consequence. This is because a lot more can be said about cultural membership, solidarity, and communication once the importance of conflict is acknowledged as an integral and intrinsic component of culture.

Consequently, there are two broad types of studies about culture. The first denies the communicative and solidarity aspects of culture and emphasizes instead the contradictions and class antagonisms that are sought to be hidden, or veiled, by cultural bravura. The other stream of scholarship highlights membership, solidarity, and bonding, but does not pay enough attention to the issue of cultural conflict, dissensions, and struggles over legitimation. The need to overcome this divide becomes all the more palpable once the nation-state is featured as an important anthropological phenomenon. Small-scale societies bound by, what is loosely known as tradition, do not apply as much analytical pressure perhaps, as the nation-state does, on the study of culture. In order to feature communication, dissension and membership within a single analytical perspective I found the notion of *root metaphors* particularly useful. Metaphors have the ability to create memberships without strict adherence to rules of grammar.

I am grateful to a large number of colleagues and students without whose help and encouragement this book would not have even been conceived. I must begin first by thanking my colleagues and students at the Centre for the Study of Social Systems, Jawaharlal Nehru University. Their support has been invaluable and always very positive. In particular, I should like to thank Professor Yogendra Singh for his role as mentor over the last two decades and more. I am also deeply grateful to Professor Aswini K. Ray who succeeds in generating discussions on a wide range of themes with candour and bonhomie. Aswinida is always willing to give the most serious consideration to the most untenable propositions that some of his friends may bring along. I am indebted to Professor Majid H. Siddiqi for being a kind of an intellectual conscience keeper for me. Professor K.L. Sharma has been a good friend and a staunch colleague. On numerous occasions he has, at short notice, covered up for me in the line of duty so that I could pursue a fellowship here and a sabbatical there. In fact, my years as a professional academic would not have been as pleasant had it not been for the friendship and consideration of my colleagues in the faculty.

I spent a few years in-between teaching in the Department of Sociology, University of Delhi, and realized, almost instantly, how lucky I was to be in the midst of intellectuals like Professor André Béteille and Professor J.P.S. Uberoi. I had known them earlier as my teachers, but now I cannot only call them my friends but also great sources of academic inspiration. When I was a student in the seventies, Professor Uberoi was my tutor for three terms in succession at the Department of Sociology, University of Delhi. That seemed very painful then, but now in hindsight I think I was extremely fortunate. I am further indebted to Professor Béteille for introducing me to John Rawls and demonstrating how important his contributions are for sociologists. I hope this book reflects my sincere appreciation of this fact. There are times when I diverge from Professor Béteille's views, but the truth is that much of what I say was initiated in interactions with him. It is only because I have taken his lead on most matters that I can afford to disagree with him on a few.

I was also extremely lucky in getting the Fulbright award and the Shastri Indo-Canadian fellowship in quick succession. I learnt a lot from the months that these grants allowed me to spend in the United States and in Canada. I hope that shows in this book, for I feel truly enriched by this experience. It was particularly apposite for me to visit North America, because in India and in Canada and the United States, issues of affirmative action, multiculturalism and minority rights are matters of public as well as academic debate.

The best part of being able to spend time outside my country has been my good fortune in meeting some wonderful people with exciting minds. Professor N.J. Demerath not only made me feel very welcome in America, but he provided me with all the essential leads towards understanding American society and politics. If some of my friends think I have become something of an

Americaphile after my stint in the United States, then it is Professor Demerath who is responsible. He led me to the right people, to the right literature, and to the right restaurants. He also did me an invaluable favour by reading an earlier draft of the work. His suggestions were very helpful and by taking them into consideration I have probably saved myself from a lot of embarassing criticism. Professor Arjun Appadurai did all he could to get me started in the University of Chicago with such efficiency and ease that it was truly remarkable. But I am also grateful to Arjun for articulating a position on nation-state and diasporic loyalties with such elegance that I knew exactly what I was up against. In a sense, Arjun's work helped me to focus more clearly on my own project and prodded me to get on with it.

The Shastri Indo-Canadian fellowship brought me to Toronto, Canada where I have many old, tried and trusted friends from my previous visits to that city. Professor Milton Israel gave me perfect academic and social support, much more than what one can expect, even from friends. His house is a haven for all sorts of stragglers from India, a true *sarai*. Professor Stuart Philpott has always been a firm and unwavering northern star. He helps me get my coordinates and feel absolutely at home in Canada. Intellectually, however, his measured comments and careful observations are very unsettling. They unfailingly make me pause and re-think what I thought was a finished product. In retaliation I have dumped all kinds of work on him, but he takes them on quite ungrudgingly.

A good part of this book, particularly the first three chapters, were first drafted at Professor Gavin Smith's suggestion. Gavin's intellectual energy has constantly goaded me into different, and often very difficult, areas of anthropology. He has also been very willing to share with me his wide-ranging expertise from peasants to petty commodity production. The question of social membership, over which I toil in most of this book, is an outcome of my long discussions with Gavin, most often in Kensington Kitchen. Professor Krystina Siecohowicz generously gave me a lot of her time and guided me in my understanding of native Canadian affairs. That I made demands on her during the summer break must have been very difficult for her, but she never showed it. Dr. Hira Singh has never ceased to be the epitome of hospitality and generosity, and I have never ceased to take advantage of him.

If it had not been for Hira this book would have taken longer to finish.

The academic contribution of all my friends, in India and abroad, is co-mingled with so many personal favours that it is difficult to draw the line and separate the personal from the professional. So if they don't like this book I hope we can still be friends. I promise to take responsibility for all the errors and shortcomings of this work. That should help!

Dipankar Gupta

Part One

From Sentiment...

─── ❄ ───

Chapter I

Introduction: Culture, Space and Social Membership

Culture and Root Metaphors

If there is one concept that involves sociologists and anthropologists alike, then it is 'culture'. As is well known, the understanding of culture is riven with differences. This has not been altogether negative, for it has helped both disciplines clarify some of the issues that such a conception must take on board. The problem of culture change has been much more acutely problematized as a consequence. This has led to the realization that cultures are not monolithic blocks that are oblivious of and neutral to considerations of power and politics. Cultures indeed express power relations, albeit in a veiled manner, and evoke emotions strong enough for people to die and kill for. It has not been easy to accommodate all these features in any single analytical conceptualization of culture. This does not mean that the attempts at doing so should be given up. We are much more fortunate today for at least we now know the areas that just cannot be overlooked in such a study. Perhaps the single most recalcitrant issue in the conceptualization of culture is the reconciliation of tradition with modernity. This brings to the fore the notion of internal differentiations within any culture, and the existence of multiple levels of saliences and meanings that are present in these differentiated segments. While multiplicity can help to take into account change, whether from within or without, it makes it very difficult to figure out how cultural communication can take place with all this heterogeneity around. It is true that cultures must communicate, but it is also true that this communication cannot presume a consensus, or a unified set of meanings. Finally, if any conceptualization of culture must include change, differentiation, and multiple saliences, can we be analytical at all in our exercise?

To acknowledge these difficulties takes us several steps forward. A clear look at these issues forces us to examine the distinction between culture and artifact, and by extension, between culture and, what is generally called 'learned behaviour'. It will be our contention, in the following pages, that much of the difficulties associated with the study of culture can be sorted out if culture is examined on the basis of *root metaphors* that govern interactions between people. Culture is primarily *practice* in the pursuit of a 'good life'. The good life is not conceived individualistically or solipsistically. When the conception of the good life is accessed through root metaphors it involves interactions with other people. As semiologists have clarified, a metaphor to be active must involve others—a community that minimally understands what the metaphor is all about. We also know, thanks again to semiologists and linguisticians, that metaphors have multiple meanings without being equivocal. A multivocal *regnant set of meanings* of root metaphors allows us a perspective on culture that is neither individualistic nor consensual. The multiple saliences in the regnant set of meanings arise from varying locations of actors and groups in society.

That cultural practice, as interaction, takes place in space, across diverse structural locations and within them, is what separates culture from artifact. Artifacts are not space sensitive, nor do they involve relations with other people around root metaphors for they can be transported wholesale from place to place without compromising on the finished product. Artifacts in their nativity often involve culture. In the first place, root metaphors may inform how a certain article should be produced in terms of social relations between people. Second, the articles may also be vehicles for root metaphors, in the sense that they express social distance and membership. Clothes, arms, hunting gear and vehicles are often used with this purpose in mind. Root metaphors have cathectivity because the good life that they recommend is not based on means-ends rationality. Root metaphors are adhered to because they are good in themselves. The notion of purity and pollution, as in the caste system, is a root metaphor, the significance of colour differentiation is a root metaphor in racist societies, and the various injunctions that inform the division into estates are root metaphors in feudal societies. We shall go into these matters in greater detail later, but a foretaste of what characterizes a root metaphor was perhaps necessary at this juncture.

In developing this theme in the following pages and chapters it is hoped that the difficulties in situating conflict, tension, multiplicity and power in the conceptualization of culture can be, at least partly, overcome. While working towards such a resolution it becomes quite apparent that cultures need not always be small-scale, and in confined spaces, but can include such large memberships as that of the nation-state.

The relationship between root metaphor and culture is very central to our study and will be discussed at some length in this volume. Without getting ahead of our argument it is worthwhile to admit at the start that this exercise was occasioned by the appreciation of the important role that nation-states play in contemporary societies. This is not simply in terms of politics and governance, areas to which nation-states have traditionally been associated. Nation-states influence our self-conscious awareness of who we are as a people with culture(s). It is only by grasping the cultural and sentimental dimensions of individual nation-states that we can enter into an informed debate on their respective structures of governance and politics. This book is devoted to these twin aspects of sentiment and structure with respect to the nation-state, but mediates them through the optic of culture. It is, therefore, all important that we now turn our attention to the conception of culture and how root metaphors can help in this direction.

Culture, Space and Nation-state

Culture is meaningful to the extent that it informs the way people interact with one another. There are various forms of interaction, but in general these take place in defined spaces and in bounded locales. This is what gives space a cultural significance even though, superficially, only geography is involved. One early indication as to why the nation-state is an important cultural phenomenon is the manner in which territory is sacralized and not seen simply as lineaments on a map. The linkage between culture and space, it will be argued here, is an integral one. Culture is enlivened in space such that without space there is no clear conception of cultural membership. This point will be pursued and extended to include the cultural membership of the nation-state and the territorial space such a membership, of necessity, connotes. The coupling of the sentiments of a nation and the structures of the state together bring about the nation-state. To see one side and not the other gives an incomplete understanding of modern, sovereign nation-states.

It is necessary to recall this connection if one is to understand how territorial alignments of a nation-state significantly alter the scope of prior cultural affiliations and memberships. Incidentally, many of these memberships may have deep and hoary roots in the natural history of that society. An analysis of this theme should help comprehend the tensions in contemporary times between the demands of citizenship and the contrary pulls of communitarianism. How community sentiments are expressed in modern nation-states cannot be fathomed without factoring in the specifics of the nation-state in question. Not only will there be a wide divergence between theocratic, fascist and liberal nation-states in regard to how community ties and associations are expressed, but within each of these types there are bound to be further variations. These variations arise from the contingent circumstances and historical peculiarities of each nation-state. Therefore, no matter which way one looks at cultural practice, especially as it extends to public life, it is impossible to ignore the reality of the nation-state. To be a practising Hindu in contemporary India, or a practising Anglican in England today, is quite different from what it used to be in medieval times. A practising Hindu lived by caste norms in dealings with other people, and the practising Anglican had a duty to go to church and not consider Jews and Catholics to be at par. In fact, John Locke in his *Treatise on Tolerance*, was rather severe on those who did not believe in God and did not attend service. If India and England have come a long way since then it is because the identity of being a Hindu or a Christian has been considerably modified by one's membership in a nation-state.

The politicization of culture is then not an afterthought, in fact it never was. However, the contemporary politicization of cultural identities cannot be understood isolated from the nation-state and its metaphors. The modern liberal democratic nation-state goes the furthest in trying to accommodate diverse cultural identities within it. The structures it must necessarily institute to be able to do so constitute the challenge of our times. Social anthropology should not shy away from participating in this gigantic intellectual churn. It must be prepared to move away from viewing cultures in isolation, or as exotic wholes. This may have been a credible approach in the past, but it makes little sense in contemporary times. The advantage of anthropology is that it heightens an awareness of the hold that symbols and metaphors have in social life. This is why the co-existence of multiple symbols and cultures within a nation-state creates a tension that needs to be addressed.

There are various routes to examining this tension. One option would be to say that only certain societies have the necessary cultural equipment for citizenship (Gellner 1994). The other might well be to argue that citizenship is a fallacy, and that only the community is 'authentic'. In such cases the civil society is seen to be synonymous with community (Kothari 1988a). Hence the call to return to tradition—albeit in a 'non-traditional way' (Arato and Cohen 1993: 202). Both these views are exclusivist and culturological in the sense that they do not help to assess the efforts that different nation-states are making towards reconciling multiple cultural identities within their respective territories. In addition, these positions ignore the historical thrust of modernization. While Gellner would calmly exclude the developing world from this drive, Kothari would be quite happy to advocate a return to a romantic tradition. There is also a third alternative which believes that nation-states are historically *passe* as cultures nowadays are no longer linked to space. Appadurai argues such a case with respect to diasporic movements (Appadurai 1996: 169).

Non-spaces

There is yet a fourth alternative which would emphasize the existence of non-places, such as airports, national highways, and one might add, supermarkets and apartment complexes (see Augé

1995: 34). Augé believes that anthropology should pay attention to such non-places as this is the sign of our times. For Augé such non-places are analytically significant as they do not arouse membership passions like cultures do with their spaces. In a sense Augé is really emphasizing the emergence of non-places within what used to be cultural spaces. This is a very useful insight which will be repeatedly used in this book. Where Augé errs is in his assessment that non-places are beginning to rule the world. In coming to this conclusion he does not pay enough attention to the reality of the nation-state and its territorial possessions that are culturally laden. The illusion that the nation-state is withering away is probably an outcome of the success of the nation-state in some developed economies. The bases of legitimate governance are so fully internalized that instruments of coercion are never fully visible. Control and co-ordination are exercised through a variety of structures that are not obtrusive. Paradoxically then, it is in those societies where the structure and sentiment of the nation-state are most deeply seated and metabolized that intellectuals believe the nation-state to be an exhausted and wasted theme. While in countries where the nation-state is yet to consolidate itself through its structures of governance the presence of the nation-state is hardly ever in any doubt.

Though Marc Augé's statement about non-places can be read as if there are no worthwhile cultural spaces left, I think it is possible to use his insight in examining how liberal democratic structures can be instituted to build fraternity within culturally diverse nation-states. It is important to bear in mind that modernization brings about such non-places, and this cannot be emphasized enough. Nevertheless, such non-places can be figured in a more vivacious and livelier fashion if seen in conjunction with the cultural membership of the nation-state, and in relation to existing traditions that manifest themselves in contemporary cultural identities. In order to achieve a certain consistency in this task, we shall coin the neologism 'non-space' in place of Augé's 'non-places' to heighten the importance of culture and its spaces.

It is true that international airports and highways aspire to a universalism that is peculiar only to itself. The signs and protocol of these non-spaces are designed to appeal to all which is why they are nobody's prerogative. It is still true however that these non-spaces are inclined towards western sensibilities. The number of travellers from South Asia and Africa who are routinely lost in airports is an indication of the western slant to these non-spaces. Even so these non-spaces function largely on the basis of technical competence instead of being initiated on pre-existing cultural norms and root metaphors. This allows people of diverse cultural backgrounds to participate in these non-spaces without any serious threat to their respective root metaphors. Non-spaces allow cultural metaphors to slide in and out with relative ease for they do not essentially challenge the aesthetic core of cultures. This should not be surprising as non-spaces are designed on means-ends rationality. The means are with respect to specific, unambiguous and de-limited ends, and are not extendable. Root metaphors, on the other hand, are not means-ends oriented and have ambitions to cover ever expanding areas of social life. Non-spaces thus cohabit with spaces, and the two together have added dimensions to our modern day lives. It would, therefore, be quite an exaggeration to suggest that such non-spaces have taken over contemporary societies. Undoubtedly supermarkets, airports and apartment complexes are beginning to look very similar in different parts of the world, yet cultural differences and spaces still survive.

Non-spaces, in short, are indifferent to root metaphors. They invoke instead a universalistic non-discriminatory organizational logic that is open to all. Membership in non-spaces does not demand affectivity as much as it does affective neutrality. It is of the kind that one can switch in and out of without any schism in the soul. It is therefore necessary to nuance Parsons' pattern variables (Parsons 1951: 66–67) if we are not to be misled into dogmatic assertions of dichotomies. The general interpretation that Parsons has encouraged with his pattern variables is that as one gets more affectively neutral, universalistic and collectively oriented, one naturally must give up on affectivity, universalism and so forth. Even though there have been significant advances in the growth of non-spaces in countries like America, nevertheless the Gallup poll of 1997 found that 95 per cent of Americans said they believed in God, 73 per cent in an afterlife, and 41 per cent said that they attended church at least once a week. Interestingly, these features are almost identical to an earlier Gallup survey in 1947 (see Silk 1997). Non-spaces can therefore grow alongside existing cultural spaces, and also proceed abreast with the emergence of new kinds of memberships in freshly formed cultural spaces. The development of Christian revivalism and fundamentalism in America is a good indication of this trend. It has also been suggested that the reliance on such cultural memberships often makes the transition to impersonal bureaucracies and corporate economies less harsh and alienating (see Mingione 1991: 55–61).

Non-spaces emerge in certain defined aspects of social life, but it needs to be mentioned that such calculated rationality, or what Alasdair MacIntyre would call 'emotivism' (MacIntyre 1981: 14–18) often only displaces affectivity to other levels without eradicating it. Thus if the job market is based on affective neutrality, there is every likelihood of such a society attracting Christian evangelists on television. If neighbourhood solidarities and commitments are decreasing, loyalties to nationalities are probably replacing them. To concede that non-spaces are uniformly flat and non-exclusionary, is also to say that they do not arouse commitment. Social life gets its resonance from the principles of inclusion and exclusion, or, in other words, from social membership. Memberships become lively only when there are non-members around. This distinction makes little sense in airports, supermarkets and bureaucracies where it is not a question of membership or non-membership. After all airports have transit passengers, supermarkets have customers, and bureaucracies have employers and employees.

At the same time caution should be exercised in not routinely equating certain architectural constructions as non-spaces. The temptation to do so is especially strong when these constructions are 'modern' ones. It is not the building or the architecture or the technical facilities available that make for non-space. For a true non-space to emerge root metaphors should be irrelevant. It is necessary to underline this point as root metaphors can enjoy a considerable round of success in seemingly modern establishments fitted with the latest technological equipment. What, therefore, separates space from non-space is the premise on which social interactions are based, and not the physical nature of the surroundings.

This point can perhaps be best made by looking at apartment complexes in different parts of the world. An apartment complex, unlike an airport or a supermarket, is not a place where people enter into and exit from without spending any length of time. As an apartment complex is where people live, where families are reared, where primary socialization takes place, it can never be a true non-space, no matter how modern the structure. Surely, there are certain technical aspects common to all apartment buildings which impose a certain kind of uniformity, but root metaphors continue to exist and literally come out through the cracks. Notions of hygiene and cleanliness differ from culture to culture, even the conception of noise varies between residents who come from diverse backgrounds. Gender and inter-generational differences show up in a variety of ways—from the use of water, recreational facilities and the employment of domestic help. This is why, in spite of architectural similarities, there is a vast difference between living in an apartment complex in New York and in one in Mumbai. This is also a reason why migrants are often not welcomed in apartment buildings where one set of root metaphors have a near monopolistic sway.

Root metaphors can also thrive on economic differences, though that need not always be the case. When they do, then memberships thus formed on the basis of wealth recommend differential lifestyles and interactional systems appropriate for the different classes. An examination of factors that enhance 'snob value' will reveal root metaphors at their base. Erving Goffman (1961) pointed out how as one went higher up the social scale there were fewer and fewer people one could backstage with. This is also what makes it difficult for the *nouveau riche* to join the set because they lack familiarity with the rules of membership of the upper classes.

It is, however, a fact that economic differences do not signify varying cultural memberships in the same fashion all over the world. What may be considered a vast economic and cultural gulf in one society need not appear that way in another. In west Uttar Pradesh (India) for example, the substantial landowner and the middle peasant lead somewhat similar cultural lives and share the same cultural space in spite of their class differences. Elsewhere in India, the economic distance between a substantial landowner and a middle peasant would have signalled a vast cultural gulf as well. In rural west Uttar Pradesh, on the other hand, the rich and the not-so-rich lead rather similar cultural lives, recreate in the same fashion, and value the same things that money can buy. Between these classes space is not separated in any meaningful way. The interactions between these classes is continuous and unmarked. Together they form a phalanx of the 'landed people' against the landless. But the distance between the landed and the landless is culturally significant and semaphored through the root metaphors of caste (see Gupta 1997: 40, 60, 108).

In a slightly different vein the same point can be reinforced by taking an example from Canada. In pre-industrial Quebec, where the French-speaking Quebecois were primarily *habitants* (or peasants), the educated few such as the doctors, lawyers, and even political thinkers, all came from this class. These professionals and members of the Quebecois literati had not yet been estranged from their roots which is what accounted for their remarkable appeal in 19th century French Canada. As Lord Durham noted in his *Report on the Affairs of British North America* that the professional Quebecois

> was separated by no barriers of or pride or distinct interests, from the singularly ignorant peasantry by which he is surrounded.... The most uninstructed population...is thus placed in the hands of a small body of instructed persons, in whom it reposes confidence, which nothing but domestic connections and such community of interests could generate (in Lucas 1912: 33).

This scenario changed quite dramatically once industrialization came to Quebec. Around 1920, in the years following the First World War, Quebec society gradually began to exhibit a clearer delineation between the bourgeoise, workers, peasants and capitalists. It is in this period again that the Catholic Church's exhortation of 'agriculturalism' and a rural way of life was challenged in practice by a large section of the Quebecois (Ouellet 1969: 59).

The further one progresses on the road down industrialization it is possible to witness yet another transformation. According to T.H. Marshall class-based cultures which were so prominent in feudal estates may, in modern societies 'dwindle to a minimum.... The working classes, instead of inheriting a distinctive though simple (sic) culture, are provided with a cheap and shoddy imitation of a civilization that has become national' (Marshall 1963: 89). Though Marshall may have exaggerated the sublation of class-based distinctions in western societies, it is true that a great degree of cultural homogeneity has been arrived at as a result of advanced industrialization. The spaces that existed earlier between classes and ethnic communities have been eroded to a significant extent in contemporary industrialized and developed societies. As can be easily attested (from scholars as diverse as Vance Packard and Hebert Marcuse), there is a greater commonality in commodity consumption between different classes and communities than was the case few decades ago. If there is also greater mobility in these societies it only suggests that there is an increased readiness for non-spaces to be more accommodating of people from diverse cultural provenances.

In this process the nation-state too has played an important role which cannot be relegated to the background. It is true that the emergence of nation-states is co-terminous with industrialization, but they nevertheless possess a driving force and logic of their own. The impact of nation-states on the opening up of hitherto bounded spaces, and in this process the creation of fresh cultural identities, cannot be overlooked. This book is concerned with issues of this order which is why an attempt is made here to understand the nation-state in terms accessible to anthropology. In order to proceed with this task it is perhaps best to start with a discussion on the anthropological conception of culture.

Chapter II

Space, Non-space and Site: Root Metaphor and *Lex*

Conceptualizing Culture

It is often difficult to recall Edward Tylor's omnibus definition of culture without suppressing a smile. For Tylor, culture was knowledge, belief, art, morals, law, customs, and any other capacity or habit acquired by a person as a member of society. This rather generous and cumbersome definition however held on to an important insight which cannot be shaken off even today. What Tylor successfully emphasized was that culture is acquired by virtue of being a *member* of society. Culture cannot be gathered from afar, but through active social engagement among those who are members of a culture. Culture is not just learned, nor passed on as an artifice. Culture is really about experience and interaction with other members. This aspect of Tylor's understanding of culture is very significant and is often lost sight of. When Kroeber recalled Tylor in his monumental work *Anthropology* (1967), it was to underline that culture was a product of people working in interactive settings (ibid.: 8–10). This was also why he insisted that culture was superorganic and could not be understood outside of the density of social interactions (ibid.: 254; see also White 1967: 17). It is, however, possible that too much is being read into Tylor and Kroeber for neither of them really clarified how membership is arrived at; or what separates one kind of interaction from another; or when memberships should be distinguished from associations.

Today there is a general disdain towards a definition of culture, or even a clear delineation of what does not constitute culture. Culture is seen as an ineffable, though not unreal, phenomenon. This has led to descriptive studies of culture (Geertz 1984), where a certain understanding of culture is slipped in without any overt definitional claims being made. Descriptions frequently depend on laying out the specific and differential logics of diverse cultures. What is being encouraged in this case is the search for particular grammars (Uberoi 1969: 125), or dispositions of culture (Geertz 1984: 11–13, 94–95). This search for cultural consistency can also be witnessed in Louis Dumont's analysis of the Indian caste system (Dumont 1970). Consequently the emphasis on textual sources (ibid.) or on 'cultured' informants (for example, Radcliffe-Brown, see Kuper 1983: 41–42), grew without paying enough attention to the fact that as cultures are born, transmitted and transformed in experience, they do not exhibit pure qualities or effortless grammatically consistent elaborations.

As textual sources and cultured informants are by definition inflexible, it damaged the way in which culture was broadcast in mainstream anthropology. Culture in such cases is quite often not what people do, but what they have locked up in their heads. When culture is about what people do with other people, that politics becomes an obvious feature of such interactions. This political aspect is often hidden from view, or when acknowledged, examined as an oddity in its relationship with culture. Politics and power are rarely viewed as aspects of culture, but as external phenomena impinging upon it from the outside.

Culture and Politics

Edmund Leach had observed in the *Political Systems of Highland Burma* (1964) that rituals were not empty inherited traditions, but a mode of expressing power (see also Rapaport 1979). Thus a Hindu wedding ritual, for instance, marks out the superiority of the bride-taker over the bride-giver. Likewise, a mourning ritual, among other things, also separates the chief inheritor from the rest of the family, and the men from the women. John and Jean

Comaroff provide a very graphic account of how in post-colonial times 'politics often masquerades as culture' (Comaroff and Comaroff 1997: 11). The belief in witchcraft took a new turn as the anti-apartheid movement came to a climax. The Comaroffs argue that it were

> young men, not people in authority, who felt most moved to execute 'instant' justice. They marked Nelson Mandela's release from prison...as a sign that reason and right had triumphed at last, with a furious spate of witch burning—often to the august chanting of freedom songs (ibid.: 12; see also Gluckman 1963: 128 ff.; Lan 1985).

To come back to the politics of everyday ritual, the compulsions to follow rituals in a certain fashion depend to a great extent on *who is watching* (Kuper 1983: 16). Rituals in a village have greater resonance than in a city. This, as Marriot has pointed out, is because the village is where the interactional nexus matters most, because people there are all too watchful and have long-term memories (Marriot 1959). In the village too cultural space is dense as root metaphors embed multiple aspects of social life. In urban areas the cultural space is not absent but compared to the village, less dense, interspersed as it is with non-spaces. In these non-spaces associations matter more than memberships based on root paradigms.

Consequently, the performance of Hindu rituals, or any other ritual for that matter, in different locales will have a different flavour. Not only does the site favour a greater attention to certain details, to the exclusion of others, but the political compulsions too will be different. A Christian wedding ritual in Kerala will be vastly different from anything in England, and so on. The facility with which Catholics and Protestants can marry in America is still unimaginable in many parts of advanced western Europe, including England.

The element of conflict within a cultural space need not always be caused by the strivings for material wealth and social distinctions as we understand them in most contemporary societies. Victor Turner's description of symbols in Ndembu rituals makes this point very vivid. In N'kanga, the puberty ritual for girls, the Mudyi tree symbolizes domestic relations where breast feeding, nurturance, and the bond between mother and child are made salient. That the Mudyi is a latex tree makes it easier to use it as a symbol for these purposes. From breast feeding to domestic relations, the Mudyi tree is extended to symbolize matriliny, succession, and indeed the values that emphasize the unity and continuity of Ndembu society (Turner 1964: 21–25).

Everything so far seems to say that there is complete cultural consonance. The milk tree stands for nurturance and the fact that the chief is the mother of the people, and so on (ibid.: 25). Contradictions make their presence felt at the contextual level. During the course of the puberty ritual women dance round the tree and taunt the men. The novice's mother is separated from other adult women and debarred from the ritual site. When the cassava porridge is announced women rush to be the first to grab the spoon. If the first woman is from the village of the novice then it is believed that she is lucky for she will find a husband nearby. The Ndembus are matrilineal people but live virilocally, and this produces a certain degree of tension between married couples. Rivalry between villages and lineages is also manifested between phases of ritual in public dances and beer drinking (ibid.: 44). This is why Turner concludes that different interpretations arise in different action situations and these interpretations are not always in concordance as they are shot through with power considerations (ibid.: 27–29).

Root Metaphors and Regnant Sets of Meaning

Before any attempt is made to understand culture either definitionally or essentially it would be a good idea to remember Wittgenstein's aphorism: *Don't think but look*. The most significant thing about culture is that it is to be understood in terms of social interaction. To believe as Geertz does that culture provides a guide to human behaviour (Geertz 1984: 44) is far too general. It guides some kinds of action but not others, especially not those in what we call non-spaces. Further, if the Geertzian position were to be followed, there is hardly any need for looking at cultures in dynamic terms. Culture, according to this rendition, is a stabilized phenomenon without much scope for internal strains and dissensions. The fact that Geertz employs terms like 'computer's program', 'blueprint', 'recipe', or 'a musical score' (ibid.: 250) to explicate his understanding of culture is itself suggestive. These analogies strongly imply a kind of cultural determinism and cultural grammar.

A better option would be to examine culture in terms of 'root metaphors' and their regnant sets of meanings. Metaphors are after all disrespectful of routine language and therein lies their power and appeal. Thus one might say that the root metaphor of caste is the hierarchy of purity and pollution, but there is no single straight, unified, 'grammatical' rendition of it. This leaves open the issue as to how this metaphor is actually realized in diverse settings. This is how Stephen Pepper, who was probably the first to use the term 'root metaphor', saw it (Pepper 1942). These root metaphors, as with all metaphors, are polysemic or multivocal, but not equivocal. There is a range of meanings that polysemy allows, but as Paul Ricoeur points out, the most literal meaning hovers over them all like an *eminence grise* (Ricoeur 1974: 12, 32–33). This point can be made more accessible with the help of an example provided by Melville Herskovits. Herskovits drew our attention to the fact that there are at least 315 variants of the Cinderella story, but in all of them the central factors are more or less the same (Herskovits 1965: 392).

If culture is seen through the optic of root metaphors then that presumes a membership of those for whom the root metaphor is meaningful. There are times when these metaphors become strident and are blazoned on one's consciousness, and at other times they lie quiescently. Moreover, it is not as if there is one root metaphor for each culture. There are several root metaphors in every culture because human beings in live social interaction do not lead one-dimensional lives. As there are significant overlaps between the bearers of these metaphors it is possible to draw membership groupings—though these are rarely exclusionary (see also Herskovits 1965: 415). This is because there are root metaphors at different levels of generality. Thus a defined set of people may belong to a certain caste as against other castes, and then again they might at another point of time identify themselves as belonging to the category Hindu against non-Hindu, and so on. Even so cultural membership cannot be simply left at the level of root metaphors. Culture, as Parsons insisted, was primarily affective. These root metaphors are then just not another linguistic device, but are symbols that evoke cathectivity, partisanship and aesthetic commitment.

Why do root metaphors evoke affectivity? Why do they generate such strong partisanship and intense loyalty? These metaphors, by viture of being metaphors, can address a diversity of aspects which is why they can be made to work in a variety of settings. That they can be constant companions over vast stretches of existential experience enhances one's commitment to them. In the case of culture the matter gets more intense because these root metaphors recall a defined space from which they get their original meaning. If in that space the metaphors can realize themselves multivocally, as metaphors should, then that is what accounts for the commitment towards them.

Root Metaphor and *Lex*

A plausible way of demonstrating this would be to take up contrary cases as control instances. It is possible to say that even bureaucratic norms can be seen to function metaphorically, as these norms too are capable of multiple interpretations. However, when looked at closely, these norms differ from root metaphors in one very significant respect. The range of interpretations they afford is parlous and limited because they are constrained by other norms in the package and do not stand alone. Unlike root metaphors, which are effective singly, and do not require back-up from other like-minded metaphors, the norms of non-spaces call out to other norms on the principle of 'elective affinity'.

In this case any interpretation of a single norm must ostensibly be in consonance with the accompanying norms. Michael Oakeshott made this point very effectively in his understanding of rule-governed practice. Rules do not stand alone, but come in a package. He referred to this package of rules that call out to each other for mutual reinforcements by the latin term *lex* (Oakeshott 1975: 129). Further, '*lex* should be as exact, as little doubtful, and as economical as may be, ...the conditions it describes and prescribes *should not conflict with one another...*' (ibid.: 128). He reiterated this point a little later when he said: 'The systematic character of *lex* is a relationship between the prescribed conditions of conduct themselves, in virtue of which they continuously interpret, confirm, and accommodate themselves to one another, and thus compose a self-sufficient (although not self-explanatory) system' (ibid.: 129).

The fact that the *lex* is not an independent metaphor does cramp the variations in possible interpretations of it. Further, the fact that these norms in elective affinity stand in a sort of syntagmatic relationship with one another does not encourage norms to function as independent metaphors. It should be borne in mind that root metaphors that constitute any culture are not necessarily logically related to one another. That is how cultural grammarians would like it to be, but there is little reason to yield to this essentialist view.

Moreover, the office space in a bureaucracy is very different from cultural space. The interaction in a bureaucracy is based on a subscription of rules and norms which do not require prior affiliations for their comprehension or compliance (Weber 1968: 1111). The ability to interpret metaphors and acquiesce to their regnant meanings requires prior socialization. Without this socialization the specifics of the metaphor's connotations will be lost. Denotations, on the other hand, tend to be univocal and hence do not require immersion into a specific form of socialization without which connotative appreciations are impossible. It is at this denotative level that the *lex* is most comprehensible.

Metaphors create a membership of those who can see words and symbols as metaphors without being limited to their obvious and overt literal rendition. As *lex* is largely denotative, its deciphering does not require any specific conditioning. The ability to speak a language does not necessarily mean that one is also equipped to comprehend and appreciate the many metaphorical liberties that one can take with it. This is why there is the frequent complaint that translations are always inadequate to appreciate the richness of a literary text. The membership that cultural root metaphors create is of those who can interpret these metaphors in terms of a regnant set of meanings that resonate within a certain space of social interaction. This membership is not based on universalistic criteria, for a specific prior socialization is a necessary requirement to be able to interpret the root metaphors in terms of a certain regnant set of meanings.

Conversely, it is possible to say that a bureaucracy can be a universalistic space for the norms are universalistic. Membership to it is open and does not require prior identification with any interactional set. Thus a bank will give loans not on the basis of family connections, but on the soundness of the investment profile of the borrower. An employee, likewise, will be hired on the basis of a universalistic statement of qualifications without recognizing any other connections or attributes, whether ascriptive or otherwise.

A bureaucracy is said to be modern not because the physical locale of its activity takes place in structures that are associated with modern styles, nor because a bureaucratic establishment can be generally well-appointed, even plush (recall our discussion on apartment complexes), but because it functions along universalistic norms. Though Korea, Thailand and Indonesia give the impression of being modern, multi-national business transactions in these countries are still conducted along non-universalistic lines. In Indonesia it was, till recently, most important to be a family member or friend of Suharto to become prosperous. Not surprisingly the Peregrine Merchant Bank of Hong Kong collapsed when it gave a huge loan simply on the basis of the fact that the borrowers were from the Suharto family. The root metaphor attached to the notion of *guanxi* favours unquestioning loyalty to the leader and reliance on family connections. This creates cultural spaces within what should be *lex* ruled non-spaces. A true non-space should not yield to non-universalistic loyalties and memberships that spring from family ties or informal networks.

Lex and Non-spaces

The bureaucratic space is open and not bounded as the case is with cultural space because officials in a bureaucracy can leave one bureaucratic organization for another without any great trauma. In fact head hunting organizations which look out for top executive slots search for suitable candidates from a wide variety of organizations. The assumption is that if one has mastered the rules of the game it does not really matter where the person is placed. This is particularly true of information technology (IT) professionals worldwide. At lower levels too typists and managers freely move from one bureaucracy to another in search of better pay or job satisfaction. As bureaucratic spaces are technically open to all on universalistic principles it is necessary to separate them from cultural spaces. By being universalistic in their orientation bureaucratic spaces belong to nobody in particular (see also Bourdieu 1984: 314). Hence it may be appropriate to use the neologism non-spaces when we refer to them.

This of course is an ideal construction. Rarely do modern bureaucracies adhere to such an ideal. Nevertheless, it cannot be denied that there is a pronounced disposition towards this end. This tendency is often held in check by the superior personal access some people enjoy because of prior memberships whose appeal has not yet become defunct. In the Asian case, as has just been pointed out, non-spaces are continuously invaded by cultural spaces, which is why mobility from one bureaucratic organization to another is not easy. The *chaebol* system in Korea, for example, is an assertion of space even though it is made up of business agglomerates. In this case certain *chaebol* houses (Hanbo, Sammi, Kia) have a preferential relationship with the government. Huge amounts of public funds are directed towards the growth and development of these conglomerates without taking into account their actual capabilities and entrepreneurial performance.

Such favoured treatment on the basis of the public exchequer looks good from a distance and gives the illusion of progress. Yet the truth is that it does not encourage universalism, even though, as in this case, it is not as if ascriptive ties are involved. Non-universalistic factors need not always be those associated with the accident of birth, but may also arise from informal networks. When these dominate a seemingly modern organization they encourage the growth of cultural spaces. This is why there is excessive loyalty to a firm, a leader, and so forth in East Asian business organizations more than in those in the western hemisphere. In Asia, consequently, movement from one organization to another becomes difficult, for the ties with a particular enterprise or firm are not based on purely universalistic criteria where rules and procedures matter most.

Occasionally there may be a vast stretch of space where certain root metaphors have precedence. The fact that there is such a uniformity over a large area makes it appear as if it were non-space. This illusion occurs because there is a great degree of unanimity between members which allows root metaphors to live invisibly and unostentatiously over a large geographical area. Cultural spaces need not be geographically small, nor always interspersed with other cultural spaces. Non-spaces, like spaces, have nothing to do with geographical size. They are distinguished by the domination of rules and procedures and not by idiosyncratic metaphors. *In non-spaces then there are no members but associates.* These associates have a high degree of mobility, a trait that cultural membership does not allow. Metaphors, on the contrary, encourage a high degree of cathective solidarity of the socialized. This naturally forecloses the option of moving about freely in diverse cultural spaces.

Very often sheer hubris obstructs an awareness of the cultural bias behind what can be mistaken as non-space. As was pointed out earlier the mere existence of a modern apartment complex does not mean that it is actually a non-space. A true test of a non-space is the universal criteria of associateship. A seemingly modern and highly technical construction does not necessarily make for a non-space. The real issue is whether or not people interact in this zone along emotivist considerations (recall MacIntyre 1981: 14–18), or on universalistic lines (recall Parsons 1951: 66–67). Further, one should not confuse uniformity with universalism. If residency in an apartment complex demands that certain kinds of food aromas be condemned as offensive then that space is not a non-space even if all those living there agree on this account.

Root Metaphors and Space

A non-space is considered to be so when it can draw its interactors from a variety of provenances as long as its stated universalistic criteria are met. A cultural space is different, for its members cannot be shuffled about. When the Partition of India took place the refugees who crossed over from west Punjab (now Pakistan) were both urban and rural. The urban migrants faced great trauma and hardship because they had to start life anew, find jobs, retool themselves, make fresh connections, and so forth. It is not surprising then that for the urban migrants the remembered space of what used to be their home is poignant and loaded with political significance. The rural refugees, on the other hand, were settled in collectivities. Entire villages were re-located and the refugees carried on with the jobs they had pursued in pre-Partition Punjab. Not only did they continue to remain farmers, they had their old friends, neighbours and relatives with them but in a new geographical locale. Their cultural space had not been disturbed in spite of migration as much as it had been for the urban refugees.

This difference between the urban and rural refugees of the Partition still resonates. The urban refugees continue to recall the brutalities and deprivations that they had been subjected to. Consequently they are inclined towards Hindu cultural and political organizations which seek to avenge the creation of Pakistan. The rural refugees have long overcome angsts of this order. Though they too lost their family members following the brutalities that followed the Partition, they were able to right themselves much quicker in their new geographical setting. The locale had changed for them but not so much their cultural space. From west Punjab villages of Pakistan they were now settled in the rural areas of Indian Punjab and Haryana. Their cultural space remained more or less intact. Their memory of the Partition is not tinged with as much anger and hatred as it is with the urban refugees. Nor can the Partition be used as a potent political symbol for the rural migrants as it can for their urban counterparts. This once again illustrates the distinction between pure geography and space.

It is possible to construct another scenario that demonstrates the link between commitment to root metaphors and space. The internationalist ideology of Marxism never really found any large-scale commitment till it was transformed first by Lenin and then by Mao, into a credo with strong nationalist and territorial overtones. In both cases territory was uppermost. The orthodox Marxian position which is internationalist is dismissive of patriotism, and for that reason it led to the 'many absurdities in Western intellectual perceptions of the Soviet system' (Gray 1988: 39). Further, the displaced patriotism professed by Bernard Shaw or the Webbs, or indeed the legion of Marxists in India, United States, and elsewhere, were incomprehensible to most. It is only after communism was linked to patriotism and the nation-state that it began to gain in symbolic energy. Beginning with Lenin's stance to pull Russia out of the First World War, to the manner in which protection of socialism was linked to saving Russia from Hitler, to the long Chinese anti-Imperialist struggle against Japan, communism thrived only when linked to patriotic space. As long as Communism was spelt out principally along Internationalist lines it found little mass support.

A major reason why socialism was de-linked from space and place in classical renditions was because it was believed that proletariats had no nation, only capitalists did. This is what led Raymond Williams to observe: 'A new theory of socialism must now centrally involve *place*. Remember the argument that the proletariat had no country, the factor that differentiated it from the property-owning classes. But place has been shown to be a crucial element in the bonding process...' (Williams 1989: 242). The language of international socialism which seeks to communicate to all, ends up by not communicating to anybody. When it does, then it is purely as a technical artifact among deracinated intellectuals and fails to arouse passionate loyalty, or aesthetic commitment, the way the root metaphors of culture do.

Cultures are enacted in a space with all its dimensions. Cultures thus become palpable realities and ostensible facts. Cultures are not locked up in remote empyrean recesses but are enacted and need to be expressed in a variety of existential settings. This obviously presumes a space: no space no cultural enactment. The longer the duration of a certain cultural space the greater is its identification with that culture. This also allows certain voices to consolidate themselves as regnant meanings of root metaphors. These voices have to do with the specifics of the cultural locale or the space. The specifics of the space and its diacritics are reflected in the various preferred innuendos and vocalities of the root metaphors.

The development of Francophone culture in Quebec can serve to illustrate this point. To quote Marcel Rioux,

> the people of New France (Quebec—D.G.) began to distinguish itself from the metropolis (old France—D.G.); they draw in on themselves to create here on American soil, another French speaking people. French institutions are modified, habits change and another *mentality* is born—a new kind of human being will appear, the French Canadian *habitant*. This man lives within an institution as unique as himself (Rioux 1971: 14).

Abbe Groulx put the same idea across more dramatically when he said:

How much more then would life in the new world...by the quality of spirit and will which it demanded, not modify profoundly the early colonists of New France? The transformation was rapid from the first generation on. When this *heritage* is no longer isolated or restrained to a few families but has spread to a great number of the same species, it constitutes a *race* (Groulx 1938: 235).

As we read through Groulx's race-oriented period piece what emerges clearly is that over time a favoured set of voices of root metaphors emerged in Quebec that reflected the empirical specifics of their surroundings. The *seigneurs* after 1760, i.e., after the British conquest of Quebec, were also vastly different from the *seigneurs* of old France. They did not have the symbolic authority, or command the allegiance that their counterparts did in the old country. Even the Catholic Church which could never realize its ultramontane ambitions in France, found ample room for it in Quebec, helped (ironically) by the British authorities. Mgr. De Laval, the founder of this persuasion in Quebec, succeeded in having the Bishopry of Quebec nominated directly by the Pope in Rome. Gallicanism in France would not have permitted such hierarchical and clerical pretensions there, but the move won greater support in faraway Quebec.

The voices thus favoured are outcomes of the peculiarities of the space of cultural enactment. Likewise, the metaphor of purity and pollution will manifest itself differently in India and in those of Indian origin in diaspora. For the same reason there would be significant differences in the expressions of Protestantism in America between the eastern sea board and the southern provinces. As cultures interact in space any alterations on this account have to be reflected in the regnant meanings of root metaphors. Such changes, or alterations may arise from a variety of factors such as technological upgradations, migration or epidemics. In this process some root metaphors may die out and others may step in, or, as is more frequently the case, a certain set of interpretations of the root metaphor are replaced by other interpretations. This is why it is difficult to separate a culture from its space. When such a link is established over long periods of time the difficulty becomes very significant.

Diaspora and Vicarious Space

For a fuller understanding of cultural space it is necessary to introduce the concept of *vicarious space*. 'This is how we do things at home' is a powerful draw in many diasporic settings. In these instances again a certain political point is being made. The interlocutors in this case need not just be the family, but also neighbours who belong to the host culture, and to other diasporics of the same background. A space, nevertheless, is recalled, which not only authenticates rituals, but also establishes co-ordinates with real and virtual neighbours. This space that is now being recalled can be termed as *vicarious space*. Though the diasporics are far removed from the land of their origin they imagine a set of cultural interactions that continue to take place in what used to be their home. The recall of vicarious space has little to do with what is happening in the old country in the meanwhile. It has much more to do with what is imagined to be happening there. Besides vicarious space, there is the reality of the existential setting of the diasporics in a faraway land. This land is where home is at present and in the future, but does not quite feel like it yet. This is why the imagined stolidity of vicarious space acts as an effective point of reference for diasporics struggling in unsettled conditions in distant sites.

It is the creation of vicarious spaces which authenticates cultural enactments and practices when they are taken out of their original setting. Without this aspect cultural enactments would cease to resonate and would become a pure spectacle for ticketed audiences. In diasporic settings certain significant and subtle alterations take place. These alterations of course recall a vicarious space, but must perforce take into account the new site of a cultural enactment. This new site sets out to create complementary, or surrogate, spaces. But as these sites will have different people, different pressures and different predicaments, the cultural enactments must necessarily be modified.

Diasporic cultures give good evidence of this. Very often they are condemned as being fossilized and retrograde versions of the original. But in fact they are actually modifications of the original and this transition had begun at the point at which a culture went out of its traditional space into a fresh site. If they appear to be backward and less progressive than what the culture at home has turned out to be it is because there is a temptation to make such comparisons on a very selective basis. The basic point remains that these diasporic cultures too are a manifestation of transformation, and testify to the polysemy of root metaphors. The trajectory they have taken is different from the trajectory that the metaphors have taken back home.

In history there have been many occasions when important temples, or institutions, which mnemonically and even indexically recalled a cultural space, lapsed from popular consciousness. The much disputed site in the north Indian town of Ayodhya is a good example of this. In Ayodhya a 16th century mosque and a Hindu temple dedicated to Lord Rama existed at roughly the same spot. Besides sharing a common plot of land they had another feature in common. They had both lain in obscurity and suffered from neglect for decades, if not for centuries. They were not important elements in the popular consciousness for neither the temple nor the mosque were active cultural spaces. This however was completely reversed when in the late eighties the Congress party and the Hindu-oriented Bharatiya Janata Party (BJP) revived this site and gave it religious and sectarian dimensions replete with contesting root metaphors. The BJP insisted on destroying the mosque in order to re-sacralize the temple and launched a successful nation-wide movement towards this end. This aroused the fears of the minority Muslim community which gave the Hindu sectarians greater charge. From dust-laden obscurity Ayodhya sprang to life and became a cultural space.

Wittgenstein had once said that the only way language can express sensations is by invoking a factual basis. Thus expressions like 'pins and needles', or being 'gnawed by hunger', or the 'head is throbbing like a hammer'. In the case of root metaphors and their regnant sets of meaning the analogy holds to the extent that these metaphors cry out for 'space'. This explains to a significant extent why contestations between rival root metaphors, say those of different religions, usually fight over symbolic areas. Ayodhya is just one of several instances. For example, in the sectarian clashes in Karnataka, the disputed site was an Idgah where the Hindus attempted to prevent the Muslims from saying their prayers. The case of Palestine is another illustration. Root metaphors stoutly refuse to live in the clouds or in the intellect. They demand that their regnant sets of meaning be realized in practice so that a site can be declared a cultural space.

Site, Space, Context

Space is not simply context either. Context is a predicament that affects both space and non-space, though not in the same way. The separation of space from context is not always easy to discern because it is generally assumed that nothing really changes so long as there is no great disjunction—the diasporic make-believe. When there are significant transformations in space, then cultural en-actments are thrown into considerable confusion. It may recall a vicarious space, which in this case will not be a land faraway but one that has just slipped away in time into the future.

When there are protracted periods of instability, space is replaced by a series of sites that are constantly being overwhelmed over time. A stable space does not develop. If, after these phillipics, stability returns, then, site gradually becomes space. Under these conditions it is also possible to nostalgically recall a vicarious space in the past when things were just so, as justifications for the present. This invention will not be a faithful copy of what actually existed, but what is convenient to recall. In which case then the original condition is constantly being reinvented as each site stabilizes into space. The original condition of a cultural enactment then is a sociological and historical one and should not be mistaken to be an absolute point at the core of an essentialized culture. The original space then is what the cultural performers think it is. Once again the merit of the aphorism 'don't think but look' pays dividends.

Among diasporics the movement from space to site is so dramatic that it is much easier to understand the analytical and empirical transition from space to site to space again. Thus for a certain period of time the Hindus in Trinidad might have recalled their respective villages in India as vicarious space while Trinidad only served as a site. Over time Trinidad became space in its own right as there were constant and repetitive accumulations of preferred vocalities and interpretations of root metaphors that were partial to the specifics of Trinidad. Space therefore is the constant attempt to overcome the transitoriness that exists in sites. This is also reflected in cultural enactments which pretend to give the impression of timelessness and would never accept its recent, let alone provisional, status. Space therefore attempts to escape the contingency invested in sites and contexts.

Cultures have to do with space and membership. Cultures are enacted in space by people who are in the know. It is impossible to think of culture without membership, but can we conceive of membership without space? Alumni gatherings are built on remembered space, diasporic unities on vicarious space, transhumance as among the Nuers on calendrical space, and so on. At each point space is not an empty abstraction but refers to some concrete enactments in geography. There are, however, certain memberships which do not have a strong sense of space. The culture of the stock market defies a concrete space. Tokyo, New York, London mean little except that share prices are rising and falling on gigantic monitors.

But are these locations not like sites with contextuality as an overt characteristic feature? In business and enterprise it is context that is predominant. One of the significant differences between *lex* and root metaphors is that the former has much greater agility in adapting to different contexts. These shifting contexts may be brought about by the rise and fall of interest rates, political uncertainty and even natural catastrophes. Thus while space tries to deny context in order to establish the suzerainty of its root metaphors, non-spaces acknowledge context in order to fashion interventions that would be most appropriate. This is contrary to Ramanujam's view that modernity is lack of context while tradition is bent over with it (Ramanujam 1990: 55). The reverse is probably more accurate. Space cannot yield to context without subjecting itself to a violent end. It must be supremely lofty and dismissive of all context-related pragmatics. Casuistry is usually a way out of a tight spot for root metaphors, and it is their polysemic attribute that allows them to do so with relative ease. To recast Ramanujam it would be better to say that modernity implies a relative lack of root metaphors, whereas in tradition it is root metaphors that abound.

Reliance on the stability of space is usually the hallmark of a declining enterprise in contemporary times. This is as much true of family concerns in India as it is of financial and industrial institutions in Indonesia, particularly under Suharto. In Quebec the same trend manifested itself but in a somewhat different fashion. As Jacques Brazeau points out, in the case of Quebec there were cultural factors involved that initially inhibited an immediate large-scale absorption of the Quebecois in the techno-managerial sectors of Quebec industry. With the growth of corporate enterprise the scope of communication changed 'from a regional to a national and even a continental basis (Brazeau 1964: 299). The rural Quebecois were still rather closely wedded to their root metaphors and their concomitant spaces to be able to operate on a 'continental scale'. Little wonder then that established renditions of root metaphors have to be eschewed and purposively kept out in context-driven business enterprises. When this is seen in conjunction with the fact that the rules of *lex* have to be backed up by, and be consistent with, supplementary norms (quite unlike root metaphors) it helps comprehend why factories, businesses, and bureaucracies do not excite membership commitments.

Root metaphors dominated family run business establishment in times of closed markets. In Mughal India the *karkhanas* (or manufactories) ran on lines established by feudal demands. The masters or owners of these *karkhanas* were not searching for profits in an enterprising capitalistic sense, but were making money in a closed economy protected by their feudal patrons. Obviously space emerged and with it a certain kind of 'business culture' that was characteristic of pre-capitalist societies. In such cultures space was an integral aspect of the cultural enactment. Memberships in traditional business communities of this sort did enliven space, whereas associations in stock markets or in modern factories do not. This is, of course, a pure type portrayal of non-spaces. Impurities can be kept out for the time being, but we will discuss them shortly.

Cultural Space and Geography

Space, as may have been noticed, is not a neutered geographical entity through which cultures pass in nomadic nonchalance. The very fact of enactment in a specific locale succeeds in culturalizing space such that space and culture act together to substantiate the root metaphors of a culture. When spaces include buildings, monuments, temples, memorials, the cultural factor becomes all too obvious. In fact these obvious cultural spaces connote larger and more inclusive cultural memberships. Even in medieval times temples signified a cultural zone of the Hindus. Alliances were often forged among Hindu chiefs and princes to protect these lands from Muslim occupation. The Sikh shrines in different parts of India make accessible the history and diacritics of Sikhism to the believer. The wailing wall for the Jews and Mecca for the Muslims are further examples of cultural space. Without these spaces neither Islam nor Judaism would be the same.

The reason these spaces are very important for respective cultural practice is because they are mnemonic of the total cultural space of which they are a part. In keeping with the fact that human beings everywhere are uncomfortable with fluidity and lack of fixity, there has always been a search for permanence. This striving for permanence is best expressed in root metaphors which is what mnemonic spaces hope to represent in a horizontal and syntagmatic fashion. In a concentrated, shorthand form they express most vividly the regnant interpretations of root metaphors specific to the space. To take the wailing wall away from Jerusalem and reconstruct it in lower east side New York, or to relocate the Sikh Golden Temple from Amritsar to Southall in London, will simply not do. Replicas can be transported to different sites but the original is a concentrated reminder of the founding space and its regnant interpretations of root metaphors. This is why temples and shrines recall these regnant interpretations sharply. As syntagmatic emblems they are just doing their job.

Desecration of these emblematic representatives of space also grieviously offends diasporic believers whose sites are still looking back to gain legitimacy. Once a site is established over a long term the original space may not be recalled with any degree of passion. The new sites now function as spaces. The Zoroastrian (or Parsee) community in India does not want to reclaim lands in Iran from where they originally came. Their space is now in India and more specifically in certain regions in western India. The Indian Christians, in most part, are not as closely linked to either the Church at Canterbury or to the Vatican. Those spaces mean little to them. The same cannot yet be said of Mecca or Varanasi, or the Golden Temple. But the future is always there to dissolve the certainties of today. In this sense, time can function as an effective despatializer. It cannot however remove the need for the coupling of space with culture.

The connection between time and space is important. If time is just the irreversible slipping away of seconds and minutes, then it is of little consequence. But if social transformations are taking place in time, then even the original space is threatened in terms of the regnant interpretations of root metaphors that had stabilized there. The pressure of changing circumstances and relations between people puts pressure on the regnant interpretations of a specific space and introduces a new materiality to culture. Perhaps the same root metaphors might remain but with a different set of interpretations. A new space will then have come into being. It is in the process of becoming that time shakes space, but once space re-establishes itself, time becomes a secondary feature and is blanched off its sociological referents.

Space, Time and Modernization

This allows a more acute understanding of what modernization does to space and therefore to culture. Modernization, as it is generally understood, is a rapid thermodynamic engine on hot rails. Consequently, time past becomes distinctly different from time present, and time future is already round the corner promising further transformations. These changes destabilize space even when geography remains stable. Modernization can also be characterized by an awareness of history as opposed to awareness of tradition. History is the rapid transformation of space by time and tradition is the re-assertion of space outside time. It is possible to recast Heidegger's notions of being and becoming in precisely these terms. Becoming is the consolidation of space while being is its destabilization by time.

In fact, as the engine of modernization gains in momentum and approaches advanced capitalism there is a superfluity of time (Augé 1995). Before one is fully aware of the circumstances of the present, the future is already upon us. Events become historical much before their 'time'. The Beatles are now history, so is Elvis Presley, the Emergency in India, and even Watergate. Time is always snapping at one's heels and running away with events. As events and relations are changing rapidly it is possible to look back and say, 'that was history, and that is now well behind'. In traditional societies the situation was quite different. Past and present merged such that no great discontinuities could be discerned. Even when invasions took place, or foreigners entered the domain of cultural space, once the situation stabilized, the older regnant interpretations of root metaphors often re-asserted themselves; or, at most, a new set of interpretations of the established root metaphors arose to take care of the new situation.

Myths, tales and folkloric songs are good examples of this. Levi-Strauss led the way when he said that myths are machines that suppress time. He should have perhaps gone on and said that this denial of time helped to preserve the sanctity of space. In India we find numerous instances of how the presence of the Muslims is incorporated into the Hindu mythic narrative structure with minimal change in the regnant interpretations of root metaphors. The Prophet Mohammed is on one occasion seen as another deity of the Hindu pantheon, and even the English are seen as continuations of earlier regimes of kingships (Gupta 1996: 154, 160).

With modernization things are not really allowed to settle. Some root metaphors lose their vivacity and powers to invoke regnant interpretations, and other root metaphors take their place and call out to different spaces. This is often seen as a species of cultural deracination. It however only appears that way because attention is often not paid to the root metaphors that are replacing the old ones, and the new culture spaces that these new root metaphors are enacting. The fears of being deracinated are highest among those who are self-consciously holding on to what is slipping away. In such circumstances there is a deliberate effort to remember and not to forget. Chances are that when put under this sort of strain the capacity to learn something new will also be limited (see Douglas 1995: 16).

Networks and connections of non-space have an in-built mobility that frightens the standard bearers of culture. The social intercourse of non-spaces can be built anywhere. The materiality of these connections do not come from the regnant interpretations of root metaphors but from norms that are in elective affinity with one another. Inter-subjectivity evolves around the internalization of these norms and not on passionate avowals of root metaphors and their regnant interpretations.

Regnant interpretations, as was emphasized earlier, require time to stabilize in order to establish space. Once locked into a set of regnant interpretations an estrangement from cultural space is very traumatic. On the other hand, if events move far too swiftly for regnant interpretations of root metaphors to stabilize, then estrangement from space has little consequence for the person. This is when the term 'deracinated' seems particularly appropriate, for now we have people who have no roots, and do not belong, as it were.

In order to appreciate why culture involves root metaphors which in turn invoke space, a quick look at contemporary American society might help. The hyphenated American, such as the German-American, the Anglo-American, the Polish-American, is a well-known and often quoted phenomenon. But it is really the American half (or the right side) of the hyphenated identity that rally root metaphors in any depth. Though no society presents the kind of futuristic deracination that was sketched in the earlier paragraph, the American case can be used to appreciate how awareness of one's heritage in hyphenated identities is not the same thing as cultural membership in space.

The American notion of heritage is very idiosyncratic. The latest census strategy there goes by the rubric 'self-identification'. Cultural background is no longer ascertained by actually verifying the backgrounds of parents and grandparents, but by asking the respondent's opinion on the subject. The respondent might choose to self-identify as Irish whereas there might only be one-sixteenth Irish in the person. Perhaps there is more Scandinavian in the blood stream, but it is really up to the respondent and there the matter ends as far as the census enumerator is concerned.

It is not as if those in charge of the census in America have capriciously introduced the strategy of 'self-identification'. The fact is that there was little else to do. Frequent migrations and inter-marriages have knocked the bottom out of cultural spaces and their situationally regnant interpretations of root metaphors (see Sanjek 1994). Today self-identified Italians, Belgians, Anglo-Saxons and Germans freely inter-marry. While they call themselves Germans or Finnish or even Italians, they have no longing to return to Germany or wherever, nor do they see those spaces as the original inspirations for their more localized sites. Germany or France is no longer vicarious space for them. Being of Belgian or French or Italian or German heritage has nothing to do with the actual Belgian or French or English living in their original homelands. For the hyphenated American it is a diacritic that means little in real terms for it leaves no impression on the space that they live in. Among the well-to-do it might probably occasion a vacation to where they originally came from, but they would go there as tourists and in all likelihood be rather relieved to get back home to America.

For the Afro-American, though, the situation is somewhat different. The American Black cannot identify with Africa either and does not want to be transported back to that continent. But while American Blacks too may have diverse blood streams, any self-identification with White blood ancestry would be both criticized by the Black community as a sell out, and laughed at by those outside as a desperate attempt to 'pass'. Blacks, rich or poor, have their racial identity in common, no matter if their skin colours are of different degrees of lightness (see Russel et al.). In spite of substantial Black economic mobility, Blacks continue to live in Black neighbourhoods, for that is where they feel accepted and at home (Sanjek 1994: 115). This is in spite of the fact that many of the upwardly mobile Blacks may believe that their destiny is not bound to the fortunes of the Black majority (Dawson 1994). White residential enclaves in the suburbs of America would generally be hesitant to accept Blacks in their midst.

The Afro-American can then never quite merge into White 'spaces'. To a significant extent this accounts for the distinctiveness of Black culture. This culture is constantly bolstered by its enactment in specific bounded locales (see Dawson 1995). These locales then become encultured spaces in which certain lifestyles, modes of interaction, conceptions of propriety and a distinct sense of identity and self-hood develop. For White Americans such distinctive spaces do not quite exist for which reason they are not so much conscious of being White, as being American. Their whiteness is heightened in their self-consciousness only when they enter Black neighbourhoods—into Black spaces. White areas which seemed like non-spaces suddenly become spaces when forced to interact across its established boundaries.

Conflict, Choices, Metaphors

Culture then is not just learned behaviour (see Kroeber 1967: 8, 252), but subscription to spatially enlivened root metaphors. This subscription is generally ascriptive in character, though it is possible for it to be adoptive as well. As the endorsement to root metaphors is generally ascriptive, it is not linked to efficiency, efficacy, or means-ends rationality. A root metaphor is therefore learned behaviour of a very special kind. This learned behaviour cannot do without an accompanying space. Material and physical entry to a certain encultured space begins the process of adoption and is the necessary condition for it.

To say space is to say encultured space. To say culture is to simul-taneously enunciate a space where certain meanings of root metaphors have become regnant. Thus to speak of culture as an analytical category is to say that root metaphors are enacted in space such that certain interpretations of them become regnant. Culture, therefore, cannot be seen independent of enactment, space, and the domination of certain meanings of root metaphors over others. It is possible to enact outside of space, as in teleconferences or in non-spaces. But as has already been discussed, interactions in non-spaces do not privilege root metaphors with their regnant meanings as they do institutional norms and rules. To repeat a point already clarified: institutional rules of procedure are not like root metaphors. Their polysemy is limited, but more importantly, unlike root metaphors, they do not stand alone but need other rules to back them up in elective affinity. In the case of the root metaphors of any culture it is difficult to always see any logical connection between them. They stand on their own and demand loyalty on the strength of their independent cathective powers.

The fact that root metaphors are not logically connected to one another—contrary to culture grammarians—allows for a degree of variation, even in pre-modern societies. As Mary Douglas once pointed out '...individual members of a culture hold very different views on cosmology' (Douglas 1978: 89). Variations exist the moment it is acknowledged that metaphors are involved. As metaphors allow multiple interpretations the possibility of conflict too is analytically implicated. As a culture is bound in practice by the overlapping subscription to discontinuous and separable root metaphors and their regnant sets of meanings, it is not possible to discern the lineaments of a culture by introspection, or on purely analytical grounds. It is only by looking at how enactments actually take place that cultural boundaries can be drawn after the fact. Hence the worthy Wittgensteinian aphorism: 'Don't think but look.' If these enactments give no room for the emergence of diverse meanings then we would not have root metaphors but largely procedural rules of behaviour in elective affinity. A disproportionate reliance on texts often yields a consistent story, but one that is also prone to caricatures. Such caricatured portrayals abound in anthropological works. In South Asian literature, for instance, it is not at all uncommon to find statements like the 'Indian "ego" is undeveloped', or that the Indian's 'grasp of reality is "relatively tenuous"' (see Ramanujam 1990: 46). Bourdieu's conception of *habitus* also encourages the tendency to typify cultures and see them as meaningful wholes. The dispositions that a certain habitus favours bring about conformity leaving little scope for dissensions and conflict (see Bourdieu 1977; see also Bidney 1953: 31).

Bourdieu's habitus and disposition are not the same thing as *interaction*, as we understand it. When interaction between individuals is emphasized the lack of concordance at the cultural level cannot but come through clearly in demonstrable fieldwork conditions. This counters the drift towards typifying cultures, for too many inconsistencies come to the surface when interactions are focussed upon. This is why root metaphors are useful. They can account for dissensions and multivocality through the variety of regnant meanings attached to them. This allows communication to take place without a unified and consonant set of meanings. Behaviour, habitus and cultural capital by themselves are unable to accommodate this very essential characteristic of culture, viz., the ability to discourse and disagree.

The fact that we are in the realm of metaphors when we discuss culture effectively means that we cannot seal off the factor of conflict in the emergence of a regnant set of meanings. The element of conflict can be illustrated even by taking one of the most inflexible institutions known to society, viz., the caste system. If the notion of purity and pollution as the basis for status marking were not a root metaphor, then any attack against the status of a particular caste could only be launched by denying the validity of the purity-pollution metaphor altogether.

This is however very rarely the case. In most of the known anti-Brahmin movements, for example, it is not as if the caste system was being attacked, but rather the supremacy of the Brahmin was being denied. Even in the case of lower caste mobilizations, different interpretations are provided of the root metaphors, but they do not always deny the subscription to the principles of purity and pollution. In other words the emergence of 'untouchability among the untouchables' (Desai 1976) as a social reality can only be possible once the polysemic character of root metaphors is taken into account.

The element of conflict which resides in the root metaphor of purity and pollution also allows for the emergence of horizontal solidarity between castes for political purposes. The castes that thus come together may not still eat with one another, let alone confront the question of inter-marrying, yet they activate the caste metaphor as a justification for their alliance. Agrarian castes can come together with non-agrarian castes against other agrarian castes as in Gujarat; powerful landed castes can align with Muslims as in west Uttar Pradesh; different artisan castes can make common cause with non-artisans as witnessed in the assembly of the Telis (oil pressers) of Orissa; or a section of the so-called untouchables link with the landed castes against other so-called untouchables as in Marathwada in Maharashtra and Belchi in Bihar. In all such cases it has been the caste metaphor that has been actively used to cement such alliances. The contemporary unity between the so-called 'Backward Castes' brought about by the Mandal Commission recommendations is yet another example of the manner in which multiple meanings can be teased out of the caste metaphor. Once again there is a grand political alliance between castes who, on other occasions, think very poorly of their allies, would not marry into their families, and not even share the hookah (a standing swivel pipe) with them.

The regnant meanings of root metaphors become active in all these cases in a defined interactional setting or space. It is difficult then to think of culture simply as an intellectual or philosophical phenomenon with enactments playing little or no role at all. This is why the standard distinction between text and context is so important. Text is inadequate for two reasons. First, it generally favours a single interpretation of a root metaphor and is ignorant, often intolerant, of the other meanings a metaphor acquires in enactment. Second, a text is not space bound. It can be transported across space like an artifact.

When a text, like a medical text, becomes an important aspect of cultural space, it is because the text also informs on matters relating to who is a good doctor, what backgrounds do good doctors come from. The regimen in medical texts are also about how to lead a healthy life, what foods to consume, hygienic considerations, and so forth. But these are adhered to because of the charisma of the doctor or the author of the text. All this is true when a text (such as a medical one) is infused with root metaphors. What makes a medical text cultural is the manner in which doctors and patients are designated, and how they interact with each other. This last aspect is where the root metaphors are most active. The same treatment, or therapeutic regimen, without an acceptance of the role of the patient and doctor, would make the text a mobile piece of artifact. This would imply that a patient grounded in root metaphors of a certain kind, of which the medical text is a part, would be loath to treatment being offered by an alien doctor no matter how closely that doctor may have mastered the medical texts. When no such hesitation exists then we can say that the medical text has now become an artifact. Ayurvedic, Unani, and Chung-I drugs can be produced anywhere in the world and administered by anyone. Those who take recourse to such nostrums without paying too much heed to the root metaphors that originally accompanied them and gave them credibility, do not often realize how far they have moved away from the original space. Medical texts thus become artifacts cleansed of root metaphors which insist on how inter-relations between people should take place, in this case, at a *minimum*, between the doctor and patient.

It is not surprising therefore that the pressures on western medicine to develop into pure non-space technology are resisted by the root metaphors in different societies of how doctors and patients should interact. Western medicine is criticized for its excessive technological dependence primarily because this runs counter to the root metaphors that still uphold a certain kind of doctor-patient relationship. The fact that this quality of interaction may not be necessary now is not seriously considered. The bedside skills of the doctor, the doctor's moral character, and, in traditional India, the caste and sex of the doctor, are elements that matter. The protocol of medical investigation is not free of root metaphorical considerations either. The manner in which women should be examined is different from the way men are. This often extends further into a diversification based on status and ascriptive background. A medical text is not knowledge free of root metaphorical considerations for they embed themselves into it. For the same reason, and from a different angle of vision, when medical texts are sublated of root metaphorical concerns they no longer attach themselves to particular cultural spaces. Deracinated thus they are free to roam the world, and join the association of artifacts and artificers.

Culture Against Artifacts

Artifacts include not just texts, but also dress, culinary preparations, and even literary styles. In a manner of speaking they can all be seen as texts of different sorts. A pure textual analysis is typically unconcerned with practice and social relations (see for example Schnudson's critique in Schnudson 1997). It is instead more interested in internal evaluations of the texts. These diverse texts are often viewed as cultural elements which is why there is so much imprecision in the understanding of culture and in the manner in which notions of cultural hybridity are formulated.

A little reflection will tell us that dress, food, and other popular markers of culture need not be spatially limited. There are Indian restaurants in London, and there are Pushkin lovers in Calcutta. Clothing styles of diverse provenances can be found in different parts of the world. It is not as if there is no cathectivity involved in these aesthetic preferences. A lot of affect goes into them yet they are not culture in themselves but artifacts because defined encultured spaces are not essential for their production and reproduction.

While culture is deeply committed to space, artifacts are not. They are notoriously promiscuous and can freely roam diverse locales. As they are free agents they are liable to fall in with other metaphors elsewhere in other spaces. Instinctively there are bound to be some misgivings in not granting artifacts the status of culture. It does offend popular conceptions, no doubt. After all clothing styles, eating habits and preferences, the appreciation of certain texts and literary styles are often considered to be the hallmarks of culture. David Bidney put it rather well over four decades ago when he said that 'no inventions or culture-objects *per se* are constituents of culture' (Bidney 1953: 27). According to Bidney:

Artifacts, 'socifacts' and 'mentifacts' are, so to speak, 'cultural capital' [notice the term—D.G.], the surplus which results from cultural life, but in themselves and apart from their relation to the adherents of a given culture they are not primary or constituent elements in social life (ibid.).

This instantly provides us with a clue as to where one goes wrong in identifying culture too closely with artifacts. Take the question of temples and churches. Another building can be built to look exactly like any important temple or church without it being the actual space of social interaction. Unless this now becomes the site (recall our earlier distinction between site and space) for a new set of social relations, the sheer fact of the building or edifice itself will have little in common, culturally speaking, with the original. Then too, as was mentioned earlier, the original space needs to be vicariously recalled till this site becomes space in its own right. In fact, an existing temple can be taken down brick by brick and transported elsewhere and still would not arouse the awe and reverence that it did in its original space. So the materiality of culture is not gross matter—stones, cement, spires, clothes, spices. The materiality of culture does not come from 'matter' in the most obvious sense, as it does from the actual social interactions through the medium of root metaphors.

In the process of this interaction artifacts enter into the picture in order to realize regnant meanings of root metaphors. Clothing styles distinguish the rich from the poor, the upper castes from the lower castes, the landed classes from the others, and so on. Culinary practices also do the same, so do the appreciation of different types of literature, art, music, etc. While these artifacts are used to illustrate diverse meanings of root metaphors they are not root metaphors themselves. This is why it is often the case that the items that go into class distinctions change but the distinctions continue to remain, and so do the root metaphors through which they are justified and enacted. Raymond Williams made a similar point when he said that '(t)he strongest barrier to the recognition of human cultural activity is this immediate and regular conversion of experience into finished products...into formed wholes rather than forming and formative' (Williams 1977: 128–29).

It would not do either to emphasize artifacts and interactions (not behaviour) at the same time. This is what Clyde Kluckhonn did when he said that culture was equally a 'humble cooking pot' or a 'Beethoven sonet' (Kluckhohn 1962: 20), as much as it was 'interaction between two pairs of human beings (man-child, husband-wife)...' (ibid.: 23). In his piece 'The Concept of Culture' which conjures a discussion among intellectuals (anthropologists heavily represented), culture comes across as pots and pans, cutlery and crockery, sonatas, learned behaviour, knowledge and 'socially valued habits' (ibid.: 23–26). Such conceptions of culture played a significant role at a time when anthropologists were fighting racism on the one hand, and at the same time striving to establish their discipline as something that cannot be reduced to psychology or history. But such concerns are no longer as engaging to the contemporary mind as much of anthropology and sociology has accepted the limitations of racist and biological explanations. Second, anthropology and sociology are more confident today of their intellectual legacy than was the position till about the forties.

The banding together of interactions, habits, behaviour and artifacts should also have been a period phenomena and not continued late into this century. Today the movement of artifacts across spaces is so commonplace that it forces a conceptual distinction between the 'humble cooking pot' and ways of interaction. The English middle class today affects a French culinary style, even eats salad after dinner like the French do. French wines have displaced liquors, such as rye, scotch and bourbon in many American homes as well. French television, on the other hand, is dominated by American serials, and popular music in France, whether Black or White, bears an extraordinary resemblance to American pop genres. If cultures were artifacts, then the globe is one, but this is still far from true. When culture is a carryall that comprises, in equal measure, interaction and artifacts, then the thrust not only gets diluted, but also misdirected.

Till recently the Bharat Natyam dance of India was something that was performed by low status and low caste temple dancers, or Devadasis. With some modifications of nuance and a major transformation of costume, the same dance is now something that upper caste south Indian women learn as a matter of acquiring basic marriageable qualifications. Even 50 years back a sign of being upper class in some circles was to practice vegetarianism and in being teetotallers. In many of the same families today things have changed so much that these taboos are no longer in effect.

Class distinctions, however, still remain but the manner in which they are semaphored have changed. In instances such as the ones just mentioned, the same item, or artifact can be used in one case as a sign of superiority, and on other occasions may have no such connotations at all.

When artifacts enter into the marking of status distinctions, or in other forms of social relations, then they get a certain spatiality. But this spatiality is on account of the social relations and not on account of the artifacts. In some parts of India only upper castes wore turbans. Subservient castes were allowed to wear a head cloth, but nothing more elaborate. This distinction of turban versus head cloth is now no longer that relevant. During India's Independence movement hand woven cloth and the Gandhi cloth cap were supposed to signify anti-Imperialism and partisanship with the nationalist cause. These items are still in use but carry no such significance (see Tarlo 1996: 11–16). Artifacts thus represent matter and not materiality the way social interactions do. Certain artifacts gain cultural salience when they give meaning to root metaphors in social interaction; they gain a certain cultural salience which is purely episodic and extrinsic in character. Once these elements are not required in the same way they can be preserved as *objet d'art*, or as museum exhibits, and they will arouse a different kind of interest altogether. This is why artifacts are capable of being freed of space and becoming geographically mobile.

A silk Kancheepuram sari can be worn by a western woman in New York and it will still be such a sari. In Tamil Nadu, however, it used to signify, till quite recently, upper caste status. Anybody can enjoy Indian food in London, or a dance performance, or the Vedic texts in Paris or New York. They have a completely different salience there because in these other spaces they are used to denote different things. Perhaps the donning of a sari, or listening to Carnatic music, or reading the Vedas is a sign of a kind of cosmopolitanism which has very little to do with the various meanings realized with the root metaphors of Hinduism in India. Or take Peter Mayle's much read *Tojours Provence*. This book is not so much about provencial food in South France as it is about 'humble patrons and peasant-like cafe owners' (James 1996: 87). Allison James contrasts this with 'global food' that 'vicariously imagines America' (ibid.: 82), wiping out the consideration of cultural space.

Clothes, food, music and literary appreciation thus have different resonances in different spaces and in that sense can be 'neutral' to root metaphors.

On occasions the adoption of 'artifacts' can lead to peculiar, and from a certain perspective, even hilarious consequences. John and Jean Comaroff record the manner in which the Tswana people of South Africa donned European clothes. A man would wear a jacket with one sleeve for he had probably run out of material, or he could even have sleeves of different colours. Or a person would have pants on 'big enough to contain all the furniture in the wearer's house' (see Comaroff and Comaroff 1991: 241). Obviously this upset the European colonizers and missionaries and they blamed native susceptibility to disease on their partial adoption of western clothes (ibid.: 243). It was very much later, write the Comaroffs, when European dress and comportment 'pervaded the public sector, laying out an aesthetic of civility and an order of values that positioned whole populations in a "hierarchical socioscape"' (ibid.: 267).

Once culture is clearly separated from artifacts it brings about a critical enrichment of Pierre Bourdieu's conception of cultural capital as elaborated in his essay 'Forms of Capital' (Bourdieu 1985b: 243; see also Bourdieu 1984). A close examination of the three forms of cultural capital (embodied, objectified, and institutional) reveals Bourdieu's tendency to lump artifacts and culture together. The embodied form of cultural capital is about long lasting dispositions. This would include tastes, deportment, and so forth. This is truly the cultural level for it is here that interactions are necessary and these interactions take place along root metaphors. These root metaphors dictate how to pursue a 'good life' in terms of manners, dispositions and habits that are to be cultivated to *separate* oneself from others who do not lead that kind of 'good life' (see Bourdieu 1984: 56). But objectified and institutional capital are of a different order and do not immediately signify interaction. Objectified capital includes artifacts like books, instruments and machines. Institutionalized capital refers to educational credentials which are standardized. In these latter forms of cultural capital there is no emphasis on space and enactment. The apparent stolidity of objectified and institutional capital can be overcome by viewing them in an interactive sense too. That is, rather than being awed by the 'thing', the 'artifact', it is more relevant to see how these artifacts are employed by root metaphors in interactional settings. What is cultural capital in France will not be the same elsewhere in the world. This is why it is important to understand cultural capital along with social capital for it is through the latter that interactions and social networks can be highlighted (Bourdieu 1985b: 251).

In Bourdieu's earlier work *Distinctions* culture is more blatantly acquisition, consumption, style, taste, with little emphasis on the interactive dimension. This is what allows Bourdieu to say that some have low culture and others high, and only a few are culturally 'pedigreed' (Bourdieu 1984: 63). To deny culture to large sections of society, and to evaluate culture as high or low, rich and parlous, is in line with popular middle-class prejudice that equates culture with artifacts. Culture cannot be understood in a parcelized or in an hierarchical fashion. Cultures can be contentious, but it would be an abomination to speak in terms of 'more' or 'less' when discussing culture. In other words, there is no alternative other than to see culture in terms of interaction through root metaphors.

Thus while we can say that there are various categories of cultural capital, it is necessary to immediately add that the items that go into each vary a great deal depending upon the root metaphors of different cultures, along with their regnant sets of meanings. Deportment, table manners, choice of friends, the use of certain instruments, and institutional recognitions all vary from culture to culture. What is prized in one culture is not in another, and in fact may be positively abhorred.

We can now see a curious analogy between geography, text and artifact. A point in geography is not space till it is encultured by enactments of root metaphors. The same geographical conditions can be found in different locales but that would not be the same space in different cases. Kerala and Bengal both lie by the sea and yet in terms of space, they are quite distinct. Srinagar in India shares many climatic and topographical features with the Alps, but the spaces are different. Likewise, food, clothes and artifacts mean different things in different spaces. A text too, it is often said, can be read in different contexts, or, as puritans are known to complain, out of context.

Limits of Hybridization: From Site to Space

As long as practices such as wearing a sari or cooking a curry are not significant in semaphoring interactionally regnant meanings of root metaphors they can be considered as acultural aesthetic choices. It is therefore easy for a Aggarwal Hindu, or a Jain to eat meat, or for Indian women to wear western clothes, once they leave the space where both slacks and meat eating carry pejorative connotations. Being a Hindu woman in America, or an enterprising Aggarwal in England enlivens different sets of meanings of the root metaphors of Hinduism. These are common enough occurrences and they are often considered to be outcomes of cultural hybridization (see Gupta and Ferguson 1992: 7). If we separate artifacts from culture, and site from space, then it is possible to understand such phenomena in more dynamic terms than what the concept of 'hybridization' allows us to.

Hybridization conceals the fact that the observer is partial to one set of regnant meanings that root metaphors have acquired in space, and further to the association of artifacts with what they are supposed to originally signify. The fact that the same root metaphors can have different meanings, or that the same meanings can be manifested through different artifacts is not quite entertained in this perspective.

Root metaphors when transplanted struggle for survival in alien, perhaps even hostile, surroundings. They cope by recalling vicarious space, but the reality of the site they are in now compels them to search for new meanings in their root metaphors and even to adopt new metaphors. The extent to which the host culture (including space) accommodates the new culture (with its vicarious space) will determine the length of memory for the vicarious space and the need to draw fresh meanings from its root metaphors. Closure of spaces, like non-accessibility (whether supported by law or not) to clubs, restaurants, voting booths, universities, or certain kinds of jobs, will result in placing the root metaphors and its vicarious space in a hostile relationship with the host culture and its spaces. In this face off the root metaphors of the diaspora peoples will obviously develop newer meanings, or at least meanings that are no longer significant in the original space. Consequently, the artifacts used to signal these meanings may be quite different too. At any rate the trajectory that the transplanted root metaphors have embarked upon, is not a hybrid, but the gradual and deliberate attempts to *consolidate site into space*. In this process not only are new meanings of root metaphors generated, but they are semaphored by a different set of articles than what are easily visible and available in the original space.

To take the argument further, it is also worth noticing that the observer who relies on the notion of hybridization also suffers from fallacies similar to the believer in witchcraft who mistakes the metonymic for the metaphoric. In voodoo, magic spells are cast on a person by subjecting the person's hair, nails or items of clothing to violence, such as by sticking pins into them, or by burning them, in the belief that the real person, wherever that person might be, is going through the same process of becoming either a pin cushion or a charred piece of ember. Likewise, it is only by mistaking artifacts for culture that the term hybridization can be sustained. The fact that alternative sets of artifacts are being used, or that artifacts of different original spaces are being employed, does not mean that the culture that they are lending their gross matter to is hybrid. Instead of hybridization attention should be paid to how site gradually legitimizes itself into space.

The notion hybridization conceals a variety of possibilities. For instance, the same root metaphors may now employ different ingredients for their realization. This is usually what first generation diasporics go through. Thus marriage ceremonies and other significant rites of passage are conducted in the host countries with substitutes for what would have been the real ingredients at home. The priest may be a colleague in the office, the temple may be the town hall rented after hours. Even the festivities may appear to be distant from the way they are conducted at home. But there is still a strong underlying similarity. Very often Hindu marriages in North America or England culminate with disco dancing. While this may seem a departure from traditional culture, the fact is that it is just the physical movements that are western, and little else. The parents are still around making sure that their children, particularly, their daughters, on the dance floor are abiding by traditional norms of propriety regarding inter-sexual contact. Thus the adherence to root metaphors which govern relations between the sexes is still very much in place even while swaying to the beat of western popular music.

Hybridization also darkens from view the possibility that the root metaphor may now encourage a set of meanings that never really found expression earlier. Caste loyalties still remain among diasporic communities without the usual restrictions on commensality and inter-dining. Marriages between castes are still not favoured, though economic and other social interactions are not governed by caste norms. Incidentally, this tendency is found even in urban India today.

There is a third possibility. This can be understood in terms of switching between root metaphors of diverse origins and provenances. Thus there is one set of metaphors adhered to at home and another set in the work place. This variety too can be found in urban/modern sectors in India but is most strongly visible and felt by diasporics. In a sense, all cultures are hybrids of one sort or the other. No culture lives in isolation for there is a great degree of overlap in the spaces enlivened by root metaphors. To use the term hybridization to refer particularly to diasporics, gives the impression that cultural boundaries are firm and unambiguously drawn at home. As cultures are always in the process of transformation, the pace may be slow or fast depending on their material surroundings, it is more fruitful instead to scrutinize how a 'site' gradually legitimizes itself into 'space'.

Indeed, it is equally essential to pay attention to how vicarious space is pressured into *becoming* a site till it re-establishes itself into *being* space once again, albeit of a different sort. Though this dialectic is constantly at work, the results are not always dramatic and easily discernible. This is what makes the 'being' of a certain cultural space apply inertia on the 'becoming' of a site. Cultural spaces act as brakes through the medium of the root metaphors which are hard to replace as they carry such cathectivity. They slow down the process of new space formations by first secreting other sets of regnant meanings. It is only when the site has deviated significantly from its original space that the root metaphors finally yield their grip to new root metaphors with their regnant sets of interpretations. Rapid urbanization often creates situations of this kind. A new urban space may develop in the same region where a non-urban space thrived, and with perhaps the same people too. The pressure that the original space was put to was because the nature of interaction between its members underwent rapid transformations. Raymond Williams' *The Country and the City* (1973) is a brilliant illustration of this phenomenon. The longing for the good old days of one's youth is also a yearning for a return of the certitudes of root metaphors that have since become ineffective, and have been bypassed either by other root metaphors or by the compendium called *lex*.

Root Metaphors and Political Ideologies

One last point before we move on to the next chapter. In many ways root metaphors are akin to political ideologies. Indeed, the ideologies of racism, fundamentalism, and casteism draw directly from root metaphors. One might also say that the ideology of democracy rests heavily on the root metaphor of individualism, or egalitarianism, without being identical with them. When political ideologies have inspirations of this kind they arouse a great degree of commitment and people are often willing to die for them. Max Weber in his classic essay, 'Politics as a Vocation' (Weber 1948: 120) distinguished between politics of commitment (which we believe draws on root metaphors), and politics of responsibility (which is rationally arrived at). Therefore, not all political ideologies have root metaphors at their base. Some may even consciously shun them, such as in the politics of economism. This latter kind of politics does not arouse people to lay down their lives for it as the politics of commitment does.

There are other distinctions too between political ideologies and root metaphors. These are not easy to draw as a root metaphor with its regnant set of meanings is also akin to ideology as it has practical and interactive consequences. A root metaphor is also political in so much as it distinguishes, separates, and hierarchizes people. What then distinguishes a political ideology from a root metaphor is the contextual element. A political ideology is primarily contextual, at certain times it has an appeal, and at other times it may not. Hindus in post-Partition Delhi were deeply antagonistic to the Muslims and yet found the secular Congress party a better option than the Hindu right wing organizations that harped on hatred towards the Muslims (see Gupta 1996: 25 ff.). Subscription to the Congress did not in any way undermine their attachment to the root metaphors of Hinduism which they pursued in other walks of life.

A political ideology is largely dependent on context for its salience, whereas root metaphors are not context sensitive in the same way. This is why root metaphors need to ballast themselves in multiple levels of social life, from birth to marriage to death. Political ideologies have a more defined focus and are, therefore, condemned to ride the waves of contextual ebbs and flows. No doubt political ideologies, especially the triumphant ones, affect root metaphors, as root metaphors affect political ideologies. Even so they are conceptually and empirically separate and separable. As political ideologies are focussed on capturing the public instruments of physical coercion they tend to become ineffective when handling issues within families, neighbourhoods, religious denominations, and between friends. In these large regions of social life root metaphors are more evident than political ideologies are. This is in spite of the fact that there is power play within families, religious denominations, and so on. But the concern in such instances is not with appropriating the weapons of physical coercion. If a root metaphor has to depend on physical coercion to win over its adherents then it is not a root metaphor at all. Physical coercion is often used to enforce one set of root metaphors over others, but not internally. If that was the case then there would be no root metaphors at all. This is why though politics and root metaphors inter-weave, political ideologies, as such, are distinct from root metaphors.

Chapter III

Root Metaphors and Regnant Sets of Meaning

Root Metaphors, Social Order and Conflict

A closer look at root metaphors reveals that all of them have to do with the establishment of a moral social order. In most contemporary societies this order is brought about through the enforcement of the principles of hierarchy and separation. A moral social order at the root metaphor level is concerned with notions like what is a *good life*, how is it to be led, what is just and unjust, and most importantly, how all of this is to be realized in social interactions. The conception of the good life is thus intimately associated with relations with other people in society. This good life is not something in the abstract, but is spelt out in concrete terms. The 'this worldly' aspect of root metaphors may often be concealed by appeals to a higher authority, but that should not deflect our attention from the fact that this higher authority is invoked with reference to matters on the ground. In spelling out the conception of a good life, it is necessary to detail the kinds of social interactions that are in keeping with moral probity, justice, and so forth. What makes a root metaphor different from abstract and lofty moralizing is detailed in operational terms. Root metaphors are not solipsistic but recommend a set of 'this worldly' norms which are principally interactive in character. Each of these aspects of a good life are signified through root metaphors with their regnant sets of meanings. It is through these meanings, often at variance with one another, that root metaphors spread their influence over diverse sectors of social life, and appeal to different sections of the population.

That cultures can be apprehended through root metaphors should not be interpreted to mean that root metaphors are always unifying in their scope. Very often cultural metaphors, including those of religion, are considered as instances of social unanimity. To view culture, or religion, as being homogenous or leading to homogeneity is reading too much into Durkheim's *The Elementary Forms of Religious Life* (Durkheim 1912). There is no doubt that Durkheim favoured such an explanation. What should be retained and defended in Durkheim's work on religion is the way symbolic memberships are arrived at. Durkheim, however, saw this symbolic relationship in a far too uncomplicated way. Probably his case studies from afar of communities like the Arunta led to this simplification.

In all fairness, the burden of consensus in examining culture is not limited to anthropologists with an overt Durkheimian inclination. Jurgen Habermas' detailed examination of communicative action is not free from this bias either. According to Habermas participants in communicative action act within a common cultural tradition (Habermas 1985, vol. 2: 208). His definition of culture is along similar lines for he calls it 'a stock of knowledge from which participants supply themselves with meanings' (ibid.: 138). This is why for Habermas socially integrative and expressive functions which 'were at first fulfilled by ritual practice pass over to communicative action; the authority of the holy is gradually replaced by the authority of an achieved consensus' (ibid.: 77). Likewise, a society for him consists of 'legitimate orders through which participants regulate their memberships in social groups and thereby secure solidarity' (ibid.). This is probably his most Durkheimian statement on the subject.

In this chapter we will present a view of culture that is participatory, that communicates, that is enacted, but is not one that is premised on consensus. It therefore leaves open the question of legitimacy as it allows for the co-existence of several complexes of root metaphors with different sets of regnant meanings. This implies that there is no necessary grammatical coherence about culture. Legitimacy is then a question of power and the assertion of one set of meanings over others. Legitimacy, in the Weberian sense, or in the sense Habermas understands it, dissolves these internal contradictions in culture. Without appreciating these differences neither cultural dynamism nor cultural stasis can be properly understood. As we shall try and demonstrate, root metaphors and their regnant sets of meanings allow us to appreciate conflict while there is communication. Root metaphors also provide the basic justification for cathectivity and affect to characterize culture. Further, as metaphors can be understood, interpreted and acted upon by those in the know of what these metaphors signify, they also connote membership and with that social space.

The difficulty lies in the way symbols are generally understood in the studies of culture. The cross is supposed to symbolize Christianity, the hammer and sickle communism. In each case the symbol arouses deep passions and a flood of meanings (see Barthes 1983: 10–11). Yet in the understanding of symbols it is never boldly emphasized that the same symbol can have different and often contrary meanings. It is for this reason that the understanding of religion through symbols is prejudiced in favour of a unified set of members with clear boundaries. Fredrik Barth's treatment of ethnic boundaries is of this kind. In his view ethnic boundaries are rather unproblematically maintained by 'signalling membership and exclusion' (Barth 1981: 204).

Given the general tendency to view symbols in this fashion, the term metaphor is much more appropriate if the effort is to accommodate diversity of meanings, and a problematic membership. The usage of metaphor instead of symbol is primarily to emphasize the existence of alternate and conflicting meanings that symbols often sublate. Otherwise a symbol too is connotative, like a metaphor, and would have done just as well for our purpose. But, by using root metaphor instead of symbol it becomes much more convenient to drive home the point that subscription to a root metaphor does not by itself lead to a situation of homogeneity within. Cultural boundaries in this case get harder to draw as diverse meanings are given to certain root metaphors. In addition, any given population lives on a variety of root metaphors. This leads to cross-cutting memberships.

In each case, if the root metaphor is to have resonance, then the regnant set of meanings that the metaphor generates should be known to members of the culture. Knowledge of the other meanings in the regnant set does not mean subscription to it. The awareness is important because it is reflected in the way people behave with one another (see also Kleinmann and Kleinmann 1991: 279). It is not that the awareness is always equal, or symmetrical. The extent of mutual awareness is a function of power. The White population of America may not be fully aware of how the non-White Americans look at individualism or Christianity. Likewise, the so-called upper caste Hindus could be equally ill informed about how the poor and depressed castes look at purity and pollution. What binds these subaltern people to the elite and affluent members is their common subscription to certain root metaphors even though the meanings that these metaphors receive at different ends may be quite different (see also Dirks 1994). Further, for them to relate to each other in practice, some awareness of the alternatives within the regnant sets of meanings is necessary if only for the purposes of maintaining control.

At this point a further clarification is required. Awareness of other meanings of a metaphor could be partial, incomplete and even incorrect. Yet the fact that there are other possible meanings is never quite ignored, though never fully appreciated. Subaltern and marginal people might conceal the meanings they give to root metaphors and keep these meanings to themselves, yet, they exhibit them from time to time, often in a disruptive fashion. Peasant rebellions, jacqueries, caste clashes and race riots are spectacular demonstrations of alternate meanings. Not only do different root metaphors clash against one another, but so also do different meanings given to the same metaphors by different sections of the population. There are sufficient instances of what can be called inverse racism and inverse casteism to demonstrate that the same ideology can be used at either end of the social scale. Peasant movements and jacqueries very often do not question the moral economy of the pre-modern agrarian world but resent the actual personages in despotic positions. It is for this reason that Marx believed that a working class movement under working class leadership would in all likelihood degenerate into a petty bourgeois movement.

There could also be more quiescent manifestations of meanings of root metaphors in literature, art, folk songs, popular tales, and so forth. Though the superior classes may pretend complete ignorance of the alternate meanings given to root metaphors by the subaltern and marginal people, they must take these into account in moments of tension if not in times of quiescence. Even in some of the more blatant cases of resistance and revolts, certain root metaphors remain in place. This should act as a corrective to James Scott's exaltation of everyday resistance (Scott 1985). The fact that alternate meanings are given to the same root metaphor does not challenge the metaphor, but may challenge the other meanings of it, along with those who hold them. Most importantly, as we mentioned earlier with Paul Ricoeur's help, a *root metaphor cannot stray too far away from its most literal meaning*. This is ultimately what makes communication possible in spite of disagreement. This also inhibits the range of a rebellion or a movement of political resistance. Revolts functioning within the ambit of a ruling set of root metaphors would be of a different order from those in which there is an unambiguous shift from one set of root metaphors to an altogether different set.

This is why it is important to emphasize that culture is a matter of power. Through culture and rituals, relations of super-ordination and subordination, distance and proximity, are manifested, albeit in a sublimated form. Rituals are also used to 'express oppositional political values and structures' (Dirks 1994: 487). This is what makes it even more difficult to live in cultural solitudes. As long as culture is understood primarily in terms of its unifying features its political aspect can be ignored. One need not necessarily be a conscious Durkheimian to do this. As Edmund Leach also complained, definitions of culture generally assume homogeneity for they emphasize learned behaviour, or sharing the same broad general beliefs, or simply a system of symbols and meanings (Leach 1982: 43). All such definitions, according to Leach, assume a homogeneous and unstratified society. This traditional anthropological bias comes through even in many modern understandings of culture.

If cultures are understood *via* metaphors then the all too ready predisposition to see cultures as if they should always 'operate in a manner acceptable to its members' (as in Geertz 1984: 11–12) is questioned. This is where Turner (1964) scores over scholars like Geertz. Nevertheless Turner's use of *root metaphor* (Turner 1974: 26) needs to be deliberately elaborated upon if it is to apply to cultural spaces more complex in their inter-relationship than among the Ndembu. In societies that are internally stratified and differentiated, the political aspect is uppermost in the level of culture. This political element in culture is better captured through the use of the term 'root metaphors' for, once again the emphasis is on alternative and contested meanings. These meanings are generated from actual experience. The fact that the same root metaphor is pressured to be so prolific, heightens our awareness of the divisive and fractitious nature of social relationships on the ground.

Individualism as Root Metaphor: Superstardom versus Success

Individualism as in America would assert that a good life is one where individuals are able to realize themselves. This value is prized above all else. Individualism as a root metaphor is not quite the same as the individualism that emerges in some renditions of liberal philosophy. In the case of the root metaphor of individualism the individual is supreme. According to this metaphor, America is for the intrepid who can fight desolation, savages, and superstition to win a continent. An American is a person who is self-supporting and self-sufficient. An American is entitled to own a gun for that is how the west was won and that is how this victory can stay consolidated. In America too, there is a great display of religious individualism. This may not be a recent phenomenon for many trace this tendency to Roger Williams and Anne Hutchinson who challenged the Puritan establishment in Massachusetts as early as the 1630s (see Bellah et al.1985).

One indication of the way the individual is held in high esteem can be gauged from the way Americans consciously exalt 'rags to riches' biographies. This is quite in contrast to the European situation where a lot of stock is still set by family connections, especially when these connections have to do with wealth and nobility. The rags to riches syndrome is reflected in other spheres of American life as well. There is an undisguised distaste for ceremony, and also for social manners that defer to status privileges. The belief that individuals can make it on their own by sheer grit, determination and hard work is reflected in their legislative acts, judicial precepts, and in the way the Americans, as a people, are generally suspicious of programmes such as those of affirmative action.

Casual attire as fashion, consumerism, fast food, making of sport superstars, and the innovations in the Hollywood film industry, all demonstrate, in one form or the other, the regnant sets of meanings in America that are derived from the root metaphor of individual freedom. The fact that rags to riches stories are prized lores is just an instance of the pervasiveness of this metaphor. The difference between America and European countries, such as England and France, can be gauged from the way Europe is still not quite swayed by the individualist metaphor prevalent in America.

The regnant meanings given to individualism in America favour members of a certain class, no doubt (see Tamir 1993: 143), but it is not as if the root metaphor of individualism is subscribed only by that class. Even though they are members of the under class, American Blacks too are deeply moved by the metaphor of individualism, but they often give it a meaning that is different from the ones the Whites give. For the Blacks individualism would be manifested in sport and music, and not necessarily in the fields of high finance or industrial enterprise. As both music and sport are open to people who must have pure talent, before they can be trained to be superstars, individualism among American Blacks is expressed in fields that do not require intellectual training as much as pure talent (see Peery 1994).

Even in these fields, Blacks tend to excel in those areas where pre-training is a negligible requirement. There are therefore very few Blacks in professional ice hockey, for here it is essential to learn how to skate before the basics of the game can even begin. Likewise, in music Blacks are rarely ever violinists, but are horn players, pianists and guitarists. These instruments can be self-taught. The meaning that individualism receives in these circumstances is different from the meaning it gets in more literary or moneyed contexts. As Blacks must depend on sheer talent to enable them to realize the metaphor of freedom, the manner in which this metaphor is expressed is not very respectful of established styles, and in fact may even be quite ignorant of them. Jazz, soul, and rock and roll, have all been quite unmindful of conventional norms of propriety. In music halls and sport arenas it is possible to be iconoclastic and occasionally succeed (see Russell 1998: 17; also Lemeille 1995: 31).

This would however be very difficult, and highly exceptional, in core areas of social and economic life. In these fields, unlike sport and music, one can be financially secure (and thus successful) and do well without being a superstar. In industry, bureaucracy, education and finance where not every player is a millionaire or blessed with the necessary talent pertinent to the respective field, individualism is expressed after an endorsement to the prevailing styles of functioning. The fierce abandon and the pouring out of guts above all else, as can be found among successful Black athletes and musicians are absent in these core areas.

Successful financiers and educationists rarely, if ever, cross the line that governs the accepted. Individualism is practised by staying well within the parameters of what is proper and what is legal. Musicians and sport personalities are more prone to legal misdemeanours than those in other branches of life. Successful Black bureaucrats or educationists behave very much like their White counterparts do in trying to realize their individualism. Individualism among those who belong to the upper reaches of the core areas is expressed by early departure for college, a conscious severing of residential ties from their natal home, and experimenting with alternative lifestyles. The behaviour preferred here is promoted by social relationships that are 'conformable with higher levels in production hierarchy' (Granovetter 1985: 486). Blacks do not necessarily give the regnant metaphor of individualism these meanings. There may be a larger proportion of Blacks who have criminal records (see Lemeille 1995: 24), but this is not because of experimenting with alternative lifestyles. Blacks do not go off to college that often, and rarely leave home because that is expected of them when they reach adulthood. Many of them just run away.

It must be remembered that the scope for Blacks to express their individualism is thus limited by whether or not they possess what is known as pure raw talent. For those who are not fortunate enough to be gifted in this manner, individualism has little attraction. Though Blacks live with Whites it is often possible to discern two distinct cultural spaces. The fact of contiguity does not allow these spaces to emerge with clarity, but the distinction nevertheless exists. This is one of the reasons why successful Black men tend to marry light-skinned women (Russell et al. 1992: 69, 95, 108, 117; see also Sanjek 1994), and hope to move into a different cultural space. They would now like to participate fully in the regnant meanings that Whites have given to the root metaphor of individualism. They no longer want to live on the edge amidst the wild dithyrambics of Black spaces (see Dawson 1994). If, added to this, they are somewhat light-skinned and can pull if off as Whites then the ambition is complete. The phenomenon of a Black being mistaken to be racially White is known as 'passing', and it is not uncommon for many Blacks to aspire for such misrecognition (ibid.: 73). It is rarely all that easy to 'pass' and it often extracts a very high personal and moral price.

On the face of it there is just the root metaphor of individualism, but not only is it capable of multiple expressions in a variety of fields, but can also have different meanings in different sectors of social life. The salience they get in music and sport varies significantly when it comes to finance and industry. Likewise, in the world of education, individualism demands a kind of guarded indulgence on the part of society so that it can pretend to a species of anarchism and eccentricity. Though the market is a strong force in every realm of American life, it is filtered in differently for those in different structural locations in society. This is what gives individualism a varied set of meanings. None of these meanings can ever stray too far from the most literal meaning of the root metaphor. It is the individual that is paramount.

Admittedly there is a great deal of stylizing that has taken place in the American illustration so far, but root metaphors are about style and stylization. Cultures are self-conscious about styles. The root metaphor of individualism, like other root metaphors, is about how people interact with one another. The emphasis on informality, the addressing of one another by their first names, the need to be self-supporting and not to look for assistance, whether from family, friends or the state, and the equality that is so manifest among partners in American marriages, all give evidence to the vitality of the root metaphor of individualism in that country.

Individualism has also received a variety of political expressions. In a large number of instances individualism has been equated with the market principle. Robert Nozick can be seen as an articulate exponent of this position (Nozick 1976). Individualism has been given other meanings too. It has been argued by an impressive number of scholars and public policy makers that to establish this ethic it is essential to realize it in substantive terms, i.e., in terms of social citizenship. This alone would help realize the principle of equality of opportunity more fully (Rawls 1971, 1974; see also Marshall 1963: 74–81). In the quest for equality of opportunity attempts are made to negate the inequalities of birth so that everyone gets an equal chance. There is a marked shift in emphasis from duty to individual rights in such instances (Marshall 1963: 73).

This point of view has been given policy dimensions in the affirmative action programme in America. According to this programme, negative accidents of birth should be neutralized so that nobody gets handicapped simply because of being born in unfortunate circumstances. In Chapter VII, we shall discuss these issues in greater detail, but suffice it to say for now that the root metaphor of individualism can receive diverse meanings which can be politically contentious.

But in both these regnant meanings given to individualism, what keeps the most literal meaning in the forefront is the fact that Americans of all major political hues are against the 'quota' system. The quota system according to them, takes away the fundamentals of individualism and introduces group rivalries which are not compatible with the spirit of American democracy (see Sowell 1990: 105–6). In India, on the other hand, democracy has been expressed through the quota system in the reservation policy for Scheduled Castes and Scheduled Tribes introduced after Independence. Quotas received a further boost again in 1990, when the Mandal Commission recommendations were implemented which extended reservations to include the Backward Castes as well.

As can be seen quite clearly, the fact that a root metaphor is subscribed to does not mean that conflict is out and harmony prevails. Far from it. It is true, by definition perhaps, that the notions of freedom and individualism allow for greater conflict at every level. From the family to the office to the arena of sports, conflict is endemic. This is as it should be in social life, whether or not the root metaphor is that of individualism. Human beings are different, and there is always the perennial desire to do better than others. The struggle for material wealth and/or social prestige generates competition among individuals at various levels of social life. The fact that people can understand one another through regnant sets of meanings of root metaphors in no way precludes the existence of conflict. A cultural space does not mean that there are no contrary opinions and ambitions.

In a hierarchical society of any kind, conflict is bound to exist. Where different strata and classes have different and divergent sources of income and of want satisfaction, conflict and tensions will necessarily be present. In the case of the root metaphor of individualism, conflict is admitted in its various regnant meanings. In other root metaphors, such as of the caste system, conflict may not be openly admitted, but is very much evident in the working of a caste society.

Root Metaphors in the Caste System

Contradictions are displayed in a much more aggressive form in societies that are hierarchical and where status levels are more deeply marked than among, say the Ndembus, discussed earlier (see Turner 1964; also Chapter II). Dirks' study of the festivals of Aiyanar in Tamil Nadu is illustrative of this phenomenon. The Aiyanar festival did not happen as often as it is frequently made out to be. But when

> they happened they did not always include everyone in the village, or result in the village communal harmony.... (I)ndeed this communal harmony was disturbed not only along the so-called traditional lines of caste or faction but along developing class lines as well (Dirks 1994: 491).

Worldly conflict is abundantly evident even in caste societies, where it is commonly believed that spiritual merit counts for more than material satisfaction. This should correct certain exotic versions of Hindu culture. The ideology of caste is based on the root metaphor of purity and pollution. This metaphor has a regnant set of meanings, not all of which are internally consistent. It is true that every caste in the caste system believes in the metaphor of purity and pollution but is unable to agree on who is purer than whom. Further, there are times when caste superiority is not evaluated simply along ritualistic lines but adjudged on the basis of possessing martial and warrior-like characteristics. One is now better by virtue of possessing caste substance of strength and valour. Kingly castes and dominant rural patrons take pride in their supposed martial caste substances. This enables them to patronize Brahmin priests as service castes. Brahmins thus become clients like other service castes, though of an elevated kind.

In all cases, however, the most literal meaning of purity and pollution is adhered to. This is because in the entire set of regnant meanings it is acknowledged that castes are differentiated on the basis of bodily substances. As different castes are made up of different bodily substances, there are strict injunctions against the inter-mingling of castes. This is why there are such firm rules regarding marriage and inter-dining.

In spite of there being a consensus at this level there is a great degree of dispute regarding the relative status of castes in the hierarchy. Brahmins would like to believe that they occupy the highest position, but this is not something that the other castes easily accede to. Those castes which call themselves Kshatriyas frequently consider themselves to be superior to Brahmins. For these Kshatriyas the Brahmins are ritual specialists and nothing else (Hocart 1945: 35–44). Brahmins are members of a specialized ritual caste and need the patronage of the politically powerful land-owning Kshatriya castes. Even within the Brahmin caste cluster, there is a great degree of rivalry as to who is superior. This holds true among the Kshatriya castes too. This feature is generalized throughout the caste system. Even the so-called untouchable castes refuse to accept their humiliation (Khare 1992: 183–86). While they may believe that there are other castes that deserve to be called 'untouchables', that stigma should, however, not be attached to them.

To get a better idea of the dissensions within the caste system it is important to scan the various origin tales of each caste. In no origin tale is the admission made that the caste in question deserves to be low on account of being made up of base substances. Whether we look at the origin tales of Brahmins or the so-called 'untouchables', what is common is that they all talk of very elevated ancestories (Gupta 1992: 122–23). In the case of the poorer castes, whom we now conventionally, and uncritically, call the 'low' castes, their origin tales generally explain their fall from high status on the basis of lost wars, or because they were victims of chicanery and deceit. All this of course happened long before history was recorded. The ex-untouchables of India also subscribe to the root metaphor of purity and pollution but interpret it differently. None of the ex-untouchables consider themselves to be untouchables but believe others may be treated as such. As Professor I.P. Desai once pointed out in a brilliant study, there exists untouchability even among the untouchables (Desai 1976).

The root metaphor of purity and pollution therefore allows for a multiple set of regnant meanings. The fact remains that not all these regnant meanings get equal expression. The ones that are prominent in social life are the ones that are backed by political and economic power. This is why there is a general trend towards claiming either Brahmin (priestly) or Kshatriya (warrior) status by all castes. It is also true that there are other castes, though in a small minority, who quite forcefully claim Vaishya, or merchant caste status. Instead of limiting our understanding of caste self-identification in terms of just Brahmin and Kshatriya templates (see Burghart 1996: 37; Das 1982: 68), it is necessary to also include, at least, the Vaishya merchant caste model as well (see Gupta and Bhaskar 1970). These three models are the axes on which the extant regnant sets of meanings based on the root metaphor of purity and pollution are articulated. Understood in this fashion cultural conflict need not be seen as a 'misnomer' in the way that David Schneider argued his case (Schneider 1976: 219). Within a culture there can be conflict because a root metaphor is liable to multiple interpretations and meanings.

Over and above the three models that have been mentioned earlier it is necessary to point out that there is a possibility that many more exist. Enough research has yet to be done in this area, but it is very likely that the manner in which many tribes are responding to the caste hierarchy also demonstrates a fourth axis of meanings. In some tribal communities, particularly in east India, there is the emerging claim among tribals that their religion is the original religion of the region. From the fount of this original religion, or *adi dharm*, contemporary Hinduism is said to have evolved. According to this version then the tribals stand at the apex of the hierarchy. There could be a fifth version that is of those castes who believe that they have evolved directly from the gods, or the sun or the moon, such as those who claim to be *suryavanshis* and *chandravanshis* respectively. According to the Samkhya philosophy, the sun and the moon are manifestations of the sublime qualities of *Purusa*, which itself is far more refined than gross *Prakriti*, or matter. Therefore, the ancient *Rig Veda* declares that the 'moon was born from the mind, from the eye the sun was born' (see Embree 1988: 19).

The fact that there are these broad grids of diverse sets of regnant meanings around the root metaphors of the caste system, does not yet exhaust the scope of conflict within it. The Brahmins are internally stratified into different kinds of Brahmins. Here again, there is a great degree of rivalry as to which caste Brahmin is superior to the others. Likewise, among the Kshatriya caste cluster similar competitions exist, and between the Vaishya and Kayastha communities as well.

The root metaphor of purity and pollution spawns a vast number of hierarchies which clash against one another for supremacy. It is not as if this clash is always overt. As was mentioned earlier, sometimes the alternative hierarchies are introverted for fear of physical repression. Once that fear is removed, as it has happened with the inauguration of democracy in India, castes have come out in the open with their alternative hierarchies. What was once introverted is now often clearly extraverted.

It should also be recognized that the root metaphor of purity and pollution is again about what it is to lead a good life. Like the metaphor of individualism in America, purity and pollution informs the Hindus as to how they should interact with one another, who they should eat with, who they should marry, and who should have authority over whom. It is at this level that root metaphors operate. Very often elaborate rules are laid out for each of these aspects, but there are times, as in the American case, when the rules are quite parlous. The important thing, however, is that root metaphors must claim authority to decide what a good life is, and how this good life can be realized through social interaction.

Root Metaphors, Aesthetic Commitment and Embeddedness

It is necessary once again to distinguish root metaphors of this kind from rules of efficiency and of how to succeed and make profit, or of how to win a war. They too talk about social relations with others, and how best to strategize in an interactive situation. These rules are optional and their adoption is predicted on the basis of their success rate. Root metaphors have little to do with success or failure. They are adopted and strongly adhered to not because they succeed, but because they are intrinsically valuable. The root metaphor of purity and pollution can ideologically wage a long battle against the most tried and tested rules and procedures of making profits and winning wars simply because adherence to it is good in its own right. A root metaphor is in many ways like Kant's aesthetic judgment. In a sense its purpose is not to *demonstrate* it is better than other root metaphors, but that it is intrinsically so regardless of any empirical validation. A root metaphor can exist in splendid isolation and surround itself with a forest of meanings. While making profit and winning a war may lead to a good life, if the routes for doing so do not draw from the root metaphor, they must first and foremost demonstrate their success rate. A root metaphor suffers from no such limitations.

In this very significant sense a root metaphor shares the characteristics of Kant's aesthetic judgement, without being identical with it. In the first part of his *Critique of Judgment*, entitled the 'Critique of Aesthetic Judgment', Kant argued that the aesthetic realm has to do with purposeless purposefulness. If in the *Critique of Pure Reason* Kant managed to rescue both religion and science, in this later work he succeeded in saving aesthetics from being mauled by gross pragmatics. Root metaphors are linked to practice and are in that sense 'purposeful', though their efficacy is not measured in terms of alternatives. Root metaphors are in a sense like aesthetics because they are not adopted on grounds of success in practical life (see also Leach 1964: 11–15).

Nevertheless, root metaphors are, and must be realized in, social interaction. Therefore they are not like art either. A piece of art can exist on its own and have no practical consequences. The subscription to a root metaphor is not because of its efficacy, but once subscribed to, it has practical consequences. It finds expression in the way in which social life is ordered and, especially, in the meanings given to social interaction. This does not mean that root metaphors are the prime movers. Their attraction lies in the fact that once born they are able to give meaning to social arrangements on moral grounds.

Seen from a different perspective, root metaphors belong to the Marxian species of superstructure. It is however necessary to go further as the rules and regulations of non-spaces are also superstructural. Yet root metaphors are very different from the *lex* of non-spaces. Superstructure is thus an inclusive term and it needs to be further categorized to yield greater analytical advantage. This will facilitate an understanding of some of the crucial sociological problems of our times, especially with regard to culture and modernization.

The increasing preponderance of non-space in modern societies is another way of saying that diverse aspects of social life are increasingly being disembedded of root metaphors. This is not exactly the same as Karl Polanyi's notion of 'embeddedness' (Polanyi 1944) for his attention was on how different realms of social life are implicated in one another. In our case, the emergence of non-spaces becomes significant for we have now a set of material practices which are quite independent of any root metaphor and can survive on the basis of associational rules, or *lex*.

Some caution should be exercised at this point. Are we not exaggerating the embeddedness of root metaphors in pre-modern conditions? Is it not the case that hunting, fishing, agriculture, warfare were conducted on principles that could be isolated from root metaphors? After all, root metaphors come into play only in the considerations of a good life in terms of social relations between members of a cultural entity. But can the technologies of production by themselves be viewed quite separately from root metaphors?

When Karl Polanyi wrote about embeddedness of the economy in various other institutions in pre-modern societies the problem he was addressing was of a different order altogether. Polanyi sought to demonstrate that in non-modern or pre-modern societies economic practices took place without there being any strictly economic institution as such. Economics was 'embedded' in the functioning of other institutions such as those of religion and kinship (Polanyi 1944). This is why he believed that economists trained in the modern discipline of economics may miss out on this aspect altogether because they would not know where to look.

Keeping this in mind let us now return to whether or not one can talk of non-spaces in pre-modern times in the same way that we can about modern societies. Analytically, yes, it is possible to conceive of non-spaces, but in a real sense such non-spaces are extremely limited. In traditional India, for instance, the caste system allowed for a large variety of castes, but not all, to work as agriculturists. Agricultural practices were by and large uniform and standardized over large parts of India. The scratch plough and dependence on monsoons and the post-flood deposits of silt were generally the key agricultural factors relevant in India. It was, therefore, possible for people to move from one geographical location to another to pursue agriculture as an occupation. Irfan Habib (1963) and other medievalists have also recorded how peasants displayed their anger against a landlord by quietly slipping away to another landlord's domain, hoping for a kinder dispensation (see for Europe, Pirenne 1937: 48; Lipson 1953: 7).

While this sounds much like non-space, it is important to be aware of certain important reservations on this score. First, though a large number of castes could pursue an agricultural occupation, not all castes were allowed to do so. Root metaphors came in the way to deny certain castes from even touching the plough. These root metaphors were held by its believers to ensure a good, just and moral social order.

Gradually, leather workers, or *chamars*, were permitted in some parts of India to perform agricultural work. Only recently have members of the scavenger caste (*churas* or *valmikis*) been employed in the fields, but this is largely because the leather workers or *chamars* are beginning to look to the urban world for jobs. Pressured by this reality the same root metaphor lets out a different meaning which now makes it acceptable for those born into the scavenger caste to touch the plough. If in the past these scavengers were kept away from agricultural operations on grounds of extreme impurity, the root metaphor from the more privileged castes' point of view is that the lower, so-called untouchable castes are all the same and there is little point in distinguishing one from the other.

This reveals another important aspect of root metaphors. While root metaphors are resistant to change and to making concessions to rationality that seeks efficiency, it has to make room whenever faced with a social impasse. When the *chamars* began deserting the village, the root metaphors were adjusted to allow the scavengers to take to agricultural operations. This again demonstrates the multiple interpretations and meanings that a root metaphor may actually generate in an interactional setting. Its staying power is in fact dependent on its capacity to do so.

Though agricultural operations by themselves were by and large the same and conformed to the known tenets of technology, the fact that access to agriculture was controlled by birth, denies such a practice to be considered as one which is free from cultural space. In those pre-modern societies where the caste system was not prevalent other kinds of cultural barriers operated. Even without the caste system, medieval feudalism tended to restrict occupational specializations by birth.

By keeping trade secrets within families, competition was restricted within crafts and trades which did not allow a free movement of goods and services (Lenin 1960: 229, 234, 325; Lipson 1953: 31). A craft therefore began to be laden with root metaphors even though its actual operation could be done along technological lines known during those times. As Pirenne put it:

> (T)he manor was not only an economic but a social institution. It imposed itself upon the whole life of its inhabitants. They were a good deal more than merely tenants of their lord; they were his men in every sense of the word.... Language itself bears testi-mony to this. What was the seigneur (senior) if not the elder, whose authority extended over the family whom he protected? (Pirenne 1937: 62–63).

Similarly in the craft guilds of England an apprentice was not simply a person who learnt his skill from the master. An apprentice's moral life and bearing were also under the master's control. The apprentice could not even marry without the master's license. All this in exchange for the master teaching the apprentice the 'secrets of his craft' (Lipson 1953: 37–38).

Chris Bayly records how Bairagi and Gosain ascetic orders played an important economic role in 18th century India. Their annual cycle of pilgrimage helped them to move goods and money through the holy cities of Bihar and Orissa (Bayly 1986: 183). Businessmen too adopted a frugal and ascetic life style in order to earn a reputation for piety (ibid.: 379), without which their enterprises would be in considerable jeopardy. Technology and labour practices of all sorts were circumscribed in this fashion by root metaphors. Root metaphors framed them and performed the patrolling function that inhibited technology from proceeding along an independent trajectory.

That is why when Polanyi (1944) found that the economic life was embedded, what he actually saw was the circumscription of economic practices by root metaphors. So it was not so much that the economy was embedded in religion and kinship, but that root metaphors laid the initial conditions of economic activities. One way of doing so was by controlling who had access to certain kinds of occupations. The granting of access was not based on any tried and tested technique relevant to that craft or specialization, but on the basis of what constituted a good, moral and just social life.

The case of the Padma Saliyars is illustrative in this context. The Padma Saliyars are by caste, weavers of silk Kancheepuram saris in Tamil Nadu, India. The origin myth of this caste relates the divine sanction their caste ancestor received from the gods to undertaking weaving as an occupation (Kawlra 1997: 94). The Padma Saliyars believe that their special gift is on account of the fact that they are 'offsprings of the union of light and shadow...on both sides' (ibid.: 98). The Padma Saliyars worship their community deities, Bhavana Rishi and Bhadravathi, and claim special prerogatives to make offerings of cloth to the Shiv temples (ibid.: 102).

For the Padma Saliyars the various parts of the loom are not regarded as pure technological devices, but are made especially symbolic by linking them to the various parts of the human body (ibid.: 139). In addition, the pit by the loom in which the weaver sits must be dug in the correct fashion so that the planetary positions match the weaver's horoscope (ibid.: 144). The loom is, therefore, not just a piece of technology, neither is weaving simply a technique. Weaving is associated with holy sacrifice and the pit is seen as the sacrificial fire (ibid.: 145–46). Aarti Kawlra's work on this community of weavers provides a limpid illustration of the manner in which root metaphors invade every aspect of weaving, from who should weave and why, to the sacralization of the instruments of weaving and the loom (ibid.). Clearly, weaving silk sarees in Kanchipuram enlivens a cultural space. What was true of weaving was equally true for many other skilled practices in pre-modern times.

As considerations of such kind permeated all branches of activity in pre-modern societies, it gave the impression that economics was embedded everywhere. Even Polanyi could not ignore the fact that in pre-modern times there were always sets of practices that were largely economic in character. Agriculture, carpentry, smithy, etc., were full-fledged economic operations. Making and unmaking of kings, the appointment of sub-feudatory members of the nobility, were likewise in the realm of politics. What made it difficult to distinguish the economic from the political, as indeed from other spheres of life (such as kinship), was the existence of root metaphors that existed in an overlapping way across these various interactive realms.

It was then not embeddedness of the economy in politics or elsewhere as much as the presence of root metaphors in every aspect of life. In many cases the same metaphors which were dominant in the economic field were also to be found in kinship and politics. This is what made everything seem so inter-woven, though they were pursued quite separately by those who lived in such circumstances. The fact that these root metaphors spanned different regions is also what gave social life in pre-modern times a strong moral tone. One could not easily slip away from the pervasiveness of root metaphors no matter which field of activity one chose to, or was destined to, specialize in.

Root Metaphors, Heterogeneity and Social Change

When root metaphors are embedded in this way it is easier to visualize the tensions they face when alternative forms of technology become known. Root metaphors, to begin with, carry with them a portmanteau of meanings. Therefore, the first recourse of a new technology is to justify it within the framework of the root metaphor. Milton Singer's study *When a Great Tradition Modernizes* (Singer 1972) is an example of this phenomenon. When the European colonizers came to India, the traditional Hindus found ways and means of interacting with them once they found that such an interaction was either inescapable, or economically worthwhile.

There comes a time, however, when the root metaphor's meanings are exhausted. In other words, the metaphor's most literal meaning cannot be accommodated anywhere. Under these circumstances, either a new root metaphor comes into being, or, as in contemporary modern institutions, the root metaphor gives way to *lex*, or to a body of institutional rules and procedures. Root metaphors are therefore only as good as the practices will allow them to be. If they seem too overpowering in traditional societies it is because economic and technological innovations were largely non-existent in those times. The armies of Hannibal and the armies of Napolean were separated by over two millennia but advanced on horseback at roughly the same speed.

It is true that root metaphors often act as disincentives for change. Yet when there is a powerful need for change these root metaphors adapt to the extent they can, or else give up and fall into desuetude. Very often when tradition can be glimpsed in the functioning of many modern societies it is because the root metaphors have found new meanings for changed times. This usually happens when the traditional ruling class continues to stay in power and is not challenged by a radically new set of aspiring elites. Naturally, the old metaphors of a good, just and moral life will still hold sway. In such societies non-spaces do not emerge as freely as they do when the traditional elites have been displaced, as in most modern societies. One should not be in a hurry to designate a non-space simply on the basis of some superficial technological or lifestyle phenomenon. This should act as a caution to most students of modernization.

In any case, what this shows is that root metaphors wilt when changed circumstances demand a change in the nature of social relations. A technological innovation that can be incorporated within the existing framework of social relations will not by itself bring about any real pressure on a root metaphor. When Jan Breman (1974) found that a shift had taken place from patronage to exploitation in west India because of developments in agricultural technology, he was primarily drawing attention to altered social relations. Under the new regime of exploitation, it does not matter who the workers are or where they come from. The number of migrants to Punjab from Bihar and east India would have been unacceptable to the entire body of villagers of different strata in pre-green revolution days. Today it does not matter quite as much. One can therefore expect to see non-spaces emerging even in these regions. If the proliferation of non-spaces seems restricted now it is largely because the patrons of yore continue to be the elites of today. This acts as a brake against the dismantling of the earlier root metaphors. Instead they tend to take on newer meanings. This is why the scholarship on modernization needs to be especially alert.

David Schneider was quite right when he said that the orientation of an actor is not exhausted by 'internalized versions...of the cultural system' (Schneider 1976: 205). Besides, human life is so varied that no one root metaphor suffices to cover the entire field. While, for example, purity and pollution is an important root metaphor, other metaphors such as those of *sanyasa* (or renunciation), or the metaphors of filial piety, or non-violence, may have overlapping memberships. Again, in the American case, besides the root metaphor of individualism, there is also the metaphor of America belonging to the community of Christians. This is a strong sentiment that does not sit well with the exhortations of individualism, but it is nevertheless held by a large number of people. Even the most tolerant denominations like the Episcopalians in America have continued to retain the Nicean Creed in their liturgical services which dogmatically asserts that Christ is the only true god. The Christian pastoral metaphor of the shepherd and his flock (see Foucault 1981: 239) is yet another sub-set that has an uneasy relationship with the notions of citizenship and individualism.*

On all the significant renditions within Christianity itself, there are fundamentalist takes as well as non-fundamentalist ones. This divide too is quite emotional and laden with a lot of cathective values. As Demerath and Williams observe, Christianity has different versions in America. Both the left and the right use religion. Martin Luther King Jr., to Jesse Jackson, to Jerry Falwell have all used the symbols of Christianity to give special salience to their respective political projects (Demerath and Williams 1985: 160). Likewise in France there is the *laicite* of confrontation and the *laicite* of compromise, and both are effectively utilized by different political parties to register their internal differences (Hervieu-Leger 1998).

There is yet another root metaphor in America, which is that American society is like a melting pot. This metaphor has been expressed in a variety of ways. Sometimes the expressions are in consonance with individualism, and at other points it is intolerant of those who want to stand apart and not merge with the mainstream. A contrapuntal root metaphor to the melting pot is of the salad bowl. All these metaphors tell us about a good life, and how it should be led. The interesting detail however is that there is no reason why these metaphors, in spite of their cross-cutting membership, should be consistent with one another.

There is a strong view in anthropology that cultures make a meaningful whole. This point of view received support in anthropological literature from Malinowski, among others. Malinowski criticized A.L. Kroeber's view that cultural traits can be independent, and insisted instead on the unifying meaning that cultures possess (Malinowski 1974: 33–34, 41). Much later David Schneider recalled this position when he wrote that culture placed 'disparate parts of the social system together into a meaningful whole.... (I)t forms the unifying principle...by providing a single set of symbols and meanings.... I have called this culture's regnant function' (Schneider 1976: 204).

Schneider's position helps to clarify our own and points to the problems associated with some earlier landmark works on culture. According to Schneider cultures are unified along a principle such that there is 'a single set of symbols and meanings' (ibid.). This would imply that the root metaphors of a culture would have to be internally consistent. Unless the constancy principle is not met, cultures will not be meaningful. Even when new meanings emerge these should be 'congruent' with the established old meanings (ibid.: 205). It is for these reasons that Schneider argues that the term cultural conflict is a 'misnomer' (ibid.: 219).

Our position on this issue is quite different. We argue here that cultures are meaningful not because all its parts hang together as an internally consistent whole, but because there is a great degree of aesthetic and affective endorsement of root metaphors. Each root metaphor is meaningful in its own right, not because it is in any demonstrable sense 'better' than other metaphors, but because there is a great deal of emotional and affective investment in it. It is not as if root metaphors are in the market place and it is up to us to choose between the various available alternatives. These metaphors derive their authority not by choice, but rather because they are before choice. As MacIntyre might argue, cultural commitment arises not from a conscious adoption of a certain value system on grounds of practical reasons. In fact cultures are so compelling precisely because they are adopted for no reason at all (MacIntyre 1981: 42, 65).

Further, the root metaphors of a culture, as we have just noted, are not internally consistent; quite often they are irreducably heterogeneous. This leaves ample room for conflict within a culture. Consider the root metaphor of the four stages of life according to Hindu thought. This metaphor is often invoked to justify the good life at different points in one's biography. Again there are considerable variations on how this is interpreted (see Madan 1987). This metaphor does not always derive from the metaphor of purity and pollution. Likewise, the metaphor of filial piety that governs a Hindu's relation to living elders and dead ancestors, is not related to either the four ideal stages of life or to the metaphor of purity and pollution. The manner in which the feminine principle, or *shakti*, is a metaphor for various kinds of political revolt in colonial times by devout Hindus is a further illustration of a metaphor that can stand apart from other metaphors in the galaxy. In

America, likewise, the metaphor of individualism is not derivable from the racist metaphor of colour, or that America is god's gift to Christians. These metaphors primarily stand on their own, for which reason it is possible to launch an attack against racism on religious grounds, or attack individualism on a racist plank. To belong to a culture does not mean complete unanimity (see also Herskovits 1965: 415).

It is necessary to be aware of the lack of consistency between root metaphors especially in the case when there are overlapping memberships to them. This is an important consideration because human lives are so diverse in existential terms that they can hardly abide by the strict rules of internal consistency. As Marshall Sahlins pithily observed 'the world is under no obligation to conform to the logic by which some people conceive it' (Sahlins 1985: 138). Further, the root metaphors in turn have diverse possible meanings. These meanings are derived from actual practical engagement as they are 'burdened with the world' (ibid.). This is why cultural delineation can only take place in a discursive sort of way. It is hard to be analytical in this matter even when there is an overlapping subscription to certain root metaphors. This is because the meanings that may be derived from these metaphors need not always be the same. To be burdened with the world has this double effect. Not only are there various and heterogeneous root metaphors conjointly subscribed to, but these metaphors have diverse meanings depending upon the diversity of experience. This is why it is difficult to draw cultural lines for rarely are root metaphors and their regnant sets of meanings adhered to in discrete and mutually exclusive categories.

To be burdened with the world has a further consequence as well. Not everything that we do is governed by root metaphors. Schneider too is of the opinion that culture and religion do not provide all the material from which people construct their reality (Schneider 1976: 208). There are institutional norms, rules of procedure and technical artifices, that do not inspire such affective endorsement as root metaphors do. They could well be an outcome of choice. This is the world of non-space. The two are not to be collapsed into one, though there have been attempts to interpret non-space and institutional norms in cultural terms. This leads to the illusion that certain species of root metaphors encourage non-spaces while others do not. This ethnocentric bias needs to be corrected with the recognition that because one fact follows another there must always be a causal relation between them. Further, tastes and artifacts have a way of lingering long after the root metaphors that initially accompanied them have been wasted. This too can lead to the frequent mistake of privileging one set of root metaphors as being more conducive to non-spaces than others.

This should also correct the tendency to view people as relentless bearers of culture with little concern for practical life. This is why in anthropological monographs there are frequent complaints of the bias towards portraying 'characters' and not real people (see also MacIntryre 1981: 27–28). The tendency to miss out on the fullness of human beings and succumb to character portraits emerges when culture is seen as a unified whole. Though both Malinowski and Schneider were aware that inflexibility and characterization were largely a function of distance, their theoretical position on culture could be easily interpreted in a contrary way. This is because in both Malinowski and Schneider there is an emphasis on the unity of meaning. In the case of Clifford Geertz, however, there is a conscious and consistent endorsement of a unified principle both in terms of conceptualization and in terms of actual presentation of field material. This is why Geertz can un-hesitatingly portray 'characters' such as the anarchic Berbers, or the rational French, or the obsessive Hindus, or the tranquil Javanese, or the guilt-ridden Manus, or the activist Crow (Geertz 1984: 53,122, 130).

It is not at all surprising that for Geertz culture is uniformly acquiesced to a system of meaning. He puts this idea across variously, but perhaps it is best said when he writes that culture is a 'set of control mechanisms—plans, recipes, rules, institutions (which computer engineers call 'programmes'), for the governing of behaviour' (ibid.: 44). 'Cultures and their symbols are like genetic codes and the peculiar tone of each religion pervades areas of life...far beyond the immediately religious' (ibid.: 119).

Root Metaphors, Patterns or Habitus

In this matter, Geertz is following an earlier tradition set by Ruth Benedict who discerned patterns of culture and used terms like Appolonian and Dionysian for taxonomical purposes. For Benedict too these styles have a certain logic of their own for they lend consistency to the entirety of a particular culture. It is interesting, as Fred Eggan points out, that Ruth Benedict in her Ph.D. thesis had maintained quite the opposite point of view. In this earlier work she saw culture as made up of disparate elements that were constantly combining and recombining (Eggan 1968). Benedict's more celebrated work on the patterns of culture is a complete reversal of this position.

The partiality towards seeing cultures as consistent and unified wholes has been given a new lease of life by Geertz's elegant and persuasive literary style. It is also in ample evidence in Pierre Bourdieu's exposition of what he calls 'habitus'. To begin with Bourdieu sees culture in a manner reminiscent of Geertz. He calls it a kind of 'map' or a 'model' (Bourdieu 1977: 2). This then leads Bourdieu to talk of habitus as a kind of grammar, though not of Chomsky's variety. In habitus it is not a generative grammar that produces an innumerable number of sentences. In a habitus instead the emphasis is on *'appropriately* using an infinite number of sentences in an infinite number of situations' (ibid.: 20).

Such a position does not immediately lay claim to the view that sentences should be internally consistent, but one should not overlook the significance of the word 'appropriately' in the above quote. Bourdieu's understanding of 'habitus' takes the further step and defines it as a 'community of dispositions' (ibid.: 35). That is not all. Bourdieu's position gets harder as he progresses. 'Though the material conditions produce a habitus, but this habitus is made up of durable and transposable dispositions...which can be objectively regulated...' (ibid.: 72). Further, the habitus is a 'durably installed generative principle of regulated improvisations, produce practices which tend to reproduce the regularities immanent in the objective conditions of the production of their generative principles...' (ibid.: 78). Finally, in a typical Geertzian style Bourdieu states: 'Through the habitus, the structure which has produced it governs practice, not by the process of mechanical determinism, but through the mediation of the orientations and limits it assigns to the habitus's operation of inventions' (ibid.: 95). Sentences such as these and the use of terms like 'map', 'dispositions', 'practical mastery over formulae' (ibid.: 88) are so strongly Geertzian in flavour that it is a wonder that Bourdieu is able to accomplish all this and quote Geertz just once, and that too in passing, in his entire work.

Neither Geertz nor Bourdieu can adequately take into account the fact that the root metaphors of a culture can be quite contradictory to one another. They would also be hard put to explain away the changes that keep taking place in the cultural make-up of people due to new insertions in their lives. On occasions these may be quite drastic. When the Tukuka cult was recently introduced among the Ndembu there was an obvious mismatch between it and some of its earlier customs. The Tukuka cult was marked by hysterical trembling 'in marked contrast to the Appolonian dignity and restraint of many of the traditional ritual performances' (Turner 1974: 250). What happens now to dispositions, maps, formulae, etc.?

Root Metaphors, Cultural Spaces and Non-spaces

Before we round up this section it is necessary to make an additional point. Root metaphors should not be seen as if they belong only to the realm of religion. Root metaphors are usually given a kind of religious sanction, but as we found with the 'rags to riches' metaphor of the Americans, or the root metaphor of 'individualism', it is not necessary that they be religious in the traditional sense of the term. Bellah's understanding of civil religion precisely underscores this point. According to Bellah there are important symbolic areas of American life which are not religious *per se*, but evoke a sentiment that is similar to religion (Bellah 1967: 175). Culture, therefore, need not be limited only to the religious sphere. The important feature about culture is not belief in the supernatural, but the subscription to root metaphors which have to do with how to lead a good life in an interactional setting.

Anthropology has generally been wary of stepping out of religious belief and ritual observances in its understanding of culture. But once we relieve culture of this religious responsibility it can be seen in a wider context. The widening of the context of culture is all the more urgent in contemporary conditions, for regardless of what may have happened in history, when objective epistemologies and hierarchical order prevailed (Mannheim 1960: 12–14), today, the world over, societies cannot be constrained within limited cultural spaces. In many societies, and for many people, religion is no longer the sole source of symbolic energy. In these changing circumstances it is impossible for anthropology to ignore that culture cannot be limited to the religious sphere alone.

When culture is more than just religion, it is impossible to see culture in both secular and religious aspects of life. What becomes important is the existence of root metaphors which tell us about a good life, a just life, a moral life. Even here some caution needs to be exercised. At the risk of repeating what has been said at length earlier, root metaphors are not the same as organizational rules which also have to do with what is proper and correct. Metaphors stand alone, but the rules of non-space need each other for support. A metaphor transgressed invites punishment regardless of the consequences. The violation of a rule of non-space is punished on grounds of the consequences that such disobedience entails.

As root metaphors have to do with notions of what is a good life (which includes what is just and moral), they invariably reflect social hierarchies, in one form or another. As root metaphors have to do with what is considered to be a good life, in a hierarchical complex society they are generally about leading a good life on the principles of hierarchy and separation. As we found when discussing Polanyi's concept of embeddedness, root metaphors are to be found in many sectors of social life and not just in religion alone. Often enough they are given a quasi-religious slant, but usually what is taken to be religious is only custom.

Root metaphors can be found in core areas as in kinship (for e.g., bride-givers are superior to bride-takers), and it could also be found in bodies as peripheral to social life as alumni associations. The root metaphors of alumni associations are rather limited in their range of applicability, but they nevertheless perform two functions. The first is that they clearly separate and differentiate between the member's alumni association and the rest. The second is that the association recalls a vicarious space of the college or the school. For the school or the college to be able to function as vicarious space it is necessary that these institutions breed a loyalty to certain root metaphors which are not functional in character. The prestige of belonging to an Ivy League college does not rest on its academic skills alone. The students from a very early stage of their admissions into these institutions are initiated into certain root metaphors. These metaphors, strengthened by apparently meaningless rituals, help to emphasize that those chosen into these premises are special, and not just brilliant. Institutions which lack this aspect are unable to work up any significant post graduation loyalty. Their alumni rarely ever meet up at regular intervals.

In Harvard, to take just one example, it is the endowments from alumni that significantly account for Harvard University's financial success. The donations largely come from those who left Harvard after graduation for professional courses or to join business. These alumni are therefore not necessarily those who have excelled academically, but feel that they owe it to Harvard for helping them on to lead a good life. It is not as if Harvard or Yale provide the best in terms of education or sporting facilities. Many of the top minds have come from state universities, many of the leading sports personalities have emerged from small schools. But the Ivy League has a different appeal altogether because there are root metaphors attached to it. These metaphors have to do with academic brilliance, of course, but also with wealth and connections, associations with the elite families, the early settlers in America, and even the romance of John Kennedy lifestyles. The University of Chicago forms an excellent contrast in this connection. Faculty for faculty, expertise for expertise, it can match, or even excel, any other American university. Yet, the University of Chicago does not get endowment funds from alumni in the generous fashion that Harvard does. The reason is that, the University of Chicago has not been as successful in symbolically constructing a cultural space. It is predominantly a non-space of academic excellence.

Metaphors such as these are what sustain these institutions more than actual demonstrable results in education or sport, or routine instruction procedures. The space in which these metaphors are enacted allows alumni to enact a vicarious space in nostalgic gatherings in alumni associations. University rankings based on achievement indices of faculty and students are not tied to root metaphors but to actual performance. These rankings keep fluctuating as they are tied to actual performance and arouse no strong membership sentiments by themselves.

The metaphor of a good life need not just reflect hierarchy but can also be about exclusion and inclusion. It is true that exclusion and inclusion are aspects of hierarchy, but need not always be so. In a hierarchy, properly understood, the orders are hierarchically arranged at some depth. But the metaphor of a good life can also be exclusionary with a very shallow hierarchical depth. Alumni associations and Ivy League memberships have a shallow hierarchy as they are most concerned about exclusion rather than hierarchizing the universities in any great detail. Pre-modern 'tribal' societies are in this sense somewhat like Ivy League universities as they are concerned largely with principles of exclusion than with hierarchy. As Evans-Pritchard once said, there was law among the Nuers, but 'between tribes there can only be war' (Evans-Pritchard 1969: 61). The Nuers think they are 'God's noblest creation' (ibid.: 182) and the Kachins feel that they are the most evolved among all their neighbours (Leach 1982: 165). There is little attempt by either the Nuers or the Kachins to elaborate on a developed ladder of hierarchy. It is sufficient that the root metaphor separates the 'us' from the 'them'. As Michael Walzer notes, in some languages, like Latin, the term for strangers and enemies is the same (Walzer 1983: 32).

This indeed is what all root metaphors must do. Some in addition make further distinctions in terms of hierarchy. Root metaphors that are exclusionary and nothing else are usually found in egalitarian societies. Those root metaphors which emphasize hierarchy and divisions within its members are naturally to be found in stratified societies. Root metaphors therefore do not make societies, but depending on the type of society different types of root metaphors become pre-eminent.

Root metaphors are about a good life. The notion of a good life need not necessarily require internal stratification. Depending on circumstances root metaphors give primacy to either hierarchy or exclusion, or to both, as in the Indian caste system for example. In all cases they invigorate a strong sentiment of membership and enliven a space. It is in this space that membership becomes relevant. Those who are not subscribers to the root metaphors and their regnant set of meanings cannot participate in this space, let alone be able to recall it vicariously. In all these respects cultural space and root metaphors differ radically from non-spaces and their compendium of rules, regulations and technical procedures.

Chapter IV

Space, Territory and the Nation-state

Cultural Space and Overlapping Membership

Culture is not artifact, nor is it all forms of learned behaviour. Culture involves membership, not association. This is why culture implicates space and cannot do without it. The materiality of space is made up of interactions between members. It is the ability to interpret root metaphors in regnant sets of meanings that makes for membership. In membership, it is difficult to isolate individuals and relocate them in different spaces. The inability to interpret root metaphors in terms of regnant sets makes an alien out of a newcomer. As associations are bound by rules and procedures they are not as exclusive as metaphors are in their appreciation. Individuals can therefore move between associations and their non-spaces with much greater facility than they can between cultural spaces which are patrolled by root metaphors.

Cultural spaces are not discrete geographical units. Different cultural spaces intersect, memberships too overlap. Geographical contiguity is however a necessary condition for the intersection of cultural spaces. As cultures are enactments of root metaphors in terms of regnant sets of interpretations, geographical contiguity is ineluctable if spaces are to traverse one another. The only way such contiguity can be avoided is when vicarious spaces are recalled, as among diasporics. Geographical contiguity not only brings about overlapping sets of membership, the obverse is also possible. Contiguity also heightens awareness of, distance from, and distaste of, metaphors which are not our own (see Levi-Strauss 1985: 57).

When different cultural spaces are geographically apart it is not an analytical challenge to comprehend them. Yet, ever so often, different cultural spaces are contiguous to one another without any overlapping memberships. In these conditions, each instance will have a distinct set of root metaphors. The extent of actual interaction between these geographically contiguous cultural spaces will consequently be very low. This low level of interaction can result in animosity or benign neglect. At any rate the relation between cultural spaces becomes an aspect of foreign policy rather than one of daily quotidian interaction. It is not then just the distant awareness of root metaphors that makes for cultural space. Root metaphors and their regnant sets of meanings must necessarily by expressed in social interaction. When there is no actual interaction then root metaphors are simply lodged in the heads and are of concern only to intellectuals and dilettantes.

Just as cultures across boundaries need not always signal hostilities, there can be groups within cultures that can be hostile to one another. As long as a significant aspect of social life is around regnant sets of meanings given to root metaphors, people are said to belong to the same culture. But nowhere is it being argued that these regnant sets of meanings must be in internal consonance with one another. What is important is that there be an overlapping subscription to a galaxy of root metaphors, and an awareness of the regnant set of meanings of these metaphors, even when these meanings are not one's own and with which one is not in agreement. It is only when social interaction takes place with this package of root metaphors and their regnant meanings (which may be internally contradictory) is it possible to delineate one cultural space from another. Therefore, within this cultural space there can be oppositional meanings given to root metaphors. This is why a cultural space need not be one of convivial amity. This is particularly true of caste-, class- and race-based stratified societies.

Overlapping memberships can be of different kinds. For example, one can belong to a caste, and then perhaps also to the category Hindu. In each instance the root metaphors will also overlap, though the diacritics will be sharp enough to assess which membership is being activated. In other words, while being a

Hindu will activate the metaphors of belonging to a caste society, the metaphors of caste will play a secondary role to the root metaphors of Hinduism. In this case, while there is an awareness of what it is to have caste loyalties, the specifics that arouse attachment of membership to a particular caste may not be of any consideration for the members who have now constituted themselves as Hindus.

Linguistic Membership and Root Metaphors

Likewise, membership to a linguistic group can energize a set of root metaphors. Unlike, say the caste system, these metaphors are, however, not to be found in the language as such. These are common root metaphors among speakers of a language which is not saying the same thing as root metaphors emerge directly from language. Membership as Bengalis or Tamils invokes root metaphors that bind Bengalis as a people—'this is what we Bengalis or Tamilians are like'; or, 'this is how we do things'. Pride among a community of linguistic speakers rests on the belief that their language is superior to others. This feeling of superiority ultimately draws on the cathectivity of the extant root metaphors, derived from caste, religion, kinship, etc., that dominate the interaction which takes place among speakers of a particular language.

Membership based on language can intersect with other memberships based on caste or religion. In 1905 when Bengal was partitioned by the British along roughly the same lines in which East Pakistan first, and now Bangladesh, is separated from India, there was an all-Bengal agitation against it. This agitation brought together Bengalis irrespective of religion and caste. If at another point religion became a major divisive force, strong enough to negate the bonds of language, as in the Partition of 1947 then that must be separately enquired into. In spite of overlapping memberships, it is often the historic experience that one kind of membership is sometimes put above all others. On occasions a membership may be denied altogether by self-consciously repudiating the root metaphors that were earlier held in common. If this happens in a durable fashion, then new metaphors emerge that now sharply and exclusively separate the two spaces.

Here again the example of Bangladesh is illustrative. By emphasizing the Muslim identity over Bengali identity, East Pakistani Muslims repudiated the many root metaphors with their regnant interpretations on the basis of which Hindus and Muslims interacted in undivided Bengal. This interaction was not without tensions especially as the Muslims in that region were predominantly agricultural workers and the Hindus were members of the landed gentry and their retainers. Some metaphors were held in common, some others were distinctly different. Even if there were common metaphors it is likely that their interpretations were different. Yet as these interpretations belonged to the regnant set, there was a general awareness of them within the cultural space. Again, when Bangladesh separated from Pakistan Bengali language once again became a critical issue. This, however, did not mean that Bangladesh would like to merge with India, or with the Bengalis in India.

The political fact of the Partition created a physical separation that reduced possibilities of further interaction between the Hindu and the Muslim Bengalis. Consequently, Bengali membership will not enthuse the mass of Bengali speakers across the border like it did in 1905. Memberships can be sustained materially on the basis of interactions in cultural space. If there is no interaction, then the mere fact of being geographically contiguous does not make for the development of a common space.

Linguistic identity heightens a membership based on the common denominators of such root metaphors that are active in a language group. For instance, Hindu and Muslim Bengalis combined together effectively in 1905 because only the non-antagonistic metaphors of these two communities were enlivened. Linguistic membership is thus a sublimated phenomenon. It is dependent on unities elsewhere so that language can then coalesce them in a quick short-hand kind of way. The many similarities in the root metaphors between Hindu and Muslim Bengalis are now contrasted with the dissimilarities between these and root metaphors of other language groups to heighten the sense of membership. Though language is also an object of aesthetic evaluation it does not tell its speakers how to lead a good life. In this sense, therefore, language has no root metaphors. Linguistic identity thus depends on the extent of common root metaphors that pre-exist between the speakers. This is why the mere fact of speaking a language without social interaction does not make one a member of a cultural space. At times, language can be just an artifact, an acquired skill, in which case root metaphors very manifestly do not matter at all.

More often than not conflicts between linguistic groups emerge from economic factors. To give this economic element greater salience it helps if the different linguistic groups have incommensurable root metaphors as well. For example, in situations where the ruling class and the subjugated belong to different linguistic communities, then identities based on language become politically volatile. In Canada, the Quebecois resented Anglophone economic and political domination of Quebec but expressed it in terms of the confrontation between French and English languages. The concerted attempts by the Parti Quebecois in the late seventies to give Quebec a French visage was largely a response to the economic domination by the English in the region. The emphasis on French as the primary language in Quebec brought about a change in the nature of social interactions as the social background of personnel also changed from French to English. Those who were earlier linguistically handicapped now became linguistically privileged.

This change qualitatively affected social life in Quebec. The influence of small-town rural origins of most Quebecois officials could now be felt in metropolitan urban Montreal as well. To take another example from India, the hostility against the English language from sections of Hindu nationalists was on account of the social prestige that was attached to English even after independence from British rule. Undermining the role of English language from public life brought people of lower middle class, and of rural backgrounds to greater prominence. Predictably, this had a profound effect on the nature of social relations as new ambitions were stoked while older styles of civil service leadership and rule became ineffectual. In this case too, root metaphors that were dominant in rural society began to penetrate urban lives. In spite of the fact that there are times such as these when language can have a profound influence in terms of social interaction, it must still be admitted that language sublimates something else. If those who came from Francophone backgrounds were in every way the same as those who came from English backgrounds, if the Hindi proponents were adherents of the same root metaphors as the bilingual civil servants/

bureaucrats, then language would be of little political import. So it is not language by itself that creates membership. Language creates staunch partisans only when it signals a metonymic aggregation of root metaphors.

Geography and Cultural Space

If the materiality of cultural space is based on interaction premised on root metaphors, then what does geography have to do with it? When cultural space is created then it naturally presumes a membership of people. Geography comes in because people must exist in three-dimensional space and interactions obviously must take place in these three dimensions. But this is a very general statement. Cultural space is geographically pegged not because certain points on the map have prior precedence, but because these are locations where interactions take place around a set of regnant meanings given to root metaphors. If all the people in this set of interactions could be transferred elsewhere such that the same set of interactions could continue, then, the cultural space will remain analytically the same though it may have a widely different set of geographical co-ordinates. Recall the case of the rural Sikh diaspora from west Punjab to India after the 1947 Partition.

In the case of tribal re-settlement projects it has been noticed that the tribal population does not mind re-settlement provided they can reproduce the same set of interactions elsewhere. The northern native tribes of Canada, such as the Innu of Labrador, were lured by this promise by the European settlers and went quite willingly to the extreme inhospitable northern territories. Only when they reached there did they realize that it was impossible to reproduce the lives they knew in this geographical terrain. That is when they protested but it was too late. In India too the tribal community is not so much tied to any one geographical location, even though they may have a strong attachment to it on account of sheer familiarity. Their resentment at being uprooted so that large dams can be constructed in areas that used to be their home is primarily because they do not trust the government to re-settle them in geographical locations that will allow them to reproduce their social relations. Not every community is as fortunate as the majority of rural Sikh migrants were after the 1947 Partition.

Though these illustrations are probably apposite they will contain some impurities. After all they have not been produced under laboratory conditions. Even so, it serves the analytical lesson of demonstrating that geographical rootedness is not a necessary condition of cultural space. A specific geographical location is, however, a necessary factor given that interactions must take place in three-dimensional space. But geographical rootedness is neither necessary nor sufficient. For the purposes of comprehending cultural space it is important to note that the geographical locale is merely contingent. Cultural space must spatially exist somewhere, but that is not the same thing as being geographically rooted.

When geography contiguously places different root metaphors with cross-cutting memberships then it is hard to discern cultural lineaments. True, cultural boundaries are never easy to draw, but what is being said in addition is that these boundaries are impossible to draw in the abstract, i.e., outside of space where interactions take place. The difficulty with demarcating cultural boundaries is because no community survives on one root metaphor alone. As root metaphors address divergent aspects of social life, it is impossible to have just one root metaphor do the entire job. It is not as if the so-called simple societies can be separated from the so-called complex societies on the basis of the fact that the former have clear-cut cultural spaces while the latter do not. In both instances there is a great degree of cross-cutting and overlapping membership on account of the intersection of cultural spaces. In balance, cultural memberships are strongest when there is a greater concentration of root metaphors and their regnant sets of meanings, and weakest when there are a few distant metaphors that do not affect quotidian life in any significant way.

Cultural boundaries are thus relative in character and rarely absolute. What makes it even more difficult to make such distinctions is the shifting nature of identities, particularly during periods of high social tension. During these times, identities in moments of peace are usually cast aside for other identities which are shrill, angular, and extremely self-conscious. At such times it is all important to be a Sikh, or a Hindu, or even an Indian, and downsize those other identities of caste, region and sect (see Gupta 1997: 148–50).

Spatial Divide, Territory and Cultural Distance

To return to the example of the Partition of India. Prior to this divide in 1947, Hindu and Muslim Punjabis and Bengalis had many root metaphors in common. Their social practice gave evidence of the fact that they were aware of the regnant set of meanings these root metaphors possessed among those with whom they interacted. The relationship between the Hindus and Muslims was not always one of amity before the Partition. Yet they belonged to the same cultural space in spite of the religious difference. This is because they either shared, or as is more likely, were aware of, the root metaphors and their regnant meanings that each valued. It was on the basis of such an awareness that social interactions took place across the religious divide. It can therefore be concluded that two religious groups can live in the same cultural space even if there are divergences in their respective root metaphors. To live by root metaphors, willingly or unwillingly signifies the presence of cultural space.

This should also clarify the statement that cultural memberships can be at different levels of concentration. It is weak when root metaphors of others are thrust upon contextually subjugated peoples. It is weaker still when there is an awareness of other metaphors but which have little or no consequence in terms of social interactions. By the same token, membership is strong when there is a greater unity of root metaphors, and stronger still when there is also unanimity in the regnant sets of meanings of these metaphors. None of this takes away from the fact that multiple memberships exist, and only when there is a significant overlap in these memberships do we assume, in a very guarded way, a common culture.

After the Partition, there was the clear political demarcation of two countries. In addition, this division was also marked by deep hostilities on either side. Actual interactions between people thus became physically impossible. Without this interaction, and as time wore on, there was little practical need to know the regnant set of meanings given across the border to root metaphors which as Punjabis or Bengalis, Hindus and Muslims might still hold in common.

Gradually, even root metaphors that were held in common because of the sheer pressure of interacting constantly, may fall into desuetude and atrophy. Such a process is probably on in the case of the distance that is emerging between the Hutus and the Tutsis, and between the Orthodox Christians, Protestants/Catholics and the Muslims in what used to be Yugoslavia. The political divide will of necessity make it difficult to interact. Had such a political and spatial divide existed among the syncretic Abangan, the purist Islamic Santri and the Hinduistic Prijaji in Java (Geertz 1969: 166–68) then there would be little scope for their interaction and for their awareness and subscription to common root metaphors.

When a spatial divide, like territorial frontiers, separates communities that were earlier in interaction, the root metaphors they held in common in the past, or the operative awareness of other root metaphors, are bound to become distant memories, without any vivacity or depth. It is not as if subscribing to root metaphors in common meant that the communities lived in amity, for root metaphors are capable of alternative sets of meanings. It only implies that a working relationship can be established and this could well be fraught with tension. When root metaphors atrophy and no longer operate in practice to articulate a good life, they leave the field of anthropology. It is now left to cultural studies to excavate them and lodge them in intellectual warehouses.

In this connection it is important to note that the recalling of vicarious space is linked with an actual cultural space. The recall may be highly stylized, and may even attain mythical characteristics. In this recall geography serves as a mnemonic device to revive in memory an interactive situation in which meaning is provided by root metaphors. The vicarious space is thus dependent on experienced cultural space and cannot exist without it.

The space that we are talking about is fairly uncomplicated. It really refers to the location of interaction and not to the Kantian notion of space as an *a priori* category of the mind, or space as pure geography. Cultural space as understood here has a lot in common with Henri Lefebvre's understanding of 'experienced space' (see Harvey 1990: 219). The representation of space as in maps, diagrams, geography, is only incidentally related to experienced space but has no intrinsic relationship with it as we saw with our Sikh diaspora example. When vicarious spaces are recalled it is not exactly geography that is being remembered but the density of social interaction. The fact that this interaction must take place somewhere gives the impression that it is that 'somewhere' which is all important. When a location gets culturalized and becomes 'space', then geography by itself becomes analytically peripheral.

Geographical space is not the origin of cultural space except in a natural sense, i.e., a three-dimensional requirement for any kind of material existence. If any particular geographical locale gets culturalized it is on account of the fact that root metaphors and their regnant sets of meanings are being realized in interaction in a particular terrain. Geography is therefore a consequence of the enactments of root metaphors. As we have seen, if the actors of root metaphors are relocated wholesale in a different geographical region then that new locale too becomes, for all practical purposes, a renewal of the old cultural space.

Lefebvre talks about two other categories of space, viz., perceived space, such as in geography, diagrams, and architecture. This need not concern us any longer as we have already distinguished between geography and cultural space. The third kind of space for Lefebvre is 'imagined space' (Harvey 1990: 219). Imagined spaces 'are mental invention and comprises codes, signs, utopian places, landscapes, as well as material constructs such as symbolic spaces, particular built environments, paintings, museums, and the like that imagine new meanings or possibilities for spatial practices' (ibid.: 218–19).

At first sight imagined space and cultural space seem to have a lot in common. Both are mental constructs. The difference really lies in the fact that cultural (and vicarious spaces) are dependent on actual material interaction, and not just 'possibilities for spatial practices'. Our difference with Lefebvre gets easier to relate, for his imagined space includes built spaces, such as temples, museums and the like. The difference between cultural space and imagined space arises because cultural spaces, such as temples, etc., are characterized by dense concentrations of certain root metaphors and can also act as mnemonic devices for enacting vicarious space (i.e., as recalled space). Independent of that temples and other such 'symbolic spaces' (ibid.) are, as we mentioned earlier, merely 'artifacts'. Indeed, Lefebvre says about as much when his examples of imagined space go on to include such phenomena as museums and even paintings (ibid.).

David Harvey quite rightly says that space cannot be understood without material practice (ibid.: 203). But this statement needs further qualifications. Not all kinds of practice need a conceptualization of space as a sociological category. Practices generated and governed by *lex*, as we noted earlier, operate in non-space. In Foucault's thoughtful considerations of space there is still the inability to see space first as a site of a very specific kind before the physical aspects of geography and extension become prominent. This is why Foucault's treatment of space is dispersed over different kinds of sites (such as prisons, panopticons, hospitals and the like) without a clear analytical statement on the concept of space as such.

This might seem a little unfair to Foucault. In a significant article called 'Of Other Spaces' Foucault went to considerable lengths in his analysis of space (Foucault 1986: 22–25). In this article, he distinguished between what he called a space of emplacement from the modern application of space characterized by conflicts and oppositions. But in both these kinds of spaces it is the physical aspect that predominates. The space of emplacement is one of sacred spaces and profane ones, of temples, of urban and rural spaces and of territories. These spaces appear to conform to cosmological demarcations of celestial and supercelestial spaces. The terrestrial spaces then owe much of their qualities to being able to reflect the cosmological theory of the society.

In Foucault's formulations, there emerges a different kind of space in post-Galelian times when techniques of social control are the major concern. These techniques of social control are manifested in the architecture of prisons, hospitals, factories, as well as in different kinds of maps—electoral, taxation, cultural, and so forth. The primary concern with space now is one of control (Foucault 1975: 226–30).

As with Lefebvre, there are certain points of similarity between the notion of cultural space as is being put forward here with the treatment of space spelt out by Foucault. In Foucault, as with Lefebvre, space can also be read as a culturalized phenomenon and not just geography. This is an aspect which cannot be overemphasized. In a sense, Lefebvre's and Foucault's treatment of space can be seen as a more sophisticated version of space and time as developed by Durkheim and Mauss in *Primitive Classifications* (1963). Both Lefebvre and Foucault, the former with the concept of 'experienced space', and the latter with the use of the term 'spaces of emplacement' and 'sites of power', refer to actual interactions between people (as did Durkheim and Mauss). In Foucault's hands a study of this kind relates space, in the post-Galilean period, to the use of power. Space then is primarily about controlling people in finite, enclosed and divided sites.

In neither Lefebvre nor Foucault is space linked with membership which arises from the overlapping subscription to root metaphors and their regnant set of meanings. The diversity of spaces that emerge in these works ultimately draws its sanction from their sheer physical attribute. This is why both Lefebvre and Foucault have a vast taxonomy of spaces. This is logically necessitated by the fact that both of them appear to lack a conceptual understanding of space before they go on to list its various types. The only thing in common in all the distinct types of space in both Lefebvre and Foucault is that they are three-dimensional sites. This is why space for them is first physical and then culturalized in different ways: in representations, in cosmogony, in penal institutions, and so forth.

The procedure adopted in this study is different. Space emerges here as a consequence of membership of root metaphors and their regnant set of meanings. The physical three-dimensional aspect of space is a preliminary ontological one and not an epistemological condition. The most salient sociological feature of cultural space is that it is here that certain root metaphors are expressed in practice. This space can be taken to a different geographical locale altogether (as with the rehabilitation of the Sikh diaspora and tribal resettlement), and it can be vicariously recalled as well by diasporics.

In neither Foucault nor Lefebvre is space linked with membership of this sort for which reason the various categories of space that they mention have no intrinsic relationship with one another. Failing this the only connection they have, the only thing they possess in common, is the physical one—the three-dimensional fact of extension. By emphasizing membership to root metaphors and their regnant set of meanings we are also able to be economical in our classification of different types of spaces. After all it is not a taxonomy of spaces that is important, but the fact that there is something intrinsic about cultural space that needs to be appreciated before qualifications and gradations can be introduced. If there should be a further classification it can only be after this analytical point is accepted first.

When space is understood as a locale of cultural practices, with memberships around root metaphors, it is easy to realize why the native Indians and White settlers in America could not agree on what is territory. The native Indian population saw territory in terms of a distinct set of cultural practices which did not include actual physical ownership of geography. For White settlers territory invoked a different kind of meaning—that which was based on exclusive possession and ownership of actual chunks of earth. This literal meaning of territorial possession was absent in the case of the native Indians. Their practices did not enliven this meaning for which reason there was mutual incomprehensibility, when not downright treachery, in the signing of treaties between the native population and the colonizers in America.

In Harvey, space is a generalized three-dimensional entity where material practices must necessarily take place. As he does not function with the possibility of non-spaces, space is not understood strictly in terms of material practices that enliven root metaphors alone. Therefore industrial practice, politics, and the entire gamut of social life are considered in spatial terms. According to Harvey '(a)ny complicated system of production requires spatial organization'. Yet when he comes to the postmodern phase he calls it the 'annihilation of space through time' (Harvey 1990: 270). This is hard to comprehend because it would then lead one to believe that there is either no material practice in the postmodern condition, or that material practice can now take place outside physical space.

If on the other hand one were to separate material practices into those that require space and non-space, then the imagined postmodern condition could be hypothesized as one in which cultures and their metaphors lie unused and unrecalled and all that is left are bodies of associational rules and organizational practices. As both space and non-space require a three-dimensional setting, the mute fact of geography is of little relevance. What is also of importance is that in some three-dimensional settings it is not easy to participate from outside and move in and out of it. It is this setting that can appropriately be called 'space', or 'cultural space' as has been argued here. In three-dimensional settings that do not impose such exclusiveness of membership it is preferable to use the word 'non-space'. This would give space a sociological resonance and separate it from pure geography as well as from the Kantian notion of space as an *a priori* category.

Root Metaphors, Enlarged Spaces and the Nation-state

We are now set to concentrate on the relationship between space and non-space, and their connection with the nation-state. Non-spaces grow as the embeddedness of root metaphors recede from diverse areas of social life. The disembedding of root metaphors does not happen in one fell swoop. The areas of interaction gradually increase with technological development. This necessitates an alteration in the set of regnant meanings given to root metaphors. Localized face-to-face relations are no longer as important and dominant. In such relations social ties were multiple even if they were not amicable. But that does not mean that we have already moved over from *gemeinschaft* to *gesselschaft*. Or even if such a transition is taking place it is not as if the days of root metaphors are over. In fact, the old root metaphors may not yet have given way in most cases. They have however found new meanings. The staying power of these root metaphors will depend on the extent to which the earlier stratification system is altered, not just in terms of personnel, but in terms of actual social relations.

Technological innovations need to be emphasized for it is with the application of new technology that the enchantment of the prevailing root metaphors and their regnant meanings can be challenged. As Perry Anderson wrily notes the 'sword and the book did not block the path of the machines' (Anderson 1990: 71). Of course, conquests too play an important role in a large number of cases. Very often though they bring about a change in personnel and adjustments in the regnant set of meanings without any major alteration. Even reform movements in India gradually met with the same fate. Neither did the conquest of Hindu territories by Muslim rulers shake the root metaphors of the caste system in any fundamental way.

However, when technology does not result in changing hierarchical relations then the same root metaphors seem to get second wind with a somewhat altered set of regnant meanings. This issue need not detain us any longer as our concern here is to examine the emergence of a root metaphor, or a set of metaphors, which along with their regnant meanings, call out to a membership on the basis of a nation-state. The reason why the examination of this membership to the nation-state must be seen in relation to the development of technology is because the membership that we are now talking about demands ties over long distances that cannot be covered by a face-to-face intimacy or by relationships that can still be traced to a common interlocutor (see Marshall 1963: 75–76).

The membership to the nation-state is also based on root metaphors, but these root metaphors are general enough to co-exist with a host of other more localized root metaphors. However, this co-existence, as we shall soon see, is not without altering some of the earlier root metaphors in many important respects (see also Rousseau 1913: 140). In countries where root metaphors have become by and large disembedded from other institutional practices there is still one set of root metaphors that is to be displaced. These metaphors are the basis on which nation-state bondings are created. Historically, such metaphors emerged around the time when the strength of locally spatialized root metaphors were losing their grip. The embeddedness of root metaphors in diverse institutional settings was gradually easing out in favour of non-spaces.

In non-spaces, the root metaphors that earlier determined who would do what kind of work, or consume what kind of article, were displaced in favour of a set of rules and procedures. Unlike root metaphors the *lex* kind of rules and procedures were in place because of their practical efficacy and not simply on moral grounds of what constitutes a good life. The moral grounds of a good life are not so much about what people can actually consume, but rather on the basis of how people should interact with one another such that a moral order is upheld. Consumptions enter the picture in order to uphold such interactional details. *Lex*, or rather the set that makes up the *lex*, does not find sanction in morality of this kind, but in terms of efficacy towards a stated goal. If a particular set does not help in attaining that goal and there is a newer option available, then the transformation is easily made.

The root metaphors of a nation-state have little to do with *lex*, as a moment's reflection will show. The loyalty to a nation-state is not because of instrumental motives but because of an ineffable sentiment. To believe that there is only a calculated affiliation to the nation-state is to completely misunderstand the sentiment and pay attention only to the structure of governance, or to economic calculations. This lesson was again brought home when American economic sanctions were imposed on India for its nuclear tests in the summer of 1998. The threat of rescinding international aid to

India only stoked the fires of Indian nationalism. Thus at a time when the root metaphors seem to be having a hard time in their earlier and well-worn grooves, a new metaphor around the nation-state has emerged to give a new sense of identity. True, this new metaphor can only be effective when social interactions can take place without being limited to face-to-face interactions. This however does not disqualify it for the fact remains that it is still a membership because it is founded on root metaphors.

It is possible to have a formally recognized nation-state but without the accompanying sentiments that rally around and draw their charge from root metaphors. In such cases the nation-state can be deemed as inauthentic even though it has all the apparatuses and structures of power in place. Such a situation has been known to occur when retreating colonial powers often re-drew territorial boundaries without popular acquiescence. How does this popular acquiescence take place? Popular acquiescence regarding territory does not begin with territory but with an involvement in the project of making a nation-state. This is what binds the members of a nation-state as a community. The actual territorial lineaments are determined by the location of the participants of this project. When territory as geography is merely added on, or decreed from above, or from without, then territory does not enliven a cultural space. It is this popular endorsement of territory that replaces face-to-face relationships to bring about what Ben Anderson aptly called 'imagined communities' (Anderson 1983).

How a particular territorial map is drawn of a sovereign nation-state depends on a number of historical factors whose combination is always unique and original (Gramsci 1971: 240). In this unique combination we can discover the popular endorsement of territory that characterizes a nation-state. Once again geography is a consequence and not an originator. Even in the exceptional case of Israel, its actual territorial possessions are quite different from the notion of a Jewish homeland that initially stirred the Zionist project.

If geography by itself were to be the important factor then there would be little to distinguish a nation-state from an empire. In empires too subjects lived within geographical boundaries that were the holdings of the monarch, or of the overlord (see Balibar 1991: 890). But these subjects did not form a membership, they were simply the subjugated people. According to Perry Anderson, absolutist regimes derived their legitimacy from the dynastic principle and not from territory, as political and economic orders 'were fused in a chain of personal obligations and dues' (Anderson 1979: 39, 45). Even as late as when Napoleon launched his attack on Russia the notion of territory was not part of a popular consciousness. It is well-known how the Russian peasants initially welcomed Napoleon hoping for a kinder dispensation under him (ibid.: 345).

A nation-state, on the other hand, is born out of popular participation, long-distance communication, and large-scale supra-local mobilizations along ideologies that transcend parochial boundaries. The ideology that groups people from long distances into a community must necessarily have the ability to transcend local mires of root metaphors based on dense face-to-face interactions. The geography that becomes sacralized territory of a nation-state depends on precisely those locations from where activism of this sort has emerged. It is only after this fact that retrospectively territorial alignments are drawn. Retrospectively geography becomes sacralized. The manner in which the United States of America grew from its initial 13 colonies is an example of this phenomenon. Modern France got Savoy and Nice only in 1860, but lost French-speaking Valle d'Aosta to Italy. In India too the clear lines of territory emerged only after Partition. Prior to that leaders of the Indian national movement were willing to recognize secession and national self-determination. After Independence and the Partition into India and Pakistan, preaching secession became a crime and this measure won support from mainstream political opinion and activism in the country (Gupta 1996: 39–43).

The root metaphor of a nation-state thus enlivens a space on account of participation and not before it. It is this participation in a supra-local project that arouses a sentiment not unlike Durkheim's 'collective consciousness'. This is why the acts of the state must seem to be 'continuous with... its citizens—to be, in some stepped up, amplified sense, *their* acts.... It is a question of immediacy, of experiencing what the state "does" as proceeding naturally from a familar and intelligible "we"' (Geertz 1984: 317).

The reason why it is important to emphasize that participation invites geography is because there is an established point of view which sees the nation-state as a natural culmination of given and primordial 'ethnic' identities (see Smith 1979, 1981). In this scheme of reckoning, ethnic sentiments and communities have existed for centuries in terms of their 'ethnie'. Ethnie here stands for group origins, history, cultural solidarity and belief in its common destiny (Smith 1981: 8, 66). There is little appreciation here of the fact that the nation-state sentiment is a recent phenomenon in world history, and second, that the new solidarity that emerges among an enlarged conception of 'we' finds its expression through actual political participation in a cultural space, or territory.

If we were to examine contemporary nation-states in continuation with the notion of 'ethnie' (ibid.: 66) then the many features that go into the making of the specifics of each nation-state would be lost. Instead we would be subscribing to what John Hall aptly calls the 'sleeping beauty' theory of nationalism (Hall 1993: 4). Implicit in the 'ethnic' theories of nationalism is the assumption that at some point this dormant but fertile imagination was awakened with a 'big bang' and from then on there has been an infinite flourishing of nationalities and ethnic consciousnesses.

It is not surprising either that the ethnic view of nation-states and nationalism cannot take into account territory, the culture space of a nation-state, and participation. Instead the primordial and near 'natural' ties of blood, dynasty, family, language and religion are seen as all important. The fact is, as Benedict Anderson has pointed out, the making of a nation cannot be easily regressed into primordial entities. The manner in which the English and French languages gradually gained precedence at the expense of the other spoken languages in both England and France is a pointer to this fact (Anderson 1983). As Ernest Renan put it: 'No French citizen knows whether he is a Burgundian, an Alan, a Taifale, or a Visigoth.... There are not ten families in France that can supply proof of their Frankish origin, and any such proof would always be essentially flawed...' (Renan 1990: 11). Likewise Benjamin Franklin stressed in his tract, *'Information to Those Who Would Remove to America'*, that though Americans were of European origin, European values are 'a commodity that cannot be carried to a worse market than that of America where people do not inquire concerning a stranger, *"What is he?"*, but *"What can he do"'* (quoted in Kohn 1946: 274). Franklin went on to say: 'He is an American, who, leaving behind him all his ancient prejudices and manners, receives new ones from a new mode of life that has been embraced...' (ibid.: 276).

What the nation-state sentiment evidently does is that it creates a community where there was none. This is why Renan advised that one should be wary of 'ethnographic politics' (Renan 1990: 16). This new community is built on the basis of a 'mode of life' as Franklin pointed out. The adoption of a nation-state sentiment is not an intellectual position to begin with, but rather this position is an outcome of actual participation in a national project enlivening a given territory.

This new community is essentially a modern product for it is premised on participation of a kind that was impossible in either feudal or absolutist regimes. For L.T. Hobhouse, that inexhaustible source of sociological wisdom, nationalism is unthinkable without a sense of popular participation, which in turn is impossible without the development of freedom. It therefore stands to reason why antiquity was unfamiliar with it (see also Renan 1990: 9). Hans Kohn too was of the opinion that nationalism was 'inconceivable without the ideas of popular sovereignty preceding...' (Kohn 1946: 3). Further, he said that this idea of popular sovereignty can only occur once the medieval relationship between the ruler and the ruled is overcome (ibid.). A nation-state is thus born out of participation and thrives on it often by an exaggerated sense of commitment. To quote Renan again: 'A nation is therefore a large scale solidarity, constituted by the feeling of the sacrifices that one has made in the past and of those one is prepared to make for the future' (ibid.: 19; see also Walzer 1983: 420).

The past of a nation is a retrospective grouping depending upon the actuality of the community enlivened by a common nationalist goal. In this recall several things are also forgotten. It is important that the French forget the massacre on Saint Bartholomew's day, or the massacres in the Midi in the 13th century (ibid.: 11). It is important for Indian nationalists too to forget the many acts of treachery against each other by the various Hindu and Muslim emperors in medieval times. It is important that Americans forget that they fought amongst themselves in the Civil War.

Seton-Watson is right when he says that '"no scientific definition" of a nation can be devised.... All that I can find to say is that a nation exists when a significant number of people in a community consider themselves to form a nation, or behave as if they form one' (Seton-Watson 1977: 5). Perhaps Kohn put it most forcefully when he said that the 'love of the homeland is not a "natural" phenomenon, but an artificial product of historical and intellectual development' (Kohn 1946: 8). Nationalism demands an 'identification with the life and aspirations of uncounted millions whom we shall never know, with a territory which we shall never visit in its entirety...' (ibid.). Consequently this sentiment and bond of identification is vastly and 'qualitatively different from the love of the family or of home surroundings' (ibid.).

It is not as if nation-state sentiments must necessarily obliterate the love of home surroundings, rather it brings in another level of cultural life that was hitherto unknown. The love of home surroundings is layered over by the more recent 'love of the homeland' (ibid.: 8). It is said that in France 'everyone has two *pays* (countries—D.G.): each has roots in his own *petit pays* (vicinage, village, region—D.G.), and all share the destiny of eternal, potentially greater France' (Lebovics 1992: 10). If the love of home surroundings gets gradually attenuated it is not so much because of the nation-state sentiments but rather because the cultural space of the home surroundings are giving way to larger non-spaces. Nation-state sentiments are not directly responsible for this because both the development of non-spaces and the emergence of the nation-state sentiments are dependent on the forces of modernization. Neither of these could have taken place in medieval times (see Turner 1990: 194).

The participation that brings about this large-scale community is again premised on root metaphors. This makes the nation-state a cultural feature and its understanding should not be made coterminous with a study of the structures of governance. The emergence of this supra-local community arises from a common mission. It is this common mission that bonds people even when not in face-to-face communication. Further this bond is a cultural one as it is justified on the basis of root metaphors, no matter what economic calculations may have occurred 'behind the backs of men'. Patriotism cannot be accounted for in an economic balance sheet. People would die gloriously for their nation, but where is a gravestone that proudly says that the departed soul died upholding the profit margins of his enterprise? Martyrdom is typically at the cultural level where root metaphors dominate. There are therefore martyrs who gave up their lives for their religion, their language, their tribe, as well as their nation.

The participation in a common mission leading to popular sovereignty is a necessary feature for the emergence of a nation-state. Having said that, it is also important to recognize that it would be incorrect to project any one kind of mission as being more authentic than others in the making of a nation-state. The important point is that in all such cases the end result should be the popular sacralization of territory. When space is thus culturalized it becomes an unfailing indicator of social membership. The space that this participation enlivens and encultures becomes the sacralized territory of the nation-state. Sometimes the common mission can be to bring about a uniform language, or to effect a religious reform, or to overthrow a foreign power. Moreover, there could be different ways by which each of these missions could be accomplished, hence the importance of Gramsci's 'unique combination' as mentioned earlier.

The French Revolution brought about French nationalism, the unification of Germany on the basis of language brought about the German nation, the fight against Japanese imperialism spurred Chinese nationalism, and the struggle against British colonialism and the emergence of Pakistan led to Indian nationalism. The missions in each of these were quite disparate but they were all common in the sense of popular participation and in the eventual sacralization of geography as territory. Different issues were instrumental in each case. This is why there are different root metaphors for different nation-states. This is also why it is often difficult for people belonging to one nation-state to appreciate the gravity and passion that characterizes root metaphors of other nation-states (see also Walzer 1983: 33).

The root metaphors that bind commitment to a nation-state and make for a community are often quasi-religious in character. While they are not always religious, sometimes they might be, yet they seem that way because they share with religion the common feature of being founded on root metaphors. This is what creates the impression of a certain 'religiousness' in root metaphors of nation-states. Robert Bellah, drawing from Jean-Jacques Rousseau called it 'civil religion' (Bellah 1967). This term has had a successful career because it is able to capture the fact that the attachment to a nation-state shares a lot in common with religious partisanship. But Bellah made this point from the wrong end. Instead of seeing both religious and nation-state sentiments as dependent on root metaphors and on their regnant sets of meanings, he tried to explain this resemblance, not always superficial, between the two by claiming that civil religion owes its origin to religion proper, and needs to be cradled by it in its infancy (ibid.: 175 ff.). In this he was following Rousseau, but with a difference. In the first place, Rousseau, unlike Bellah was not at all sanguine that this reliance was a good thing. According to Rousseau this dependence on religion is

> bad in that, being founded on lies and error, it deceives men, and makes them credulous and superstitious, and drowns the true cult of the Divinity in empty ceremonial. It is bad, again, when it becomes tyrannous and exclusive, and makes a people bloodthirsty and intolerant, so that it breeds fire and slaughter, and regards as a sacred act the killing of everyone who does not believe in its gods (Rousseau 1913: 135, also 107).

The truth is that the metaphors of a nation-state do not promote harmony between nations, but rather highlight the distinctions between them. This is what religion does in practice with respect to other religions. Indeed this is the role of all cultures in general on account of their foundations in root metaphors. That nation-states depend on these metaphors has been widely noticed if only to comment on the fact that nationalisms can be dangerous and can arouse irrational passions. In the *Social Contract*, Rousseau presciently observed that excessive devotion to the fatherland breeds intolerance towards outsiders (ibid.: 107). But that is exactly what subscription to root metaphors is all about. As Yael Tamir notes, if nation-states were to be totally dependent on neutral structures then they run the risk of creating 'alienation and irrelevance' (Tamir 1993: 149), and perhaps irreverence too. Of course there are nation-states that thrive on root metaphors that are directly borrowed from religion. Israel is a good example. Even the Israeli Knesset is named after the 'Great Knesset'. The root metaphors of England as a nation-state also have a religious component because of the official status given to the Anglican Church. It would nevertheless be incorrect to dismiss the specifics of one's commitment to the nation-state, and not to distinguish it from religious affiliations.

The root metaphors in France however go to the other extreme and purposively deny religion any official status. The French conception of *laicite* has all the markings of a root metaphor about it. It does not translate easily into 'secularism', nor does it mean the separation of the church and state. Without denying that it also refers to these meanings, it has other meanings too. These have to do with the French Revolution and the manner in which the church's activities were controlled and supervised by the state. It is just not the separation of church and state, but a purposeful subjugation of the former by the latter (see Hervieu-Leger 1998).

Like the other root metaphors we have discussed so far (e.g., purity and pollution, or racism) the root metaphors of individualism and even liberalism, or those inspired by the Judaic faith, or by *laicite*, are all amenable to multiple interpretations. In a convincingly argued piece Bhikhu Parekh draws attention to at least three kinds of liberal stances with respect to minorities in Britain. They range all the way from the cultural assimilationists, to the cultural *laissez-faire*, to what he calls the cultural pluralist approach (Parekh 1995). In Israel, the protagonists of peace and the hawkish fundamentalists both draw their inspiration from Judaism (see e.g., Aran 1991); the *laicite* has adherents who will not budge from any of the known ways of French life to accommodate Muslim women who wear a head dress to work and to school, and then there are those in France who take a more generous view of the matter by interpreting *laicite* in less confrontational terms (Hervieu-Leger 1998).

In India the conception of territory that came alive with the Partition in 1947 found at least two important political expressions. One considers Pakistan to be a theocratic state and the other perceives it as an evil Muslim state. The first gave credibility to Jawaharlal Nehru's vision of a secular and socialist India, while the latter provides the rationale behind Hindu political parties to work up a hate agenda against the Muslims. The fact however remains that no matter where one begins from, Pakistan is an enemy and the nation-state's borders are inviolable. Ernest Renan had perceptively remarked that all nation-states are built on a grief. Therefore, 'where national memories are concerned, griefs are of more value than triumphs, for they impose duties and require a common effort' (Renan 1990: 19). One of India's griefs is Pakistan. Russia and then Iran and Iraq have been America's griefs. It is grief of this sort that binds members as patriots.

With Independence of India in 1947 came the Partition and Pakistan. As the two nation-states happened together it might give the impression that they arose from the same movement. The practices that brought about the freedom of India were, however, vastly different from those that created Pakistan. The symbolic charge for the Indian movement came out of an anti-colonial struggle, while for Pakistan it was freedom from the Hindus. The two movements with their attendant root metaphors were positioned quite differently and were consistently at odds with each other. Not surprisingly then the root metaphors of the two are distinctly different. For the national movement fighting against colonialism, it was important to bind people of all faiths, caste, and creed together to form a mighty phalanx against the British colonial presence. In this struggle it was imperative that popular participation be encouraged. This necessitated anti-feudal agitations on land reforms, and a demand for greater democratization at the provincial level (see Thorner 1981). It is through these practices that the root metaphors such as those of secularism and economic independence gained pre-eminence.

After the Partition the consciousness of territory heightened almost instantly. The grief of the Partition was deepened by the brutalities and destruction that took place on both sides of the border. This consecrated territory and seared it into India's national consciousness. The enemy was around the corner and just outside the borders. The affirmation of this cultural space and to its attendent root metaphors came from all quarters of India— including, at that time, Kashmir. Even the leaders of the DMK movement in Tamil Nadu changed their position quite dramatically. After 1952 they gave up their demand for secession from the Indian union, and announced instead that the Independence of India was not of north India alone but of south India as well.

After the Partition, as mentioned a little earlier, no allowances were made for democratic assertions of any kind towards national self-liberation. If in the past such ideas were loosely bandied about, it now became a criminal offence to espouse them. The Indian government systematically and relentlessly went about integrating the erstwhile princely provinces into the Indian union and there was a general and enthusiastic acceptance of this measure (see Gupta 1996: 15–19).

To stay a moment longer with India. In India the root metaphor of anti-colonialism which has an important spatial dimension also found expression in the planning process under Jawaharlal Nehru.

It has been revived again in recent years to justify a diametrically opposite position, that of economic liberalism. It is now argued that unless India liberalizes it cannot stand up and be counted as an economic force. While liberalization may benefit those who operate in non-spaces, its rationale is derived from the fact that it will help make the nation-state stronger, and not just benefit certain individuals. Thus even today many foreign collaborations are put under close scrutiny, and if there is an opposition to any on purely economic grounds it is always projected as a national responsibility. The other Indian grief is the historical memory of being colonized by European powers. This too has left a strong impress and functions as a root metaphor.

As the affiliation to an authentic nation-state is largely on the basis of subscription to root metaphors there is little point in trying to undermine it with rational arguments. As John Locke had observed long ago, a soldier is willing to die for his country, be blown to bits by cannon fire at the command of his superior officer, but this superior authority cannot 'command that Soldier (sic) to give him one penny of his Money' (quoted in Koontz 1981: 7, see also Locke 1967: 407). In one case it is a matter of unreasoned conviction towards upholding the cause that the uncalculating root metaphor imposes, but when it comes to parting with money the situation is quite different—now clear economic calculations are involved (see also Koontz 1981: 97).

This also explains, on the obverse side, why nation-states, in spite of being professedly democratic, cannot tolerate any dissension from the root metaphors that underpin their formation and cohesion (see also Rousseau 1913: 140). The English will not give in to the demands made by the Irish dissidents no matter how democratically they may have been arrived at, and the Indian government will not allow Kashmir to separate even if the majority community there should espouse such a demand. The violation of a root metaphor is a much more serious business than violating an order in the compendium that makes up the *lex*. If the root metaphor of territory is abrogated the entire nation-state compact stands threatened. If Kashmir were to be taken away from India, or Ireland from the United Kingdom, or Quebec from Canada then this would wrought profound unrest in the remaining part of the countries concerned. The community will not remain the same after such an act and would require a fresh round of negotiations which might in turn generate new root metaphors, and might even lead to further fragmentation. The alienation of territory is always the most painful for nation-states to bear. This is because territory signifies the cultural space within which the community aspires towards common goals.

Nation First and then State

The space that the nation-state root metaphors heighten becomes sovereign territory. This space marks the outer limits within which the more local spaces and cultures (with their root metaphors) are enacted. Some of the dominant root metaphors of the Indian nation-state are those of anti-colonialism, the metaphor of an ancient and glorious civilization, the metaphor of equality and participation, and the metaphor of Pakistan. It is worth noting that the metaphor of purity and pollution which is so important for the caste system is not present among the metaphors of the nation-state. Indeed the purity-pollution metaphor is actively contested by the metaphor of equality. It should also be noticed that these metaphors are not necessarily in consonance with one another. As Bhikhu Parekh states: 'Operative public values are not always mutually compatible' (Parekh 1995: 216). As we mentioned earlier, root metaphors when they cluster together do not do so on account of internal consistency but just because they happen to gather in that fashion.

The root metaphors of the nation-state come from a common sense of participation. It is the field of participation that designates the territory of the nation-state. The state is always a step behind the formation of the nation. When the nation is being formed as an ideological construct the state structure is still not an important consideration. Before India became independent, none of the major strands of the national movement had a clearly worked out plan as to how the state would be run after British colonialism was over.

There were different points of view that were aired from time to time. The Bombay Plan put forth by some leading business people of India was one among them. The socialist leanings of Nehru were never fully fleshed out in the years prior to 1947. The Planning Commission and the introduction of what was later known as the Mahalanobis model of statist intervention to modernize the economy were all post-Independence features. Even the territorial matter seemed somewhat hazy in pre-Independence days what with Congress party leaders allowing in those years for national self-determination and the parcelization of territory. Jawaharlal Nehru clearly said as much in a letter to Sir Stafford Cripps: 'Finally if a definite area expresses its will clearly in favour of separatism and this is feasible, no compulsion will be exercised to force it to remain in the Federation or Union' (see Mansergh and Moon 1976: 855; see also Gupta 1996: 43).

Not only were the nationalist leaders rather cavalier about territory but were not sure whether the structure of the state would be a 'Federation or a Union'. Once Independence came and the Partition happened the sense of common participation climaxed. This burnished the territorial lineaments and branded it in popular consciousness. After Partition not only was any secessionist activity considered criminal, but the easy accession of Princely India to British India demonstrated the popular endorsement over territory.

After Partition, regardless of what Hindu nationalists like Veer Savarkar had said about sacred soil stretching from the River Indus (now in Pakistan) to the oceans in the south, India's sacred soil, after 1947, was clearly quite different. The idea of territory had to take into account the new reality of Pakistan. There has never been any significant demand in India to capture Pakistani territories. In any case such ambitions, wherever they might exist, do not generate mass enthusiasm. When the Indian Army went into Lahore in 1965 there was never any intention of staying there and extending India's territorial frontier. The Bangladesh case too illustrated the hostile desire of India to weaken Pakistan, but not to snatch territory away and add it as an adjunct to West Bengal.

As the concept of territory is based on shared participation, a common grief, and a common mission, it is highly likely that a nation-state cobbled together primarily on the basis of historic agreements will be fragile in character. Historic agreements cannot take the place of strong centripetal sentiments which gird and underpin the nation-state. In the Indian case, for example, Kashmir's accession to India was the result of a historic agreement. The manner in which much of the North-East regions were forced into India was also not an outcome of sentiment welling up in those areas, but rather for military/strategic reasons. In these two regions the nation-state sentiment is predictably quite weak. In Canada the problem of making a nation-state on the basis of historic agreements shows up very clearly in the tensions between French Quebec and English Canada. Where historic agreements have been arrived at, special care needs to be taken to involve those regions in the larger membership of the nation-state. The problem lies in the fact that the membership of the nation-state, like all other memberships based on root metaphors, is unsympathetic and distrustful of all those who are not quite on the 'inside'.

This innate hostility is hard to overcome as any appeasement towards those with whom historic agreements have been arrived at can easily be undone by jingoistic politics that can whip up misplaced patriotism but with great political effect. In North America as a whole this is evident in the hostile manner in which the agreements with native Indians are looked at by the non-native people there. Historic agreements have to be supplanted over time and made redundant. The background and the necessity of the agreements need to be forgotten and sublated from popular consciousness. But that requires skillful statesmanship and a moratorium against jingoism. While the first is usually in short supply, there is always an abundance of the latter. This is why historic agreements represent fault lines within nation-states. These agreements bring together spaces that are not concentrated but dispersed. For this reason, as argued earlier, political force is a dominant presence in keeping these spaces together.

Sentiment, Structure and the Nation-state

The structure of the state emerged rather quickly in India after Independence. The dependence on the framework of the colonial state was immense as no serious thought was given to this aspect during the days of mobilization. Lenin too faced a similar problem after the 1917 Revolution when he found that most of his comrades were 'talkers-in-chief' and had little idea of how to run a stake. The NEP had to be brought in along with the czarist officials to stabilize the Revolution. All this in spite of Lenin's famous *State and Revolution* which clearly advocated the smashing of the czarist bureaucratic state machinery.

Once the nation-state and its root metaphors are in place, quite a few of the root metaphors that existed in the past must necessarily undergo some modifications by the nation-state's root metaphors. Caste activism in India, and indeed caste consciousness itself, have undergone significant changes since India became independent. Religious awareness and minority consciousness too have been significantly altered. The politicization of linguistic identities also had to bear the impress of the nation-state. It should be remembered that linguistic politics in India grew largely under the aegis of the nationalist movement, and not prior to it.

Together with anti-colonialism, anti-Pakistan, the metaphors of secularism and minority protection form the important cornerstones of Indian national sentiment. The manner in which the national movement developed and the nature of its climatic moments together forged these metaphors at the national level. To fight the British colonialists it was necessary to enlist all classes, poor and rich. The distinctions between castes would obviously be a barrier to the formation of such a phalanx. This necessitated the development of a broad-based agitation approach that changed the character of the Congress party from being a debating society to a mass mobilizer. Secularism included the Muslims too, but the issue of religious minorities received greater attention and conscious deliberation because the British were intent on playing off one community against the other. To counter such moves the national movement had to be especially sensitive to the religious question as well. All of these features show up in contemporary Indian politics as well. While there may be disagreements on what is secularism and what is anti-casteism, no mainstream political party can openly say that it is casteist or theocratic. There are different sets of meanings given to these metaphors, of course, but the conflict is really based on alternative meanings than on the metaphors themselves. The right wing Bharatiya Janata Party attacks the Congress for being 'pseudo-secular', but does not say that it will disband secularism when it comes to power. The debate over secularism in India once again demonstrates the many contesting meanings that can be drawn from that term. Even so it is worth noting that the many meanings of secularism put forward by their respective advocates are mutually comprehensible—they form a true discourse. Cultural identities such as being a Hindu or a Muslim, no longer repose in closed cultural spaces but must encounter the nation-state root metaphors and in this process undergo modifications.

Some of these processes started prior to 1947 with the national movement, but that was in anticipation of Independence. After Independence there were several major political mobilizations launched on the basis of cultural identities, and none of these could escape the impress of the nation-state's root metaphors. The movements for linguistic provinces in the mid-fifties were rationalized on the basis of deepening democratic governance, but found their fervour in the metaphor of popular participation. The nativist movements such as the Shiv Sena in Mumbai and the anti-Bangladeshi uprisings in Assam had to take into account the strong centripetal nation-state sentiment towards territory. To a large extent, this nation-state sentiment also explains why these movements gradually shifted their animus from enemies within the nation-state to enemies outside. The Shiv Sena in Mumbai began by targeting the south Indians but gradually shifted to an all out attack against 'anti-national' forces such as the communists and the agents of Pakistan. As Bal Thackeray, the Shiv Sena chief, once said: '*Pahela Rashtra phir Maharashtra*' (personal interview). Loosely translated it means: 'First the nation-state and then Maharashtra state'. In Assam too the first round of agitations were against the Bengalis from West Bengal, who, it was alleged, had cornered the better white collar occupations, to the poor peasant Muslim migrants from Bangladesh. The spectre of Muslim treachery and the threat of another partition draw deep from the xenophobia against Pakistan, and from the jingoism of territory.

Caste consciousness is not just based on the notion of purity and pollution but has the metaphor of secularism and democratic egalitarianism added on to it. In the movements for reservation, or positive discrimination, on caste grounds, the metaphors of secularism and democratic egalitarianism are invoked. It is also true that the opponents of reservation too rely on these metaphors, but that is what root metaphors are all about. They can have different meanings, which can be held by conflicting groups, and yet they must discourse amongst themselves. It should also be remembered that the movement against untouchability originated with the national movement, and the attempt to create a larger community. As these mobilizations, quite expectedly, gained sharper focus after Independence this led many to erroneously believe that they had independent, and even prior, origins, and operated solely on their internal cultural logics.

The importance of the root metaphors of the nation-state affecting a variety of practices can also be understood from a different perspective. So far, we have discussed how the root metaphors of the nation-state with their regnant meanings have affected the functioning of the other existing root metaphors such as those of linguistic, caste and religious identity. This has to be complemented by an awareness of how nation-state metaphors are embedding themselves at the expense of other metaphors in a variety of economic and political practices.

Embeddedness of Nation-state Metaphors

In all modern nation-states considerations of national security and economic well-being permeate practically every aspect of social life. These considerations can be put forward in neutral policy terms. They need to be carried to the people in a more symbolically charged fashion. Indeed, even the framing of such policies is not bereft of a 'popular moralism' that is so important in democratic societies. State craft is therefore justified and pursued on grounds of protecting the integrity of the nation-state which immediately brings to the surface the specific root metaphors that pulsate in different countries. Patriotism and flag waving are only the more obvious manifestations of the sway of these root metaphors, but they are evident elsewhere too. It could be the metaphor of preserving individualism, protecting freedom, protecting economic independence, saving secularism, upholding the nation's glorious past, and so on. In each case the group for which all of this is being activated is the nation, and the nation is located in the sovereign territory of the nation-state.

The many similarities between contemporary nation-states need to be examined in any study of modernity and modernization. In particular it is necessary to record the gradual domination of the rule of law, the development of the public sphere, and the adoption of the liberal principle in economic affairs (Marshall 1963: 76). Despite these very impressive commonalities nation-states also possess very striking diacritic features that separate them from one another. Even if individualism is present in all modern and modernizing societies under the aegis of liberalism, individualism exists in America as a root metaphor quite independent of any formal awareness of, or acquiescence to, the principles of liberalism. Individualism therefore stands on its own independent of the body of *lex* with which it may be retrospectively grouped. This is why a large number of Americans believe (the gun lobbyists, for example) that laws that contravene this metaphor of rugged individualism must be struck down. The devotion to individualism is much stronger among Americans than among the average Canadian, or French, or German, or Scandinavian. The zest the Americans display and the lengths that they can go to for the sake of defending capitalism as the American way of life is somewhat unique even in the western hemisphere. This is an outcome of their equation of capitalism with individualism. That is why there is often little hesitation among Americans in spontaneously supporting even anti-democratic regimes so long as capitalism is protected in those countries.

The fact that root metaphors need not be in harmony with one another, nor be applied consistently, can also be seen in the way the United States targets Gaddafi's Libya and Saddam Hussein's Iraq. This time, it is not because these countries or their leaders are socialist. The anger of the American public and government is stoked by the fact that both Gaddafi and Hussein are dictators. Consequently, they believe that democratic norms should not apply to them. This is what allowed at least two presidents of the United States to authorize the assassination of both Gaddafi and Saddam Hussein.

At a time when other root metaphors function somewhat shamefacedly and are receding in their ability to embed themselves in multiple practices and in multiple institutions, the root metaphors of the nation-state seem to exhibit none of these qualms. It is also true that though the earlier root metaphors may have lost much of their persuasive power they have not yet quite disappeared. Their ability to provide emotional bonding is still noticeable. The important difference however lies in the fact that their ability to embed themselves in multiple settings has fallen sharply. Without claiming that the metaphors of the nation-state have rushed in to fill this vacuum, it can nevertheless be said that the moral plane has shifted to another level. In societies which are becoming increasingly supra-local in their operations it is not at all unreasonable to suggest that a sense of moral community is now being effectively provided by the metaphors of the nation-state (see Turner 1990: 184, 211). When these earlier cultural spaces were being gradually eroded it led to the fear, especially in the early years of the industrial revolution, that morality would disappear and let loose anarchy and anomie (see Nisbet 1970 [1961]). These fears were particularly pronounced among 'people of culture' as can be gauged from Carlyle's apprehensions in the 'English Question'. With the benefit of hindsight we can now see that all morality was not lost. It was this same process of modernization that produced the root metaphors of the nation-state at about the same time. These metaphors provided a stabilizing influence and ushered in a new morality with a new and more enlarged cultural space.

This is something that empires, whether feudal or absolutist, could never do. This was not because of want of trying but because empires never enlivened a space around root metaphors that were shared in common. Consequently the root metaphors in those periods that were enacted in practice were largely local in character. It was the local that was replicated and magnified at higher levels. The relations of subjugation and patronage at the level of the village was enlarged to the level of the chiefdom, which was then carried over and enlarged at the next level, and so on till it reached the ultimate authority at the emperor's court. This is what gave medieval polity its segmented character and its perforated allegiances. What happened at the higher reaches often left the local levels untouched.

This can hardly be said of any functioning modern nation-state. Now policy decisions, alternations in emphasis between root metaphors, all leave a significant impact at the lower levels of the political structure. Should health care be the state's responsibility? Should education be subsidized only when non-denominational? Should abortion be allowed? Should landless workers have the right to the land they till? Should the style of the majority religious community be the 'way of life' of the others in the nation-state? All these are profound questions and all of them depend quite significantly, though not entirely, on root metaphors for their justification.

Economic rationalizations for these issues are to give a semblance of debate, but the questions are all really moral in character. The impact of decisions taken on any of these issues cannot be isolated and will affect the society as a whole.

The emergence of the nation-state as cultural space, technically called territory, does not mean that the other spaces should necessarily collapse. When such a tendency is found it is not because of the power of the territorial space. It is rather because the practices of the society are progressing to a level where the earlier root metaphors cannot embed themselves meaningfully in most institutions any more. If the metaphor of the nation-state is able to embed itself at various levels it is because it enlivens a larger space which is not incompatible with the scale at which modern day operations take place.

Nation-state, Space and Non-space

Can we think of a world of pure non-space? Many scholars already see signs of it in postmodernity or supermodernity. While it is true that there are international economies that flit between locales can it be denied that concrete practices still take place within sovereign territories? Can it be denied that these concrete practices cannot be conducted independent of the laws of the land which in turn are conditioned by the root metaphors of the nation-state concerned? What is more reflective of reality is that within the cultural space of a nation-state there is a greater degree of freedom from prior metaphors which were local, or even parochial, in their dispensation. As the nation-state metaphors enliven a larger cultural space, mobility within this space becomes much easier. Other root metaphors, even when they exist, no longer come in the way in any effective fashion.

One can now be more affirmative and say that there is a proliferation of non-spaces now because the space of the nation-state embraces a greater commonality than any root metaphor could muster in the past. A root metaphor is not just a belief but is one that has a regnant set of meanings through which material practices are realized. Indeed it is possible to go even further. The skills to operate in non-spaces are becoming increasingly generalized on account of what Marxists call the socialization of the means of production.

When qualified migrants are allowed ingress they can start functioning in these non-spaces without having to first immerse themselves in the root metaphors of the nation-state to which they have come. This is the advance that modernity has made possible. Even though many migrants still hold on to their land of origin and recreate vicarious spaces they function efficiently in the non-spaces within their host nation-states. They are legal residents of an alien country whose body of *lex* they abide by, but whose root metaphors they generally do not subscribe to. Their sense of community is drawn from an alternate source—the root metaphors of their original 'homeland'. It is therefore not uncommon that such efficient workers in non-spaces should frequently invite the wrath of the host population, in spite of being law abiding and productive. Even so it is undeniable that the scale and technology of production has tended to universalize skills irrespective of nation-state boundaries.

In most cases this would lead to the disembedding of some root metaphors from institutional practices. Modern bureaucracies and industrial organizations are free of root metaphors of purity and pollution, or of race and ethnic origin. It is possible that in some instances these might be present but it is not as if their presence is either necessary or consistent. Even the modern embeddedness argument that Granovetter presents is not about root metaphors but about the 'widespread preference for transacting with individuals of known reputation...' (Granovetter 1985: 490). The reputation of individuals is not based on grounds of family or traditional status. Gavin Smith's correction of the contemporary advocates of flexible specialization is also an important reminder that past economic practices have not been wiped clean yet. Homogenized work experience is still a fiction (Smith 1991: 223; see also Mingione 1991: 111). What is equally relevant for this study is that the existence of regional specializations also demonstrates that it is not the product but the interactions that people enter into in order to produce that is important. The production of a seemingly modern technological component need not mean that the producers are functioning in a non-space.

These amendments notwithstanding, the fact remains that to a large extent economic activities take place without the embeddedness of root metaphors even when workers labour in multiple sectors of the economy. This is certainly quite different from a premodern situation where ascriptive status would play a dominant role in considerations of all social and institutional relationships. If, however, the dependence of the rural world is still very dominant on the urban worker then it is difficult to ignore the possibilities of embeddedness of root metaphors in a worker's life. After all the rural and the urban exist as a 'cultural divide' (Smith 1991: 21).

The fact that the old root metaphors with their localized zones of influence have ceded a lot of ground thus allowing modern institutions to come up is a very significant development. What is often overlooked, however, is that the root metaphors of the nation-state continue to lurk behind the applications of these universalized technologies. While an American and a Canadian university will resemble each other in a great many details there will nevertheless be certain subtle differences in the university systems in these two countries. Remember the two countries are not just neighbours but also have a great deal in common in terms of foreign policy, aesthetics, sports, and in terms of religious denominations. In spite of these very significant areas of similarity the differences too are noteworthy, especially for our purpose. These differences are not of the kind that make it impossible to move from one system to another, but when such moves are made some amount of reorientation is still required.

A professor in an American university is alert to the fact that academic prestige is related to the capacity to raise funds in a much more crucial way than it is in Canada. This is where, once again, the effects of America's rugged individualism can be noticed. Further the fact that private universities have higher status than public or state universities in America is another significant difference between universities in these two countries. In Canada all universities are state funded and there are no private universities. American universities have to be sensitive to the race question, and, most importantly, to the problems and issues that the American people think are research worthy. What should not be forgotten is that American universities cannot easily overlook that America is a superpower and this is often reflected in the nature and quality of research that is conducted. The concerns of Canadian universities are obviously quite different. If they do not have to bear the incubus of race and superpower metaphors, they have those of bilingualism and multiculturalism to take care of.

The same can be said about the structure of industrial organization in these two countries. The technologies of manufacture and distribution are the same in all industrialized countries. This is why it is possible to talk about non-spaces in the first place. But we mention non-spaces in a guarded kind of way because nation-state metaphors are never completely absent. When the discussions on free trade between America and Canada began the apprehension among Canadians was that the Americans would pressure them to change their insurance and health scheme measures. Many Canadians were therefore against such a trade agreement for they felt that it would take away from what is uniquely Canadian from Canada. Even today, in spite of the free trade pressures, Canada still clings on to its universal health care system as an emblem of being Canadian. In Canada, it is hard to find the kind of support rugged individualism has across the border in the United States.

Canadians believe that they are a fortunate people: fortunate to be in the land of plenty and relative peace. Radio and television stations routinely announce different surveys carried out by a variety of international agencies that place Canada as the world's best place to live in. Americans do not see themselves as fortunate people, the way Canadians do. The Americans believe that they are special people, for their country fought against the privileges of feudal stratification to emerge today as a superpower. Intercommunity relations too are nuanced differently in these two nation-states. Multiculturalism arose in Canada from trying to bridge the chasm between Quebec and the rest of Canada. This logically led to the consideration that other communities within Canada, especially the visible minorities and the native Indians, need special measures and protection. To benefit from such state supported policies is not viewed pejoratively in Canada as it is in America. Many Black intellectuals and middle-class professionals in the United States do not wish to acknowledge how affirmative action helped them in their careers. Affirmative action in America does not have staunch supporters even from among its beneficiaries. The American root metaphor of individualism is probably responsible for this. Canada, on the other hand, threatened constantly by a potential rupture between its French and English populations has to keep its multiculturalism alive for national survival. Therefore, in spite of being America's neighbour Canada cannot afford to be too American.

As the nation-state inaugurates for the first time a space larger than the locality, or the parish, or the vicinage, it allows technological applications greater room to flourish. This opening up of what were earlier closed spaces has allowed the universalization of technology. This has made it easier for people of different cultures and spaces to interact. This should not be taken to mean that the locales of technological application are always free of the root metaphors of particular nation-states. These metaphors are not obsessively present in a stark form but are often hidden behind the body of *lex*. This is why they are difficult to spot. In the past it was, if anything, the other way around. Now it is possible, indeed feasible, to independently formulate rules with technical considerations uppermost as the root metaphors of the nation-state have undermined localized and encysted cultural spaces.

In pre-modern societies the rules of economic aspirations were conditioned by root metaphors. In the Indian caste system, for example, agricultural occupations were not even to be supervised by the landlord classes. It was beneath the superior castes to be concerned about such earthy affairs. The Catholic hierarchy in Canada tried to establish in the 19th century a medieval attitude to work among the Quebecois by saying that they should not even think of entering the gross fields of accounting, engineering and the like. Instead they should aspire to be peasants, to be the palm of apostleship and to be orators like Cicero, and let the Protestants take care of the more material arts (see Trudeau 1974: 9). The hierarchy did not succeed too well in this endeavour for, by then, the technological bases were rapidly changing in Quebec (ibid.: 10 ff.).

The domination of root metaphors over *lex* works when technology is stagnant and the classes rest one on top of the other in a highly sedimented form. This is what allows root metaphors to gain so much power. When technologies are continuously being modified they must be able to function according to internal rules of transformation. In this connection Charles Sabel's study of the modern economics of flexible specialization is noteworthy. To begin with, the production units are organized in such a way as to facilitate a constant rotation of managers. No one locale is allowed to become a cultural space. Further, products are 'constructed of a set of modules, each available in a number of variants, which can be recombined into many versions of the basic item' (1989: 34). This allows the growth of intra-industry networks where information is shared freely (ibid.). In addition, workers 'are taught a full range of new equipment so they can shift jobs easily' (ibid.: 36). The contrast between a modern economic operation such as this with the Padma Saliyar weavers mentioned in Chapter III, clearly drives home the difference between space and non-space. If the root metaphors of the nation-state interfere with this process of perpetual technological innovations and the emergence of non-spaces, then stagnation will set in and root metaphors will take precedence over *lex*. But in general root metaphors of the nation-state do not play that kind of an inhibiting role, except perhaps in times of national emergencies (the term itself is important).

As the root metaphors of a nation-state make for a community that is spread over the entire cultural space, or territory, it is not essential that they be realized constantly in local settings. This allows a lot of room for the body of rules and regulations to function without constantly being held in check by traditional root metaphors which operated in closed spaces. If these metaphors dominate every aspect of organizational behaviour and interaction then it is a modern despotism or totalitarian government that we are talking about.

In the ultimate analysis non-spaces are not absolute in character but only relatively so. The latitude given to the free play of *lex* is greater in modern societies for technology has a certain autonomy within the more encompassing space of a nation-state. This makes it difficult for the non-spaces within this geographical cultural space to be completely free of root metaphors in their functioning. Yet these root metaphors are *not the first principles* on which the body of *lex* is established. This allows one to still talk of the enlargement of non-spaces as a modern phenomenon. It is much simpler now to move from one setting to another without having to orient oneself to the root metaphors of each locale. In large stretches of the nation-state the root metaphors tend to be uniform and hence become largely invisible in their effects. They merge into the background. For the migrant newcomer it is only one set of root metaphors, those that have to do with the nation-state, that the person has to get oriented to, and not, as in pre-modern times, with a host of metaphors and with a diversity of cultural spaces. Very often the migrants get by without such a submergence in the metaphors of the host nation-state. These migrants can still struggle to find a niche for themselves as long as the host society provides them with non-spaces to feed the body and lets them imagine vicarious spaces for the soul.

Chapter V

Sentiment and Structure: Nation and State

Nation-state, Unity and Difference

With the inauguration of the nation as a community the numerous cultural spaces within a geographical unity begin to relate with one another supra-locally. The intensity of this relationship varies depending on how certain spaces extend themselves. For instance, when it is a question of expressing a religious identity contrapuntally against other religious identities, then the nation-state metaphors cannot but be recalled. In these moments it is impossible to observe religion as a private affair. Any nation in the course of its history, no matter how short it might be, has had to resolve issues of identity conflict, involving either religion, language or caste. On occasions like these nation-state metaphors become salient.

For instance, Hindu-Muslim antagonisms, or Hindu-Sikh contradictions, readily activate root metaphors of the nation-state. Linguistic quarrels too do the same. We have dwelt at some length over this in the previous chapter. What needs to be emphasized again is that over time these experiences become part of the natural history of a nation's memory. To be a Hindu or a Sikh cannot be configured without these public extensions of religious memory playing a role. It is for this reason that what it is to be a Hindu demands a rooting in the territorial space of the nation-state of India. To be a Hindu in India, or a Muslim in India, or a Christian in India will be a vastly different experience from belonging to any of these denominations anywhere else in the world.

Part of the reason for the differences will lie obviously in the variations that exist in the very existential settings in which these religious denominations find themselves. Where else in the world will Hindus in such large numbers be found next to Muslims but in India? Particularities abound in different geographical locations which is why contingencies exist everywhere. These particularities leave their impress on what it is to be a Hindu, a Sikh, or a Christian, as they did even in pre nation-state epochs. It is when we come to the question of examining how contradictions between religions are worked out and resolved in modern times, that the nation-state metaphors become significant in the making of cultural identities.

In the past, i.e., before there were nation-states, the contradictions between religions were resolved largely on the basis of power. The side that won took it all and the rest 'behaved' till another opportunity arose (see Gupta 1996: 67, 158–61). Further, in the context of a closed economy with limited mobility, the supra-local factor could only be activated by little else than full-scale war. It was the principle of conquest that played an important role in medieval and absolutist epochs. In between, there were centuries of peace, but this was a medieval peace. This peace was established on a hierarchical principle depending on who the victors were and who the vanquished. There may have been no accurate historical chroniclers then, but folklorists, and a natural sense of survival, together did the job quite adequately (ibid.). Cultural diversities survived but in quietude and did not dare to clamour for attention.

Today, the situation is quite different. The supra-local context provided by the nation-state is not of war and conquest. War may have led to the formation of nation-states, but the ideological compulsions of nationalism are in no way compatible with those of the previous epochs (see also Anderson 1979: 38). The supra-local community of the nation-state is one of bonding around root metaphors and thus vastly different from medieval or absolutist regimes. Further, if a bonding of this kind is to be viable, any nation-state that has evolved beyond its crude nativity must actively seek to integrate the marginal peoples within the territory. There is, of course, the option of going theocratic or fascist. In such cases, the majority (howsoever arrived at) denies equal rights to minorities. While such options do not take away from the legal fact of being a nation-state, they undermine the aspect of collective membership.

In the United States there was no consideration for the Blacks when the Constitution was first framed. The White settler colonizers saw themselves as the single force behind the American Independence movement. It was as late as 1868, with the Fourteenth Amendment, that 'equal protection of laws' was granted to the Blacks. With the Fifteenth Amendment of 1870, Blacks got the right to vote. America could be so dismissive of the Black presence till then because the White population there did not consider Blacks to be part of their quest for national sovereignty.

In the Indian case, as mentioned before, the initial conditions of the national movement were such that the lower castes and religious minorities were involved in the mass mobilizations of the anti-colonial uprisings nation-wide. Their inclusion was not just a matter of their physical presence, but an outcome of conscious ideological articulations by the national movement on a variety of levels. In the Indian case, therefore, universal adult franchise and minority rights came together with the arrival of Independence.

The manner in which different nation-states come into being also determines how sensitive they are to the question of creating and maintaining harmony between different cultural groups and communities. Fascist and theocratic states suffer from no such constraints, but they are hardly models for emulation if seen from the perspective of the minority and disprivileged communities. If accidents of birth should be allowed to diminish one's status in a nation-state then the nation-state is still wanting in many respects. The contributions of liberal democracy, inadequate though they have been on a variety of occasions, provides a format for reconciling differences within the nation-state without sublating them by executive fiat.

The nation-state believes that it speaks in the name of all. This explains why modern nation-states are particularly embarrassed when faced with recalcitrant communities with their divergent cultural practices. This was never a problem in medieval times. A nation-state however presumes a cultural community and a sacralized cultural space (or territory). There are several ways of solving this problem, some democratic and others not. One solution, under these circumstances, is to call the marginals aliens and enemies of the territory, as the Jews were characterized by the Third Reich. Jews were portrayed as people with loyalties outside Germany, perhaps even to the yet unformed state of Israel. To do this, the Jews were first made into a homogenous unity, and then as they were the marginals everywhere that factor was used to emphasize that they owed no allegiance to the nation-state of Germany, or to any other extant nation-state for that matter. 'Statelessness', as Michael Walzer observed, 'is a condition of infinite danger' (Walzer 1983: 32).

The other alternative is to devise a variety of laws and regulations that bring in the marginals into the mainstream of the nation-state. It is possible that this effort is one of cultural assimilation as with the melting pot metaphor, or even the French metaphor of *laicite*, but could be a cultural pluralist, or a cultural *laissez-faire* one as well (Parekh 1995). At this point I do not want to go into the relative merits of each, but merely suggest that nation-states try to take into account the diversity of cultures by relying on its root metaphors. Though this is never satisfactorily accomplished, cultural identities, nevertheless, cannot be innocent today of traces of belonging to a nation-state. Often anthropologists do not take this factor into consideration which gives their accounts a certain ahistorical and idealized character. Contemporary cultural identities are not before the nation-state or after the nation-state but imbued with the nation-state.

When a quick survey is done into the pre-history of contemporary nation-states one finds that in their early and formative stages nation-states in Europe were very intolerant of marginal cultures. At that point the bonding of the majority community, howsoever defined, was all that mattered. England, which prides itself on being the mother of democracy too had a fairly murky past in the early years of its nationhood. It did not revoke the Test and Corporations Act which disprivileged the Protestant dissenters and Catholics till as late as 1828. Anglican monopoly continued in all UK universities till 1871 when the Universities Test Act became a law. All through the 18th century the Toleration Act of 1689 was in effect which permitted everybody but the Catholics, Jews and Unitarians to worship freely. It even outlawed Catholic religion for the English people. In terms of modern sensibilities, the Toleration Act could not have been more inappropriately termed. But this appears inappropriate to us only in hindsight. Toleration in the Toleration Act only referred to allowing free elections and free speeches (for male Anglicans), control of Parliament over the army, and so on.

In most cases the actual fact of living in a capitalist economy has helped to congeal nation-state sentiments on an expanding basis. The dynamism in capitalism and its ability to penetrate localized economies has given supra-localism a definite existential edge. Without capitalism actually making feasible supra-local economic operations, the supra-local sentiments of the nation-state would have been difficult to sustain no matter how excellent its start may have been.

Capitalism, Nation-state, Root Metaphors

To the question: 'Can capitalism survive without the nation-state?', the answer has to be 'yes, but...'. To the question: 'Can the nation-state survive without the instrumentalities that capitalism makes possible?', the answer is 'no, but...'. Capitalism can survive without the nation-state if capitalism belonged only to the capitalists. Capitalists, as Lenin had pointed out, are looking for markets regardless of nation-state boundaries. But capitalism is a practice that involves those who are not capitalists as well. If the roving instincts of capitalists disregard the interests of these others then the capitalist operation will face difficulties. The opposition to the capitalists will be ideologically of the kind that will accuse them of not taking national interests into account. One way or another, nation-state sentiments would surface.

Nation-state metaphors too cannot survive without capitalism in the sense that without capitalism and its undermining of local economies, economic practice would continue to be embedded by cultural metaphors that invigorate only confined spaces. This would impede capitalist operations as a variety of local cultural metaphors and spaces would constantly come in the way. As the nation-state allows for a community that is supra-local, it provides capitalist economic practices a morality it would otherwise have lacked. Further, it can rely on this morality to evade the pressures of the strictly local. This is why it was argued in the last chapter that a true non-space is hard to arrive at and one can only talk in terms of non-space in a relative sense. But the nation-state requires capitalism too inasmuch as it is now able to embed an important domain of activity on a routine basis. Economic planning, economic crisis resolution, economic prospects in terms of individual biographies, are now susceptible, and indeed yield, to nation-state metaphors. Otherwise such a significant aspect of social life would remain completely impervious to the appeals of nation-state sentiments. The relationship is therefore mutually advantageous and supportive. It is now even possible to talk of capitalist development in terms of national advancement.

Diversity, Alternatives and Integration

The coupling of nation-state sentiments with capitalism also makes for a new understanding of diversity. In traditional societies there was no conception of diversity for one could not rise above one's location in cultural space to view the entirety. Being rooted in one's own cultural space made one aware of other regnant meanings to root metaphors. It also made one familiar with root metaphors in neighbouring locales, even though one only sporadically interacted with them. But that was all. In place of diversity, traditional societies talked of strangeness, of wildness, of the lack of godliness, but never really of diversity (see also Kluckhohn 1962: 69). Distances in cultural spaces were first ontologically marked. This gave 'otherness' unworthy and questionable moral qualities. Edward Said's *Orientalism* is all about how the eastern cultures are viewed by Europeans as weak, effeminate, and given to wild swings in passion (Said 1978). It is only after nation-states triumphed the world over that the differences between culture were signalled primarily in epistemological terms.

Diversity is a positive value today because the nation-state sentiment allows an elevation above the limitations of the earlier cultural spaces. The bonding that is brought about by the nation-state's root metaphors makes it imperative not to dismiss those with whom one did not hitherto share overlapping cultural spaces. The call to respect diversity is really a very recent sentiment. To respect other cultural attributes within the overarching framework that the root metaphors of the nation-state creates is an outcome of modern times. An early glimpse of this can even be found in

Germany among the Romantics like Schlegel and Schiller (see Lovejoy 1960: 188–90). The fact remains however that diversities outside of the nation-state enjoy no such generous privileges.

Though there is a moral judgement to respect diversity, it is also a fact that the greater the diversity in cultural spaces, and the lower the insertion of the nation-state's root metaphors in those spaces, the more traditional and backward a society tends to be. Diversities therefore are not good in themselves. They are good only so far as they do not conflict with the root metaphors of the nation-state. In that sense some of the isolation of earlier cultural spaces is overcome, though it cannot yet be said that they do not exist. Their existence, however, is not such that they do not allow a commonality of membership at a different plane. This naturally means that there should be a readjustment of the root metaphors of these prior cultural spaces to be able to make allowances for a supra-local community. To the extent that such adjustments are made, diversities can co-exist within the nation-state.

Diversities which do not make room for this larger supra-local community are gradually eased out by the twin forces of capitalism and the nation-state. The nation-state's root metaphors make no concessions now, and can indeed be quite intolerant when faced with such situations. On occasions this can force a break within a nation-state, as with the emergence of Bangladesh. The eventual denouement on such occasions is not a nation-stateless conglomerate of cultural spaces, but another nation-state.

Diversities in tradition blocked movement, and encouraged suspicion across cultural spaces. Diversities can only be a positive value today if they do not carry the same features. In the past diversities did not mean alternative lifestyles, they only meant distinctive differences. In fact one can get a glimpse of this even as late as France between 1940 and 1944. After the German invasion of France, the Vichy regime under Marshall Petain, set about to emphasize French cultural purity where

> there would be no mixing of modern with antique; authenticity ruled. Groups in one region were discouraged from singing songs or performing dances that originated elsewhere. The performers had to be from the region they represented and costumed in what was deemed to be the traditional fashion (Lebovics 1992: 172).

But in a modern liberal democratic nation-state diversities are acceptable and accepted only when they promote *alternative* lifestyles and choices, as well as actively sponsor a diversity of artifacts and products of diverse traditions. Kymlicka seems to accept this position but does not emphasize the difference between closed cultural practices and open alternative lifestyles (see Kymlicka 1995: 121–23). As Tamir points out: 'Members of national communities unlike communists and vegetarians have no desire to persuade others to follow their way' (Tamir 1993: 149). In essence, then, diversities are compatible with nation-state sentiments as long as they free themselves from the past and present themselves as spaceless artifacts, or as alternative lifestyles that are open for adoption.

In the Indian case it should now be possible for Bengalis to live in Andhra and speak Telugu and take great pride in Telugu arts. Likewise it should be possible for an ex-untouchable to enter the Minakshi temple in South India, wear a silk saree, and conduct mortuary rites in the fashion that only Brahmins were allowed to do in the past. Only under these conditions can diversity be respected by, and made compatible with, the nation-state. Diversity by itself is not a virtue, but diversity tamed and opened, is certainly not to be despised. Seen this way the protection of persecuted or threatened minority communities is not prompted by the unqualified ambition to preserve their cultures as it is to with their confidence as equal citizens in a nation-state.

The above should not act as a corrective to all those who propagate the respecting of diversity as an end in itself. To value diversity in this fashion is to ignore its pre-modern provenance (see Bhabha 1990: 208). Such an unqualified support to diversity is really quite anathemic to the spirit of and to the root metaphors inaugurated by, the nation-state. As a matter of fact the entrenchment of the nation-state metaphors gradually grows with the development of capitalism which over time either effaces diversities, or presents them as alternatives that exist within the territorial borders. The earlier cultural confines in America of Irish ghettoes, or Polish ghettoes, or Jewish neighbourhoods no longer exist with the same kind of vibrancy as they did even 40 years ago. The divisions between these communities were deep enough in those days so that even the socialist movement in America till the thirties was divided into the Jerusalem Socialist Party, the

Italian Socialist Party, and so on. Today, over half-a-century later, but still within a lifetime, things have changed considerably. Even the Jews have now become 'white folks' (Sacks 1994: 83–84).

This should not be taken to mean that Irish enclaves, etc., are nowhere to be seen in America, but that their exclusiveness is fast disappearing. The only ghettoes that still persist are the Black neighbourhoods. This, as we said earlier, is an outcome of class and race. Had it been just one or the other the matter would have been quite different. The gradual acceptance of East and South Asian migrants in White neighbourhoods is quite remarkable. This is largely because class no longer differentiates them from the rest though race still does. In the case of the Irish migrants as race does not play such a distinctive role, class mobility has led to their absorption into an American way of life. In the case of the Blacks it is both race and class which are significant which is why there are fairly distinct cultural spaces governed by Black root metaphors. This diversity is not a positive feature of American society as it occludes movements across spaces and non-spaces.

This should be a pointer to uncritical endorsements of diversity for diversity's sake. What is infinitely more preferable, given the direction of modernity and the gradual ascendance of allowing for alternatives and choices, is the undermining of diversities with distinct cultural spaces. In this quest the nation-state's metaphors act as potent solvents of past diversities. Poets like Neruda, Tagore and Yeats who wrote movingly about grand nation-state sentiments (see Said 1994: 226, 232) did not qualify it by placing diversities at the same level as the 'motherland'. The attempt to accommodate diversities within the ambit of the nation-state is tellingly present in India's national anthem, itself a composition of Rabindranath Tagore.

The movement towards a cultural homogenization of space proceeds apace with the protection of diversities as artifacts. Museums, and the museum frame of mind, are widely promoted. Culture historians too go about trying to rescue arts and crafts that are soon becoming defunct. There is nothing morally virtuous in such salvage operations, for as Mary Douglas said, we cannot learn something new unless we forget something old (Douglas 1995: 16). When universities give large grants for projects such as these it is yet another exhibition of what Edward Said might call 'Orientalism'. This is an orientalisation of one's own past, but only after it has been rejected and rendered inapplicable for enactment in contemporary practices.

Inter-subjectivity, Public Sphere and *Res publica*

The dissolution of distinct cultural spaces that the nation-state encourages brings about cultural homogeneity. This tendency cannot be doubted and may even lead to a lot of anguish among people as varied as de Tocqueville and Hegel. The positive side of homogeneity is that it brings about a greater degree of inter-subjectivity (for example Schutz 1978: 134, 137), and the creation of a public sphere. This leads us from an examination of the *sentiment* of the nation-state to a study of its *structure*.

Jurgen Habermas once commented that higher levels of integration, such as those of the kind that the nation-state necessitates, require legal institutions based on moral consensus (Habermas 1985, vol. 2: 174–75). What he should have added is that this moral consensus can come from no other source than the root metaphors of the nation-state. As these metaphors are not always internally consistent they lead to diverse legal interpretations and disputes over points of law. What nevertheless comes to the fore is the emergence of a 'public sphere'. The cultural spaces of the past get privatized, like religion, and a new arena for social interactions is realized (ibid., vol. 1: 340–43).

This public sphere however needs to be understood differently from the way in which Habermas has characterized it. Thus the public sphere is not inhabited by a world that is completely rational to the extent that it keeps out 'normatively ascribed arguments' (ibid.: 340). Normatively ascribed arguments are not kept out for then the requirement that legal statutes have a moral basis will have to be dropped. The public sphere emerges because the rules of arriving at an 'achieved understanding' are agreed upon, leaving the door open for politics to determine which understanding is to gain primacy. In this sense the public sphere emerges not because there is a unanimity to keep out normative elements, but because there is a general agreement on how disagreements should be framed. The normative elements that are of significance in the public sphere emerge from the polysemic character of the nation-state's root metaphors. Debates in the public sphere are inspired by root metaphors but are constrained by rules of democratic conduct and dissent. A careful reading of Oakeshott should prove fruitful in this connection (see Oakeshott 1975). Chantal Mouffe gets the point perfectly when she, using Oakeshott again, distinguishes between the struggle for diverse political ends and the formal relationship in terms of rules for conducting politics (Mouffe 1992: 232–33). The *res publica* that thus emerges is simply the public concern and consideration for others (Oakeshott 1975: 147).

This *res publica* can only be understood if seen in the context of *lex*. For some reason Mouffe generally ignores this aspect. It is the *lex* that grants participants in the *res publica* the formal status as *cives* (ibid.: 128–29). The *lex* does not prohibit different conceptions of a good life, but it insists that they be debated over according to the rules of the game. In the days of diversity proper it would have been impossible to arrive at an understanding of either *lex* or *res publica*, as practices were boxed in root metaphors in local cultural spaces. The arrival of the nation-state metaphors frees these spaces in terms of their external dimensions, and further insists that they be compatible, if not actually conform to one another.

The moral content of the public sphere must also come from nation-state sentiments and can come from nowhere else. Between nation-states there is no ground for morality but only amoral bodies of *lex*. There is no firm basis in international morality as there are no root metaphors at that level which are enacted by everyday, routine, popular participation. Universal brotherhood or the dignity of human life are features that figure in unworkable charters of human rights. Civil rights, on the contrary, have a firm moral base as they are linked to nation-state metaphors and then to the *res publica* of the public sphere.

What the public sphere does is that it allows for a greater degree of inter-subjectivity of positions. The barriers that local cultural spaces traditionally erect become porous and frangible. This has already been hinted at when it was mentioned that diversities in nation-states must allow for choices in alternative lifestyles, where these alternatives still exist. It is this structured possibility of interchangeability of positions and inter-subjectivity that makes the public sphere so public and the space so enlarged. As the rules of enactment are not to be found in prior cultural spaces, a *lex* governed *res publica* comes into being which derives its moral basis from the root metaphors of the nation-state. This moral basis need not be constantly invoked, nor need the participants always bear it uppermost in their minds. In fact when it silently informs without being aggressively dominant that its powers are the most persuasive (this is what Gramsci's 'hegemony' is all about). It is only then that it becomes truly moral.

Diasporics, Minority Rights and the Nation-state

The vibrance of root metaphors of the nation-state and the cultured territorial space they enliven can be felt even by diasporics when they settle in alien lands. Their conduct there, and particularly their struggle for minority rights in countries of their adoption are charged by the vicarious spaces of the nation-state rather than by any subscription to universal laws of brotherhood. In this connection it is necessary to notice the timing when diasporics, as minorities, first raised their voices against discrimination. When ethnic pluralists began advocating greater tolerance between communities in western democracies like America, it was also the time when ethnic distinctions were getting increasingly blurred, and there was greater tolerance. The worst was already behind them (Steinberg 1989: 48–49). 'On behalf of our sons,' Irving Howe wrote in the *World of our Fathers*, 'the East Side (erstwhile working class migrant areas of New York—D.G.) was prepared to commit suicide; perhaps it did' (quoted in ibid.: 53).

In the days when immigrants from China, India, Africa and South East Africa had few rights in North America there was hardly any clamour from among them for equality of status. In America the Chinese were locked in filthy rooms by the dozen and denied the basic rights of citizenship. In Canada for decades migrants of South Asian origin did not have the right to vote. Still there was hardly any energetic protest from these immigrant quarters. If anything, the fight on this ground was carried out for them by benevolent Americans and Canadians. The Jews too hardly raised a voice regarding cultural discrimination against them. Hard though it may be to believe now, till the closing years of the Second World War the Jews and the Blacks were on the same side.

It was among the Jews, particularly in the United States, and in the rest of the western European world more generally, that consciousness about their identity and rights was first articulated. This agitation coincides almost perfectly with the growing demand for, and the eventual realization of, a Jewish homeland in Israel. The establishment of such a homeland gave an enormous impetus to Jewish rights all over the world. To a very significant extent the persecution of Jews by Hitler's Germany focalized Jewish identity, but it was only with the realization of a Jewish nation-state that Jewish activism in countries all over the world became pronounced. In France too where the Jews had always lived as French the Jewish identity was being stridently proclaimed. For centuries, the rabbinical model was the preferred template for the Jewish male. In their confined ghettoes in most of Europe, Jews adjusted to persecution by idealizing learning, particularly of the Torah (Professor N.J. Demerath, personal communication). The aggressive warrior-like Jewish masculine ideal developed much later along with the gradual formation of the state of Israel. This explains to some extent why Jews were not prepared to resist the Nazis, and also why Jews need not be Zionists and yet remain extremely protective of the state of Israel. It is Israel as a sovereign nation-state, and not as a mythical promised land, that gave Jews the world over courage and dignity. Vicarious spaces have a powerful emotional charge and the manner in which they were invoked to forward minority rights by diasporics proves the point.

The Jewish case might seem like an unusual one, co-mingled by the excesses of Nazi Germany, and by the extraordinary talents of the Jewish community wherever they may be located. A scientific experiment can nevertheless be conducted on a comparative basis by studying when other communities, the Asians for example, first began to demand rights in diasporic locales.

Here too we find the extraordinary coincidence of the demand for minority rights by Asians and the emergence of the nation-state in Asian countries. After India became independent and Nehru went to Ottawa, Canada, Indians began to assert themselves as a minority group which demanded parity with the rest of the Canadians. The same is true for the Chinese after China emerged from the Revolution. This holds true for practically every country in Asia and Africa. The fact that migrants could now claim their origins in independent and sovereign nation-states, allowed for the recall of vicarious spaces with greater stridency. This strengthened the demand for rights as minorities in diasporic conditions. The same Indians, the same Chinese, the same Arabs, lived incognito lives in America, and wherever else they went (see Burnet and Palmer 1988: 160). First, with the stirrings of national liberation movements in the countries of their origin, and later with the actual establishment of nation-states in the excolonized parts of the world, the diasporic population from these countries found their voice in the lands of their adoption. From being immigrants they became members of a diaspora. Diaspora, as the historic genesis of the term suggests, connotes membership. It is only by being able to recall a vicarious space of an independent, sovereign homeland, that immigrants can make the transition from seriality to membership, and become a diaspora population.

This also accounts for why there is such a strong demand for ethnic pluralism at a time when communities have actually a much better position than what they ever had before. In the period when the conditions of the migrants was much harsher than it is today, it was the melting pot theory that was doing the rounds. Now that the immigrants are much better off, it is the demand for ethnic pluralism that is being voiced from minority quarters. The capacity to recall a vicarious space, the nation-state, is what provides the minorities with their emotional and moral power.

The experiment can be carried even further. The two important communities that cannot recall a vicarious space of this sort, i.e., a nation-state that is independent and sovereign, suffer the most and their efforts are easily undermined. The first are the native Americans. They cannot claim a sovereign nation-state, or even a series of nation-states to energize their demands. The fact that these native communities are called nations and not nation-states is itself indicative of this fact. Nations can exist in the head, like so many artifacts can, but nation-states enliven a space, the sovereign territory, which can then be invoked as vicarious space for minority agitations, as the diasporic people do in America and the rest of the western world.

Blacks in America cannot recall a vicarious space either for they do not identify with Africa or even with pan-Africanism. Some of the more articulate members may contrive to espouse such an identity but it is not a feeling that the Blacks share as a community. Black politics too is extremely vulnerable on this account and tends to turn viciously inwards in moments of stress. Louis Farrakhan's emergence as a major Black leader today is probably symptomatic of this condition. Further, Blacks from the Caribbean are not akin to the native born Blacks in America. This is why there are tensions between them (see Cox 1970: 380). In fact it is widely believed that the Haitian migrants in America tend to distance themselves from other Blacks because they were the first Africans to free themselves in the colonies.

Territory as the encultured space of the nation-state is far from being an exhausted empirical and conceptual phenomenon. It would be premature to say that for the diasporic peoples the lines between the homeland and the host land are blurred (Gupta and Ferguson 1992: 10). If what we have said above regarding the emergence of the demand for minority rights among the migrant minorities is even the least bit convincing, it should demonstrate that the ability to recall a vicarious space plays a very strong role in diasporic lives. To suggest, as Appadurai does, in a set of forceful essays on modernization, that in the new global order the nation-state has become obsolete is to over-generalize from a deracinated, diasporic optic (Appadurai 1996: 169; see also Lash and Urry 1987: 300). Appadurai is probably convinced of his post-nation scenario for he believes that: 'Everyone has relatives living abroad' (Appadurai 1996: 171). This statement can seem convincing only to those who come from highly mobile and successful backgrounds.

The reality is that most people live in spaces and have relatives who live there too. Further, to believe that the rich in Mumbai are not very different from the rich in New York (Gupta and Ferguson 1992: 20) ignores the realities of living a life. Can the rich in Mumbai stay rich for one moment without the presence of the poor in the city? It is important to recognize how the rich in India relate to the poor and to the not so rich who are in their immediate environs. In addition, the role that patronage and connections play in being rich in cities like Mumbai cannot be ignored. In seeking answers to these questions the vast gulf between being rich in New York and in Mumbai gets emphasized.

In the recently held World Trade Organization conference in 1995 the countries of the Third World resented the pressure from America and the other G7 countries to negate the advantage that industries in poorer countries enjoyed because of the abundance of cheap labour. The rich of the poor countries protested, for they argued that cheap labour was their strongest selling point. The rich in the west and in Mumbai, or anywhere in the developing world, play according to vastly different scripts. To conflate the two is to be mesmerized by superficial signs of consumption and not attend to the reality of social interaction.

Sentiment, Structure and Citizenship

Anthropology can legitimately lay claim to the study of the nation-state as questions of root metaphors, cultural space and community are involved in such an examination. There has been a reluctance by anthropologists to enter this domain for it was generally felt that the nation-state has to do with structures of legality and impersonal alienating practices which are not amenable to fieldwork or to concepts that are familiar to anthropologists. This, we have tried to show, is far from true. Moreover, a nation-state cannot claim a durable or moral status if it is based only on *lex*, or a body of rules and operational procedures. The nation-state is not based foundationally on what Weber would call *zweikrational*. A completely neutral nation-state can hardly arouse patriotism. Without uncalculating patriotism no nation-state can hope to survive for long.

It is important for anthropologists to realize how a study of nation-states with their root metaphors, regnant sets of meaning and territorial spaces can give their discipline a contemporary relevance. By leaving behind the small group and its localized cultural spaces, anthropologists can contribute significantly towards the comprehension of modern, complex societies, all of which are today organized on nation-state principles (see e.g., Spencer 1997: 7–12). It may be argued that in some cases there is the structure of the nation-state without the sentiment, but it is structure and sentiment together that govern nation-states in most parts of the world.

It is true that no nation-state can survive without root metaphors whose regnant set of meanings are enlivened through practice within a cultural space. But this is really the first step. In order that nation-states survive and reproduce themselves in time it is necessary that certain policy decisions be taken so that the sentiments that bind people together can be realized in as many instances as possible. The greater the instances of such commonality, the stronger the nation-state tie will be within a particular territory. The more vivid too will be the recall of vicarious spaces by diasporics in far-flung lands.

Nation-states are built on popular endorsements of root metaphors, with their regnant set of meanings, which in practice enliven a cultural space which is the sovereign territory. This popular aspect of a nation-state can be undermined and lost sight of, for social relations are inherently unequal and hierarchical in most societies. Inequalities, when they are too sharp, offend the egalitarian principle on which the nation-state is founded (see Marshall 1963: 76, 81, 87). It is for this reason that appropriate policy measures are often contemplated which would realistically lessen the feelings of alienation that are bound to arise in a society where not everyone is actually equal in all respects, except perhaps in their patriotic fervour.

The nation-state belongs to all, rich and poor, privileged and the under-privileged. If classes and strata had been left undisturbed from medieval times by modern nation-states, then the ties of commonality would soon wear thin and snap. This is where considerations of citizenship come up. The challenges of realizing citizenship in a substantive and not in just a formal way has been the concern of nation-states ever since the early years of the 20th century. This is also the high noon of nation-state awareness, so it is only natural that the concerns of citizenship should accompany the rising tide of nation-state sentiments. All well-developed contemporary nation-states are concerned about realizing substantive citizenship, though the methods adopted may be vastly different. The important point is that such public policy measures were hardly ever entertained in pre-modern times. The warp of such policy measures relies on the woof of nation-state sentiments. Historically, with nation-states, it has always been sentiment first and policy next. Having dealt with sentiments let us now go to a study of the structures of the nation-state. In this process, particular attention should be paid to understanding what implications these policies have for realizing substantive citizenship which has always been the promise of nation-statehood from the days of the French Revolution onwards.

Nation-states are created in moments of, what Sartre would probably call, high 'fusion'. This euphoria however does not last for very long and the routine of seriality is bound to set in sooner or later. Once nation-states come into being the question of keeping it going becomes an urgent task. There is no blueprint for it in tradition, or in spontaneous community organizations. Sustaining the fraternity that was unleashed at the time of the formation of nationhood has to be accomplished by deliberate measures of statehood. The commonality that spurred the community of patriots and gave them the badge of membership, does not reflect itself in other aspects of social life.

There are vast differences in economic and cultural spheres, and this is often complicated by the fact that the two can also reinforce each other. Unless statehood comes up with policies that inform the structures of governance that can keep fraternity going, the sentiments of a nation-state will be hard to sustain. In previous sections it has been emphasized that cultural space comes about in an interactive setting. Interaction brought about a fusion of sentiments, it is interaction again that is necessary to sustain it. The state must think now in terms of structures that can overcome the extant differences between members of a nation-state and give them a commonality that is not an evanescent one.

This is where citizenship figures as an active consideration. It is through citizenship that the fusion of sentiments is sought to be sustained. Subscription to nation-state metaphors is a necessary but not sufficient condition of substantive citizenship. Through the principles of citizenship the commonality that is threatened in the inequalities of social and economic life is addressed so that fraternity can still be preserved. This fraternity is not one that must compulsively make everyone equal in every respect. It should however give the individual a chance at realizing equality. The various theories of liberalism, beginning from Locke and culminating in John Rawls are important in this context.

In the following chapters attention will be paid to those aspects of collective life in a modern nation-state that most threaten the principles of fraternity. Accordingly it is imperative to discuss what is meant by citizenship in the context of a civil society, and how minority rights and community rights should be viewed in an expanding liberal atmosphere within a nation-state. An important theme that is constantly reiterated in the remaining chapters is the reconciliation of liberal individualism with the protection and enhancement of fraternity. This implies that minority protection, the cultivation of freedom, and the advocacy of positive discrimination must be attentive to both the individual and the promotion of fraternity. It is not an easy task, but it is to this that we shall now turn.

While we discuss issues relating to fraternity, it should also be clear that the nation-state necessitates a new kind of fraternity from the ones established by custom or tradition. The sense of fusion that the project 'nation' brings about can only be consolidated by the framework of the 'state' and its structures. The fraternity that is now relevant is a fraternity that is to be constructed. Fraternity, in other words, becomes a *project*, and is not a *given* solidarity. In fact, all earlier solidarities are extremely suspect and must give precedence to the establishment of fraternity along lines of citizenship within the conditions of a civil society. These are still words, perhaps the following chapters will help substantiate our position.

Before we embark on that task it is important to clarify that the root metaphors of the nation-state mimic the root metaphors of traditional cultural spaces, but are not identical with them. Tradition, *when most tolerant*, allowed for cultural spaces to co-exist in a non-invasive sense. The root metaphors of the nation-state are not quite as quiescent and seek to actively intervene in the pre-existing cultural spaces and their memberships. With the nation-state's arrival there is a certain self-consciousness regarding how cultural spaces should conduct themselves for the larger glory of the whole. There are various ways of seeing the whole—the totalitarian and the liberal democratic are the two extremes in this regard. The totalitarian/fascist solution is a simple assertion of majoritarianism. It is the liberal democratic path which poses the greatest intellectual challenge; it is the liberal democratic option that also possesses the greatest liberating potential. It is for this reason that this book is about the structures that liberal democracy devises in keeping alive the sentiments of the nation-state.

The nation-state metaphors are not only more invasive than traditional cultural metaphors, they are also more parlous in terms of the regnant sets of meanings that accompany each metaphor. This may seem surprising at first glance. When a set of metaphors commands such a large cultural space with so many members, the unreflexive assumption generally is that the regnant sets of meanings must necessarily be more varied. In actual fact the reverse is true and with good reason. As the nation-state metaphors seek to supersede earlier cultural spaces and include them within the territorial space, the principles and sentiments for unification cannot allow for too many variations or exceptions. It is in this self-conscious drive to transcend parochial spaces that the root metaphors of the nation-state are quite different from the usual run of cultural metaphors. This again shows that logically the nation-state is not very supportive of closed spaces, nor of the kind of encysted cultural diversities that these spaces entail.

Perhaps the greatest difference between cultural metaphors and membership on the one hand and those of the nation-state on the other is that of the range and depth of commitment. While cultural membership is intense and equally subscribed to, the situation is not quite as homogenous with nation-state membership. In the making of the nation-state, while large numbers may have been involved, there are also significant chunks that were not participatory in the same sense. These are usually the less organized, less visible, less fortunate sections of the population. These categories of people become legal citizens, but are not substantively so. In other words, the root metaphors of the nation-state do not mean that all legal citizens are in a state of fraternity. All nation-states realize that the membership of this fraternity has to be enlarged, so that citizenship does not remain just a legal status. This is why there is a need for policies and structures of government. At different levels, and in different ways, regardless of whether a nation-state is liberal democratic or not, the question of substantive citizenship/membership is one that no nation-state can completely ignore. It is with liberal democracy, however, that the realization of enlarging and deepening fraternity is comprehensively recognized.

In spite of these and other differences between nation-state metaphors and other cultural metaphors, there are also great similarities between them. This is what enables us to consider territory as cultural space, and citizenship as a form of social membership. Like other cultural metaphors the root metaphors of the nation-state need to be realized in practice. It is this that calls attention to the study of structures through which the nation-state metaphors can be realized. The most important consideration of social membership of a nation-state is the realization of citizenship. This, as we said earlier, is a task of great significance especially within the framework of liberal democracy. While liberal democracy is not alone in emphasizing that citizens have diverse origins and starting points, it is probably alone in protecting the right to political differences. The range of political differences allowed by liberal democracy is quite impressive, but everywhere, its limits are set by the root metaphors of respective nation-states. A political opinion that attacks the basis of the cultural membership to the nation-state, or threatens to compromise on its cultural space—the territory—is first marginalized and then systematically pulverized. Yet, when these limits are not transgressed liberal democracy allows for several visions of the good. In this sense liberal democracy does not advocate a perfectionist view. It canvasses instead for a state of affairs where a variety of conceptions of the good can compete in the public sphere for favour among citizens.

Part Two

...To Structure

Chapter VI

Civil Society or the State: What Happened to Citizenship?

The Challenge of Liberal Democracy

The sentiments that give birth to the nation do not always bring forth a liberal democratic state. The option of a theocratic state, or a fascist state is always a live one. This possibility hovers in the background, and cannot, indeed, should not, be casually dismissed. The liberal democratic state does not emerge naturally, as it were, after the nation has come into being. This is quite paradoxical as the liberal democratic structure can alone ensure the sense of common participation that enlivened the cultural space of the nation. But, to keep the root metaphors of this cultural space alive, it is necessary to continuously engage the members of the nation to be involved in common projects. In a modern society, this effectively means the protection of the principles of fraternity whereby the nation-state is not seen as being inclined or partial to one category of people and not to the other.

Fraternity would also imply the creation of conditions where individuals have the freedom to participate in a collective and realize themselves. It is on questions of the conditions of realizing fraternity that it is important to discuss the issue of civil society. *Civil society is not a thing*, but a set of conditions within which individuals interact collectively with the state. In this process freedom is advanced, but not by acts of benevolence from above. It is rather by participation in common projects. In other words, the condition of civil society keeps altering the nature of the society, for both the state and the citizens are constantly being transformed.

This is why civil society is such an important consideration when the question of setting up structures for the realization and enhancement of fraternity becomes paramount. If the structures set up for enhancing fraternity are done without the condition of civil society being present then those structures are bound to become patronizing, static and sources of vested interests. In this chapter an attempt will be made to clarify this issue. To do so, it is necessary to wade through some of the popular conceptions of civil society which stand in the way of appreciating civil society as the condition under which the structures of a liberal democratic society can be instituted.

Civil Society Against the State

How can one account for the surge of literature on civil society these days? In India, Rajni Kothari was one of the first people to revive this concept in 1984 (Kothari 1984). Around the same time the term was also doing the rounds in western academic circles, gathering strength with each turn. Today there is a plethora of literature on this subject, and, perhaps because of it, a general confusion about what 'civil society' is supposed to mean.

It is tempting to dismiss all this as yet another fad. To do so would be a pity for it would block out the many sociological issues that the literature on the subject brings out. These sociological factors also help us understand why the term enjoys such popularity today.

It is true, as many observers have noted, that the disenchantment with the state is a major reason for the contemporary interest in civil society (Keane 1988; Seligman 1992: 12; Blaney and Pasha 1993: 3–24; Chandhoke 1995: 31; Hann and Dunn 1996: 4). In developed western democracies this disenchantment is largely because of the surfeit of consumerism leading people to wonder that happened to certain natural simplicities (e.g., Seligman 1992). Along with such consumerist excesses the state has acquired panoptic powers of surveillance akin to Foucault's dystopia.

Such powers at the top, aided in no small measure by technological support, undermine the viability of democratic participation through modern institutions. The state thus begins to resemble an incubus which cannot be shaken off. In the totalitarian regimes of Eastern Europe and the Soviet Union, this image was even stronger (see Spulbeck 1996). All of this put together explains why the concept of civil society emerged in these societies in such opposition to the state.

In countries like India, the state is not a good word either. The reasons in this case are almost the reverse of the ones in the European situation. Over the past five decades the Indian state has been unable to deliver in spite of repeated promises. In fact, some would go on to argue, things have become much worse during these years. Technological advance has been monopolized by an elite section in India. It is this stratum that controls the state and influences its functioning.

The majority of Indians, on the other hand, have only witnessed the negative consequences of technology, and in that sense have been its victims. Instead of heeding to the needs of the majority the Indian state is busy aggrandizing itself and its functionaries. It does so in the name of democracy, but in reality has scant respect for it. Instead of promoting unity the state is basically divisive in its orientation as it constantly seeks to marginalize communities and estrange them from each other (see e.g., Kothari 1984, 1988a, 1988b, 1991; Nandy 1984, 1989).

This disenchantment with the state has, however, taken different manifestations. In some cases it has resulted in a recall of sentiments and structures of the past (Seligman 1992; Kothari 1988b, 1991). In other cases, quite conversely, there is a demand for the strengthening of intermediate institutions which will realize the promise of constitutional democracies (Béteille 1996b). Ernest Gellner, in his recent contribution on civil society, also lauds the institutions of constitutional democracies of the advanced western world, but leaves behind the impression that such arrangements cannot really by exported to other shores (Gellner 1994).

The truth, however, is that it is not studies of this kind that have given the concept of civil society its second wind in academic circles the world over. The reason for the resurgence of this term is because it is generally viewed in terms of a return to a traditional moral ordering of community relations. The emphasis is now on moving away from a universalistic discourse, which is laden with technological domination, to one of moral sentiments based on shared mutuality and trust (Seligman 1992: 12).

Rajni Kothari expresses this view forthrightly when he says that civil society must draw

> upon available and still surviving traditions of togetherness, mutuality and resolution of differences and conflict—in short, traditions of a democratic collective that are our own and which we need to build in a changed historical context. This is the basic political task facing Indians—the creation of a civil society that is rooted in diversity yet cohering and holding together (Kothari 1991: 29).

If the concept of civil society today is largely charged by a return to tradition then that by itself is no minor irony. When the term 'civil society' was first referred to by Locke, Rousseau, and, then most elegantly, by Hegel, it was to inaugurate a break from a hierarchical and medieval past and a movement into a more public spirited era. In a civil society the individual is a member of a family, part of a corporation, but, most importantly, a free citizen in a constitutional republic (see Anderson 1996: 102).

When the odd study on civil society in India today does pay attention to the need for constitutional democracy (Béteille 1996b), emphasis is placed on the role of modern rational-legal intermediate institutions. These institutions could be the corporate structure of the economy, the judiciary, the municipality, the various institutions of local self-governance, the university, and so on (ibid.). For Béteille, the hope for modern Indian society lies in the elaboration and proper functioning of these rational-legal intermediate institutions.

The state, it seems, cannot be quite trusted upon to uphold the autonomy of such institutions, though it established them in the first place. Béteille finds that over the years these institutions have been internally perjured by the state's political interference (Béteille 1991). They must therefore be freed from these political imperatives if they are to stand up on their own and be true to their basic institutional logics. It is only by reviving these institutions that the promise of liberal democracy can be attained. In which case, these intermediate institutions need not be viewed as tributaries of the state structure but, on the contrary, can now be independently valorized. We are therefore in the heart of a paradox. Rational-legal intermediate institutions are independently good for constitutional democracy even if the state, which originally set them up, is not always quite so. These institutions are rather like endangered species that need to be protected from statist depredations. This has important consequences, especially for the notion of citizenship in a developing country. But more of that in a while.

Civil Society and Community Ties

The dominant trend in current renditions on civil society clearly privileges community ties based on custom over modern constitutional arrangements. In all such cases, custom, and even tradition, are primordial wells of fraternity and mutual trust. As the modern constitutional state is now suspect, it is almost natural that institutions prior to it should be viewed kindly in a friendly light. Contract theorists and later Hegel, followed by Liberal thinkers, all saw tradition as essentially irrational for it constrained human freedom. Now, however, as depicted by many modern day civil society protagonists, it is in traditional mores and customs that moral authenticity resides. Clearly this revulsion to the modern state, which goes all the way to the other side, is reminiscent of the ro-mantic reaction to the state, science and technology that Heidegger, and to some extent Husserl, popularized in early 20th century Europe.

One can see elements of this even in Jurgen Habermas' *The Theory of Communicative Action* (1985) though he does not invoke the concept of civil society in any fundamental way. Nevertheless Habermas argues that societies are characterized by system integrating and symbolic integrating functions. Symbolically integrating aspects are those such as the family and inter-personal relations which are based on consensus. System integrating ones are those that relate to political power and the economy. Traditionally, according to Habermas these two modes of integration functioned in tandem, but modern societies have uncoupled them. The 'life world' which is the zone of consensus and easy inter-subjectivity is now overwhelmed by the system integrating forces of money and power.

The contemporary conjoining of tradition with the concept of civil society sees the world in a similar way. It is against the background of disillusionment with the state that the tendency to romanticize 'society' must be positioned. As a consequence, those aspects of the society least touched by the state seem more 'civil', precious and authentic.

India provides a hospitable locale for such a point of view. Not only has the post-colonial state in India been a great disappointment, but tradition beckons from every nook and cranny of this society. The rationalist Jawaharlal Nehru was short on patience on any kind of traditional swill, but what has the Indian state achieved in the past 50 years of independence? Rather than take a jaundiced, unsympathetic attitude towards tradition one should look at it as a source of social bonding. The protagonists of civil society in India now argue that if we have lost our bearing as a nation it is because we were so dismissive of our cultural roots.

This point of view can be misread as belonging to the same species of thought which in Europe has spawned 'new social movements'. There is a major difference between the two and that should be cleared up right away. In new social movements the attention is on how to revive intermediate institutions of modernity without necessarily exalting tradition. Yet the new social movements are not concerned with the need to capture state power (for example, in Touraine 1992). These movements in Europe seek to pressure intermediate institutions to respond to popular will, and in that sense restrain the arbitrary and undemocratic use of state power. There is no focussed attempt anywhere to divorce these intermediate institutions from the state. Instead, these institutions are now being reminded that in their original condition they were supposed to be the vehicles of popular initiatives.

The concept of civil society that is generated by new social movements does not necessarily deny or even undermine the validity of modern state apparatuses. The new social movements in the west challenge unpopular state action by invigorating intermediate institutions of the state. These may be the local council, municipalities, action groups at the borough or neighbourhood level, or unions and special interest activist forums. All of these are recognized aspects and appertunances of modern democratic states. Trade unions, or interest groups, or local self-government councils were not set up to oppose the state, but are perceived as so many agencies through which the state receives its inputs from 'agentic individuals' (Seligman 1992: 5).

What is new about the new social movements is that while they oppose overbearing and unresponsive governments in power, they have no desire to question the legitimacy of the modern state, or to directly take over state power. They remain firmly rooted within these intermediate institutions and work to keep them active so that they do not fall into disuse from either complacency or neglect.

The Call for Humane Governance

What is the majority slant on civil society in India? Civil society is generally understood by Indian academics as a realm which is inimical to modernity and its creations. As the constitutional state is also a modern phenomenon it is also extremely suspect. Civil society thus lies in traditions and customs that are either before the state or outside the state. As the Indian state has failed on many fronts, the temptation to revile it and its many institutions as unmitigatedly evil is rather difficult to resist. Some of the best known exponents of civil society as embodying customary and traditional ties are Rajni Kothari, Ashis Nandy and D.L. Sheth. Their writings on this subject have generated wide ranging debates. As we will soon see the question of civil society in India draws in matters relating to affirmative action (or positive discrimination), relationship with minorities, and the authenticity of the Indian nation-state itself.

It is not easy to compress the large repertoire of the civil society experts in India, for their arguments have evolved over time and are often reactions to concrete political events. There is yet another difficulty. Very often, with the exception of André Béteille (1996b) and Partha Chatterji (1997), references and allusions to civil society are made somewhat independently of the tradition and provenance of the term in western scholarship.

The concept of civil society in India can also be read as a cultural critique of the Indian state. In critiques of this sort India's history and its peculiar cultural genius serve as points of departure. Anything that does not square with this is immediately suspect. Rajni Kothari, the leading figure in this regard, argues that the crisis of governance in contemporary India has come about because the state is insensitive to the myriad diversities of the subcontinent. Instead of being alert to these differences the state tries to stifle them in the name of political unity (Kothari 1988a: 2223). But it is not unity that it really wishes to bring about. The state's real project is homogenization—cultural, political and social.

These homogenization efforts by the state negate the culture and talent of the people and instead, foist a techno-managerial structure on them. The state's increasing reliance on the urban industrial class has led to the bifurcation of two Indias—one urban and the other rural (ibid.: 2227). It is quite obvious that Kothari's sympathies lie with the latter. It is also in rural India that the civil society functions best. It is in the villages, away from the prying and destructive eyes of the techno-managerial urban elite, that the native genius and dispositions of the Indian people can be found in their near pristine condition.

The prospects, therefore, for humane governance are remote in the modern Indian nation-state (and by extension all modern states), as it prioritizes the compulsions of the profit seeking market (Kothari 1988b: 2, 39). Humane governance, on the other hand, should give primacy to endogenous impulses and aspirations as these emerge spontaneously from the people. Instead the Indian nation-state brutally marginalizes all those who do not fall in line. It is in these marginalized zones that the true impulses of civil society lie. To quote Kothari:

> Civil society's ordering of politics and governance is, in my view, the take-off point of human governance. Such a re-entry is what contemporary social movements strive for. Human rights movements, ecology, movements, women's movements, the peace movement are all about restoring the first principles of the 'good' and the 'good life' in the conduct of human affairs. Such sources of regeneration...*lie more in the South than in the North, more in women than in men, more in the marginalized than in the powerful, more in ethnic identities and submerged civilizations than in dominant cultures* (ibid.: 3).

For Kothari then the state is quite unambiguously an alien construct. It is this that prompts him to repose his confidence in non-governmental organizations as they are closer to the marginal and subjugated people and hence better tuned to the stirrings of civil society (ibid.: 71, 109–10). D.L. Sheth too delves into the merits of non-governmental organizations for they are free from the power seeking homogenizing logic of the state (Sheth 1984: 259–62). Ashis Nandy complements this point of view by arguing that western oriented people in India first look to the state and adjust their culture accordingly. This is why the state is oppressive to those who are true to their indigenous cultural moorings (Nandy 1984: 2078–80). In a later paper entitled 'The Political Culture of the Indian Nation-state', Nandy develops this idea further. According to him the

> culture of politics has in recent years depended more and more on a mix of Indian high culture and the metropolitan culture of the nation-state. The traditional dialectic of the Brahminic and the non-Brahminic the classical and the folk, the textually prescribed and the customary practice has been bypassed (Nandy 1989: 9).

As a result, instead of diversity we now find a 'scaled down homogeneity...(and a) constant search for grand technological and organizational feats as evidence of the cultural superiority of the new elites' (ibid.).

Return to Tradition

The need to invigorate civil society with tradition gives tradition a gloss that modernization theorists, Marxists and liberals (such as Béteille) would strenuously object to. Even the espousal of minority rights by hearkening to traditional values, *pace* Kothari and Nandy, constitutes quite a novelty. To argue that tradition housed values of tolerance, fraternity and broadminded goodwill in bound to take the uninitiated by complete surprise. While such a view was aired previously from conservative and even reactionary quarters, it is now being endorsed even by zealous advocates of the 'subaltern peoples'.

In a country generally acknowledged to be the most hierarchical, rigid and oppressive among known human civilizations the claim is now being made that Indian tradition exerted, on balance, a healthy respect for people's initiatives and aspirations. The ignominy of caste, ritual widow burning, child marriages, and the subjugation of women are calmly overlooked. Even the sacredotal texts known for foisting Brahminic and male-centred prescriptions and ideologies are now seen as founts of wisdom and compassion. Ancient Hindu texts such as the *Manusmriti* and the *Yagnavalkyasmriti* which actively campaigned for a Brahminic and masculine social order are being reinterpreted as being popular in origin and accommodative of diverse points of view (see Kishwar 1994: 2148).

There is however another kind of tradition and custom which appears much more congenial, at least at first glance. Many peasant communities, such as the Jats and Gujjars of north India, have tried to come out with their own versions of a civil code. For example, the Jats gathered in 1993 is Sisana, Haryana to formulate a code that would be binding on all Jats (see Gupta 1997: 145). This gathering of Jat clan heads decided to ban dowry, liquor vends and liquor consumption, as well as extravagant marriage ceremonies. Details as to how different rituals should be conducted were elaborately spelt out. Some of this would certainly appear very laudable to many, especially the strictures against dowry and ostentatiousness.

This, however, is not all. As we read on we find that the document also endorses that women should be educated, but it severely opposes any hint that this education should make them financially or socially independent. Women's education is recommended not because this would make women independent citizens, but because they can then become better mothers and help their children with school work. Further, the Sisana document does not favour the free mixing of sexes or co-educational schools. It also maintains that after marriage a girl loses all rights to her natal home and to her father's property. If, for some reason, a marriage goes wrong and it cannot be patched up, then the offending party should be boycotted (for the full Sisana document see Gupta 1997: 200–203).

Looking back now it becomes clear that the injunctions against dowry and extravaganzas were as inflexible and intolerant as those against women's independence and inheritance. The community spokesmen not only ordained that certain ceremonies must be held, but also explicitly laid down the modalities of their performance.

Failure to comply would make the offending party liable to social boycott. Therefore, though there might be elements in tradition which look good from afar, they are not really manifestations of either goodwill or tolerance. More than anything else, tradition and custom once again come through as unbending for they can only demand complete obedience.

In communitarian renditions of civil society, however, it is only modern institutions that are wrong. Not just that, in the Indian case, even the Indian nation-state is seen as a conceptual and empirical monster. The fact that different linguistic, religious and regional communities, with their divergent notions of the social good, are boxed into a single nation-state, demonstrates to these critics the state's oppressive callousness towards marginal and non-conformist aspirations. As primordial (or ascriptive) identities define the horizon of meaning, the state must necessarily be dismantled if authenticity, humaneness and popular initiatives are to rule again. Stated in such terms, civil society resembles 'the state of nature' that Locke found so distasteful (Locke 1967). Civil society is also all about the 'heart', about 'enthusiasm' and 'natural simplicity' that Hegel so unambiguously distanced himself from (see Hegel 1945: 95, 125). Moreover, when civil society is seen as tradition the internal contradictions between communities and within communities are completely overlooked. Communities are seen as self-regulating and non-contradictory. The horizon of tradition is packed with only well-meaning individuals sworn to fraternity and principles of tolerance (see Taylor 1979: 157–59; MacIntyre 1981: 205).

Though Partha Chatterji's understanding of civil society is different from that of the cultural critics, there is much in common between them. Chatterji considers civil society to be part of modernity and modernity alone. For this reason he sees civil society even in institutions set up during the period of colonial rule in India (1997). In Chatterji's opinion, civil society has been cornered by the better off sections and members of the elite. This is why he has a negative view of modernity and all those who work and employ modern institutions. In this he is one with Kothari, Nandy and the cultural critics of the Indian state. There is of course the difference between Chatterji's notion of civil society and those of the cultural critics. But this could be seen largely as a terminological matter as their larger positions seem to coincide.

For Chatterji civil society is modern institutions for which reason, he argues, one must break out of it by relying on political initiatives which are outside of these institutions. The end result is very much the same. Like Nandy, Kothari and Sheth, Chatterji too is very critical of modernity. If Kothari and Sheth look to grass-roots movements as an alternative to the stifling technocratic managerial state, Chatterji pins his hopes on autonomous political realms to accomplish the same. It is not very clear whether in establishing the autonomy of the political Chatterji too would like to plumb the depths of tradition. In spite of terminological differences and a certain ambiguity on some points, there is an obvious similarity between Chatterji's view and those of Kothari, Nandy and Sheth. Both points of view distrust the modern state and its projects, and both believe that the answer lies outside the purview of modern institutions. The die is cast in terms of the elites versus the authentic masses.

It is also quite apparent then that Rajni Kothari or Ashis Nandy would like to preserve some of the gains of the Enlightenment with respect to freedom and dignity, but without the modern state. Therefore, while they find virtues in tradition they would not make common cause with straightforward revivalists. This nostalgia for tradition on the one hand and the desire to be free on the other is a first class contradiction they seem to be oblivious of. As Marx explained in the *Grundrisse*, it is impossible now to return to ancient Greece as we can no longer be naive enough to give up our freedoms (Marx 1973: 111).

The fact that the majority of Indian scholarship on civil society insists on being *naive* from a safe distance is what makes it reminiscent of European romantic revivalists of the 19th and early 20th centuries. This also explains why proponents of civil society in India have no sympathy for the functioning of modern organizations and institutions as they are all seen as agencies of oppression. Therefore, affirmative action is advocated in its most uncritical form without a thought as to how the well-being of intermediate institutions can be protected (see Béteille 1991 for a critique). As institutional efficiency is considered to be just a mask which the techno-managerial sector dons in order to ruthlessly homogenize the subject and marginalized population, there seems to be no need to worry unduly about it.

De Tocqueville on Intermediate Institutions

At this point it is necessary to consider André Béteille's contribution to the subject of civil society. I believe Béteille is largely reacting against the manner in which the cultural critics have romanticized the concept of civil society and linked it quite unabashedly with tradition. So far Béteille's is a rather lonely voice in the Indian debate on civil society, but his vast academic reputation, and the erudition he brings to bear on the subject, call for close attention. To set Béteille against the rest therefore seems like a good manoeuvre to get significant conceptual issues out in the open. Béteille's route to civil society is very different from the one considered so far. He recalls the classics, but finds his point of inspiration, not in Hegel or Rousseau, but in Alexis de Tocqueville's study of American democracy (de Tocqueville 1954). It is for this reason a slight digression into de Tocqueville is perhaps called for.

Though de Tocqueville's experience of America was on the whole a positive one, he nevertheless feared the excessive power that the American state had the potential of acquiring. To that end he argued that democratic associations be kept fit and in readiness so that the state could be curbed if and when the occasion arose. Absolute power should not be vested in any single authority which is why checks and balances are required. As democratic states tend to give the legislative too much power, democratic associations and voluntary organizations are necessary to exercise countervailing pressure. In this case it is not clear if these intermediate associations or institutions are agencies of the state structure, or are outside the state. It would appear that for de Tocqueville the intermediate institutions possessed a rationale quite independent from that of the modern democratic state.

For Alexis de Tocqueville intermediate institutions were coeval with the modern state, but not necessarily outgrowths of it. Instead they emerged because of the customs and manners of the people. It is in this sense that de Tocqueville found America to be unique. As its immigrant population was largely influenced by the puritanical outlook of the Pilgrim Fathers, there was a natural adhorrence towards centralization of power and other forms of aggrandizement. De Tocqueville was convinced that this popular mindset could be trusted to act as a deterrent against the American state becoming too powerful. Any time an issue comes up, local councils and voluntary organizations spontaneously emerge to debate and discuss the matter.

It is also possible to make the case that, for de Tocqueville, democratic associations functioned as agencies of the state to help realize its various goals. But these two positions are quite distinct. In one case democratic associations curb the excesses that a democratic state is prone to commit, and in the other case these associations link individuals to the state as active members of the citizenry. Of course, one never exists empirically without the other. The question really is of emphasis and direction. Nevertheless, as will be argued later, this conceptual distinction has important practical consequences as well.

Further, de Tocqueville's study presents yet another complicating factor. De Tocqueville clearly made the case that democracy required, at least in the exemplary American situation, a specific cultural make-up in terms of customs and manners. This cultural factor was therefore prior to the establishment of the democratic state. Indeed, without it any attempt towards the establishment of a democratic regime would be severely limited. This is why de Tocqueville often despaired at the efforts of the French Revolution to set up an enduring democracy. In other words, the customs and manners of the American people can also be considered as a primordial given whose natural genius led towards the establishment of a democratic society.

The use of de Tocqueville in Edward C. Banfield's work, *The Moral Basis of a Backward Society* (1958) also encourages this position. Recalling de Tocqueville, Banfield argues that only a rich associational life can be the mainstay of modern societies. A rich associational life emerges when individuals interact with one another through institutions such as local councils. Interaction through primordial institutions does not bring about the kind of associational life that Banfield is talking about. It is for this reason he does not see much hope for the so-called 'backward societies'. These backward societies may have tradition, but not an associational life that brings about enlightened self-governance as in the modern state.

To paraphrase Banfield, rich associational life comes about only through modern intermediate institutions. It is through the multifarious ties that these institutions sponsor that public trust is generated. It is this that allows the modern society and the state to function the way they do. Therefore, in the ultimate analysis, the agencies of rich associational life *lie outside* the modern state, though they are coeval with it. If anything, it is this rich associational life that then gives rise to the modern state. More recent works, such as those of Putnam, practically lift the essence of Banfield's arguments and recast it in the context of 'social capital' (Putnam 1993).

On the other hand for Locke, Rousseau and Hegel (and even perhaps Adam Smith and Ferguson), intermediate institutions of democracy were not just coeval with the modern democratic state, indeed their express intent was to link the individual to the state as free citizens. It is the modern constitutional democratic state that created free citizens. In earlier regimes there were people but not citizens. Locke's point that democracy grew out of the disenchantment with the 'state of nature' should not mean that democratic impulses were already present as a cultural given in pre-democratic societies. Citizenship, democracy and intermediate institutions therefore come together in one fell swoop.

Intermediate institutions then not only make it possible for the modern state to realize itself, they also help individuals to realize their essential freedoms. Hegel stated this position forthrightly as he saw intermediate institutions as substantiations of the ethical imperatives of the modern state (Hegel 1945: 157).

Thus while Hegel and Locke would both agree that the nostalgia for the past, as in the romantics, is highly misplaced; while they might both agree that such intermediate institutions cannot be found in the state of nature; nevertheless Locke maintained a 'hire and fire' view of the state, while for Hegel the state was the ultimate repository of the ethical imperatives of freedom. What, however, unites Locke with Hegel against de Tocqueville, is that for both of them the intermediate institutions were born of the same drive and impulses that brought about the modern state. For de Tocqueville, however, the customs and manners of Americans were democratic to begin with, and the American state emerged as a consequence.

Unlike de Tocqueville, in classical conceptualization of civil society, intermediate institutions do not stand apart from the state. This is as much true of Hegel as it is for Rousseau, and Locke. Indeed, in all such cases the valourization of institutional autonomy, whether of the judiciary or of the market place, draws sustenance from the basic axiomatic assumption that the state alone can guarantee essential freedoms to the individual. Without prefiguring this, institutional autonomy would lack a full-fledged rationale. This is why autonomy does not mean that institutions should pull in different directions. Instead their specific drives possess resonance and body because institutions emerge from the collective of which they are a part. It is only in a modern constitutional state that institutional autonomy is at once a symptom and a result of social cohesion. As such freedoms were inadequately realized in the 'state of nature', there is no longing or nostalgia for the revival of tradition in any mainstream classical exponent of civil society.

To be fair, de Tocqueville's promotion of intermediate institutions was also forward looking. But if his head was not so firmly set against turning back, one is not very sure where his heart would have led him. De Tocqueville's position on Algeria clearly furthered the forward looking view (see Richter 1963). However, when it came to the passing away of the *ancien regime* in France he regretted that certain profound human values had now been lost forever. It is this that separates him from Locke, Rousseau, Adam Smith and Hegel. Hegel was perhaps the most unequivocal of them all when he wrote that civil society is not about 'natural simplicity' (1945: 125), nor is it based on the 'superficial philosophy which teaches that the opposite of knowledge, the heart and the enthusiasm, are the true principles of ethnical action' (ibid.: 95).

Intermediate Institutions and the State

We are now better equipped to appreciate Andre Béteille's contribution to the debate on civil society in India. In a manner reminiscent of de Tocqueville, Béteille argues that the well-being of modern institutions can be guaranteed only if civil societies are understood as comprising truly autonomous bodies (Béteille 1991, 1996b). In doing so Béteille is emphasizing the need to be wary of giving into traditional solidarities and associations as they are inimical to the functioning of modern institutions. Some of these modern institutions, according to Béteille, are universities, judiciaries, hospitals and corporations (ibid.). But Béteille is not only drawing attention to the fact that traditional solidarities undermine the well-being of modern institutions, he is also blaming the Indian state for eroding the autonomy of the institutions that it had once set up. It is significant to note in this connection Béteille's overt reliance on de Tocqueville, his rather unenthusiastic references to Locke, and his studied and deliberate distancing from Hegel.

First, and quite naturally, de Tocqueville. In a de Tocquevillean manner Béteille is for upholding the institutional autonomy of intermediate institutions for that would be the most effective guarantee against a demagogic state. The Indian state, Béteille believes, has given in to mass political pressures and to sectarian and communitarian forces. Such a state would necessarily undermine the well-being of intermediate institutions, which is where civil society lies. In order to protect civil society, it is important to keep these institutions autonomous and independent of state control.

One reason why Locke is not immediately attractive to Béteille is probably because Locke, like Adam Smith, favoured a kind of minimalist state (see also Nozick 1976). Given India's late entry into the modern world, and its extreme poverty, the state in India is expected to intervene as a mobilizing instrument to alter the existing state of affairs and realize developmental goals.

Unhappy though Béteille is with the performance of the Indian state, he is not yet willing to give up on it as a vital mobilizing agency. Where Béteille is disappointed is not only with the state's inability to perform but also in the manner in which it has infected intermediate institutions with its compromising political proclivities. The issue that is then uppermost on his mind is how to protect these intermediate institutions from the pressure of mass politics.

This also explains why Béteille is suspicious of Hegel and Gramsci. In the latter case it is perhaps justifiable, as Gramsci saw civil society as an instrument for exercising the will of the state. In this connection it also needs to be said that Marx's notion of civil society is very different from that of Hegel's. For Marx civil society is rather simplistically understood as anything that is outside of the state (Marx and Engels 1969a: 38, 77). This even includes the simple family and the tribe. Civil society does not emerge in Marx with the dawn of constitutional democracy and the idea of freedom. It has been there all the time, through history.

Hegel, however, is completely different. The civil society is not worth the candle for Hegel if it does not manifest the ethics of freedom of which the state is the highest repository and the 'actuality of the ethical idea' (Hegel 1945: 155). Hegel's version of civil society talks of no greater good than actualizing the ethics of individual freedom.

It should be made clear though that this freedom is not of the kind that the hero enjoys, but a freedom that human beings can attain in association such that they can fully realize themselves (Hegel 1945: 108; see also Rousseau 1913: 62; and Durkheim 1957: 71). The majesty that Hegel sees in the state is not because of its coercive abilities but rather because it is the highest realization of freedom. According to T.M. Knox, Hegel's most erudite exegete: 'It cannot be too often emphasized that Hegel's philosophy culminates not with the state but with art, religion and philosophy, which lie beyond the state and above it' (Hegel 1945: 305).

The fact that Hegel has been loudly appropriated by the likes of Lenin or Gramsci does not mean that Hegel himself would have in any way condoned the erosion of individual freedom. In fact, it is in Hegel that one finds the most systematic rationale for the autonomy of intermediate institutions that Béteille and most true liberals cherish. According to Hegel, these institutions form part of the civil society compact as they manifest the ethical imperatives of freedom which radiate outward from the state. It is the civil society that gives freedom to the citizen. A citizen is not just a free market agent, nor just a rational-legal human being. The freedom that the state gives to its citizens is the freedom to develop socially valuable assets irrespective of the accidents of birth. Walzer is quite right when he says that 'civil society is a setting of settings: all are included none is preferred' (Walzer 1992: 98).

Institutional Autonomy or Citizenship

What Béteille's appeal for maintaining the well-being of institutions lacks is a rounded rationale that grounds these intermediate institutions in a larger perspective. It is not enough to say that if the constitutional state wants to attain its stated legal ends it must protect the well-being of institutions. The point really is how to understand institutional well-being. After all, it is possible to set high standards of institutional efficiency and well-being without taking the citizen into account. The efficiency and well-being of institutions need not benefit society as a whole. These intermediary institutions could just as well look after themselves and set up perfectly idiosyncratic norms. In fact a range of such alternative possibilities can be found in Nozick's critique of 'do good' liberalism (1976: 207–8, 247).

The fact that the Indian state has constantly whittled down institutional autonomy for sectional political advantages has led Béteille to valourize institutional autonomy as a good in its own right. This is tantamount to rejecting the state as an aspect of civil society. That would have been alright except that citizenship gets short shrift for no fault of its own. This is the unintended consequence of Béteille's position. Citizenship is the unfortunate casualty as institutional autonomy no longer needs the state for its actualization.

The interesting feature is that both Béteille and the cultural critics distrust the modern state for one reason or the other. This justifies to a great extent, even explains away, the Indian state's inaction as far as being responsible to the public is concerned. In effect, it lets the state off the hook for it is no longer pressured to perform for the welfare of its citizens, or to realize citizenship. Proceeding strictly on Béteille's lines one cannot adequately justify public funding for education, health and internal security. The state is only petitioned to stay out of the functioning of intermediate institutions after it has put in place a 'system of rational, impersonal law' (Béteille 1996b). For Béteille what counts the most is that these intermediate institutions be characterized by impersonal rules of efficiency. It does not really matter whether or not they pay any attention to public welfare. In fact, on closer examination it appears that these are not so much intermediate institutions as they are simply modern organizations.

A clear implication of this stand is that all well run organizations are good provided they are technologically forward looking, and allow the best within the respective organizations to emerge. These institutions are intermediate because they are neither enmeshed by the compromises of politics that the state is encumbered with, nor are they compelled to give in to archaic demands and obligations of traditional associations, which is characteristic of Indians in 'their state of nature'. They are intermediate not because they link the state with the citizens—with the public, but rather because they fall conceptually, in-between.

Though Béteille ostensibly relies on de Tocqueville, his real hero is Max Weber. It is a system of rational-legal authority that Béteille would like to see implemented through intermediary institutions. While a constitutional democratic state must have at its core a rational-legal framework, it is not as if it works in the same way if the direction were to be reversed. A rational-legal system does not necessarily need a constitutional democratic state. It may be realized through the market, and through facilities like the Golf Club. The most important feature of a rational-legal structure is that it should abide by rules that are not traditional, familial or particularistic. A market economy fulfils these criteria, so does a system where merit plays the most important role. To appreciate that rational-legal institutions are not necessarily democratic in character, one has only to read Nozick (1976).

From Béteille's treatment of intermediate institutions it appears that as long as these institutions work efficiently they are worthy of protection and need to be encouraged. Efficiency can be understood in a variety of ways and several of them have little to do with citizenship which as T.H. Marshall (1977) once said 'has a tendency towards equality'. If one were to go by Béteille's position then these modern institutions could well function along lines inimical to the interests of citizens in general. They could quite feasibly have a tendency towards inequality. In India we see many examples of this, particularly in the establishment of expensive private schools and hospitals. These institutions which should cater for the welfare of the citizens instead service only an affluent minority.

As the institutions of civil society are intermediate (in the Tocquevillean sense), it is not inconsistent that Béteille's notion of citizenship should be primarily a legal one. In Béteille one does not get a clear sense that these intermediate institutions are manned by those who are first citizens, and then, experts. What appears more important is that the institutions be autonomous and manned by qualified functionaries. The fact that the institutions of civil society must first and foremost give substance to citizenship is relegated to the background. In this case, it is hard to find a logical connection between institutional well-being and national or collective well-being. It is only in Hegel's understanding of civil society, as we said earlier, that we find a clear rationale for the reconciliation of the universal and the particular in an ethical community.

Civil Society and the Ethic of Freedom

In the Hegelian understanding of civil society, intermediate institutions possess autonomy intrinsically because they are aspects of a democratic state and not because these institutions are opposed to it, or have an independent provenance of their own. According to Hegel, the autonomy of the institutions of civil society emerged because the ethics of freedom permeated through them. It is this ethic that made for individual growth but, within a collective of which the constitutional democratic state was the highest expression.

This ethic of freedom, for Hegel, can be experienced in the family, in civil society and of course, in its highest form in the state (Hegel 1945). The family, civil society and state do not mark the stages in the development of civil society, as it is often interpreted. They are instead 'moments' of the ethic of freedom which beats synchronously in all of them (see also Marx and Engels 1969a: 34 for a clarification of 'moments'). At one point Hegel even says that the family and the corporation are 'the two fixed points round which the unorganized atoms of civil society revolve' (Hegel 1945: 154). The family is no longer simply an institution of sexual gratification and patriarchal oppression, but one where altruistic ties of blood and marriage are in consonance with the rights of citizens (ibid.: 148). The corporation (which is part of civil society) is not just market oriented and self-seeking in its disposition (ibid.: 151, 153), but enters into contracts according to policies which do not undermine the well-being of citizens. The corporation is thus constantly under the 'surveillance of the public authority...' (ibid.: 152). Nor is the state autocratic, bureaucratic, or demagogic. The state in which civil society manifests itself is a constitutional democratic institution (ibid.: 160 ff.). If one were to draw freely from Rawls and Dworkin, then, one might go on to say that such a state guarantees its citizens the freedom and opportunity to acquire socially valuable assets as members of a fraternity (see Rawls 1971: 102, 128; and Dworkin 1977b: 141–50).

The state, corporation and the family are essential prerequisites for the ethic of freedom to organize and reproduce itself. For example, a developed civil society even converts the church into an association like any other association, and 'brings it into the domain of the state' (Hegel 1945: 171). The church, no matter what its denomination, is not an alternative source of temporal power, but an institution catering to the spiritual needs of individuals. The disunion between the state and the church is in Hegel's view 'the best piece of good fortune which could have befallen either...' (ibid.: 174).

Hegel's position on the family and the church helps us once again to mark our distance from the communitarians. A sophisticated version of communitarianism may not demand a whole-sale return to tradition. Instead, it might contend that one must be sensitive to tradition and custom in order to recover what is best in them. It would then appear that it is possible to lift bits and pieces of tradition and append them to modern institutions. The problem then would be to bind the diverse logics of tradition and modernity and cement them together in the same society. Even sophisticated communitarians have really no answer to this question. Indeed, I believe, communitarians of all hues are not sensitive to such issues and therefore fail to problematize them.

At this point Hegel can help us again. It is not as if Hegel said that with civil society everything arises anew. Hegel did not argue that in civil society institutions like the church and the family should be extirpated simply because they originated in tradition. This is what Marx had recommended in the *Communist Manifesto*. On the other hand, for Hegel, institutions like the family and the church continue to exist in civil society, but their *raison d'etre* is completely transformed by the ethic of freedom. It is not that the best of tradition is continuing in the present, but that the present has transformed the past and forced it to work along modern lines.

In all such 'moments' the citizen is clearly the principal protagonist. In each of these instances the ethic of freedom demonstrably protects the citizen's freedom to acquire and develop socially valuable assets, regardless of traditional loyalties related to birth and creed. Even the most private domain of the family is intrinsically converted by considerations that are essentially 'public' in nature. This is yet another instance of the distance between Hegel and Marx on the notion of civil society. For Marx, the development of history involved the dissolution of the family. Marx saw the family primarily as the site of patriarchal oppression and no more (see Marx and Engels 1969b: 123). For Hegel though, the family transforms itself once it becomes a 'moment' of civil society. Patriarchy slips away, but the family remains (see also Walzer 1983: 227–42). Likewise, the church in civil society can no longer lay claim to temporal power or even command spiritual allegiance. It depends on its survival by accepting the right to choice of worship, and by tending to the spiritual needs of those who willingly associate with it.

This also clarifies our reservations against Partha Chatterji. According to Chatterji even institutions set up by colonial governments should be considered agencies of civil society. What needs to be pointed out is that these agencies and institutions can be instruments of technological modernization, but they do not involve citizens. In this sense Partha Chatterji too overlooks the close link between civil society and citizenship (Chatterji 1997: 30–34, especially 33) but the primary task of civil societies is that of constituting a community of citizens bound by the ethics of freedom and not by particulars of hierarchy and tradition, or by the rational-legal calculus of the market place.

As Béteille is quick to dismiss Hegel he overlooks the importance that citizenship gives to the ethic of freedom. It is not security, nor mutual consent—but freedom which is realized through the collective. It is this, and rational-legal instituions, that makes citizens. Otherwise one could have citizens without a democratic state. This clarification cannot be found in de Tocqueville, nor in Max Weber, but only in the writings of Hegel.

For Kothari and the cultural critics the matter is quite straightforward. As humaneness and authenticity are found primarily in tradition and custom, the cultural critics have little sympathy for the well-being of modern institutions. For them, efficiency is just a word coined by self-seeking technocrats with their heads in the western world. This is why the conception of the public is absent in their works, which are otherwise redolent with references to the masses and to the marginalized and subjugated sections of the population. The need to maintain standards of modern institutions is a laughable ambition that is sneeringly dismissed. As there is nothing civil about these institutions there is little point in upholding their efficiency. The cultural critics would instead promote a policy that would favour the deprived and the marginals to capture these institutions and make good while they can. If the better off could have used it for themselves, why not the less fortunate?

This, essentially cynical view towards modern institutions can be upheld only if one logically looks beyond the modern state and its apparatuses as agencies of humane governance. This the cultural critics do for they believe that the modern democratic, constitutional state is a technocratic behemoth out to crush the true sources of civil society. Logically then, the cultural critics are consistent. Politically, however, their position is unrealizable, and not simply because it is regressively communitarian. The horizon of communities does not include democratic values and choice, though it provides security, often of the patron-client variety. The citizen really in nowhere in the picture.

Civil Society as an Empirical or Analytical Category

The divide between the Hegelian view of civil society and those inspired by either communitarian principles or by de Tocqueville has other ramifications too. For Hegel, civil society functioned more as an analytical category which is realized in empirical institutions, whereas for the others civil society is limited to certain definite aspects of empirical reality. Hegel's civil society is a manifestation of the ethic of freedom. This ethic is also capable of realization in the corporation, the family or the state. It was crucial for Hegel to demonstrate that something as private as a family was as important an instance of the ethic as was civil society or the state. So for Hegel the ethic of freedom was not limited to a given set of institutions, nor was civil society restricted to corporations and associations. As long as any institution expressed the ethic of freedom it fell within the domain of civil society.

This is why Hegel's civil society is neither specific primordial communities nor a defined set of rational-legal institutions. This does not mean that it was a piece of conceptual jugglery entirely up in the air. On the contrary, as Hegel often laboriously pointed out, a concept was worthwhile only if it was empirically realizable. The concept of civil society too must be empirically realizable, but that is not the same as saying that it rests only in certain empirical locales. Unlike both Kothari and Béteille, the Hegelian position would not limit civil society in advance to certain kinds of communities and primordial ties, nor to a specified set of rational-legal organizations. Instead, it would find instances, or 'moments', of civil society wherever the ethic of freedom (which valourizes the citizen) is manifest. Naturally, such an ethic is incompatible with primordial communities as they cannot incorporate freedom of choice in any meaningful way. But such an ethic is not intrinsically hostile to rational-legal institutions. It needs to be recalled, however, that not all rational-legal institutions are sensitive to citizenship and to the ethic of freedom.

Letting the State off the Hook

Civil society as an ethic of freedom manifests itself in the modern democratic constitutional state by creating citizens and by upholding institutional autonomy. This fact has not always been fully appreciated in India. The gross inadequacies of the Indian state tempt one to reach out to primordial unities or to intermediate institutions. What this does in effect is to take some of the heat off the state and let it off the hook. This is rather surprising considering the fact of India's economic backwardness, and also the fact that most people in India still depend directly and indirectly on the state, inefficient though it is, at a variety of levels. This is true for the rich as well as for the poor. Therefore, in practical terms the state is still a critical mobilizing agency. In such a situation one would have expected intellectual energy to be directed towards pressuring the state rather than to letting it off the hook, either by valourizing traditional associations and communities, or by seeking to protect the autonomy of intermediate institutions as an end (or a good) in itself.

One principal reason for this outcome is the great differences that exist between classes, communities and regions in this country. This makes the idea of citizenship very hard to realize in practice. The inter-subjectivity that John Rawls felt was so essential to ingrain the basic tenets of citizenship (Rawls 1971: 102) is constrained by the immense variations in life styles and expectations. There is no viable common base on which differences can develop and flourish. Without the emergence of such a common base, citizenship will always be a privilege and not a status with an active role. It is not as if all are equal in every respect in civil society. The conditions that civil society set up do not presume a perfectionist equality of that kind. If such a denouement occurs it is all very well. The pursuit of equality of this sort is not, however, central to the existence of the conditions of civil society. What civil society insists on is that a liberal democratic society must make the condition of civil society a generalized phenomenon such that individuals have the basic requisites at their command to realize themselves in society.

Lord Alfred Marshall was right when he said that 'differential status...was replaced by the uniform status of citizenship, which provided the foundation of equality, on which the structure of inequality could be built' (quoted in Marshall 1963: 91). What still needs to be clarified is that when citizenship confers an equality of status it also makes possible through the conditions set by civil society to expand the horizons of freedom. Without this the status of citizenship would not involve any dynamism. If citizenship be-comes a passive attitude, as it would without the conditions of civil society, then the differences of birth and circumstances can never be altered.

When the conditions of civil society are examined in India, it gives the impression of hopelessness and despair. Citizenship cannot be realized by a majority of India's legal citizens in an active form. The legal title of citizenship without an active role component does not make for a fraternity, nor does it strengthen the sentiment of the nation-state. It is then that questions such as 'For whom is the nation-state?' come up. In order to realize the conditions of civil society in India, as anywhere else in the world, conditions should be such that it is possible to materially enlarge upon the scope of freedom and not let freedom be the prerogative of a few. This is where Hegel's contribution to the understanding of civil society is so important. For instance D.L. Sheth finds that 'the "civil space" for the enforcement and protection of rights of individual citizens is by and large restricted to the politically and economically organized sectors of the society...' (Sheth 1991: 34). In Sheth's opinion then it is only these economically well-organized sections that have benefitted from modernization. But Sheth stops a little too early. What needs to be emphasized is that if the benefits of civil society are restricted to these sections in spite of constitutional democracy, it just shows that the conditions of civil society are far from being in place. It is only by entertaining the conception of the conditions of civil society that the limits of mere legal citizenship can be analytically comprehended. As freedom in this case is being realized only by a minority, and not by the people as a whole, the basic ethic of civil society can hardly be said to exist in any meaningful way. It is impossible to be civil in an uncivil society.

This explains why citizenship cannot be seen just as status (Marshall 1963: 87). This would be a sociological anomaly. As Goodenough clarifies, every status has a role that accompanies it, and rights are burdened by duty (Goodenough 1965: 2, 16). A citizen then, according to Goodenough, is not a category or kind of person, but one who has roles to fulfill as part of the status that is being occupied. This role cannot be a passive role. If it were, then, it would be another way of saying that citizenship as status is a completed product where nothing else remains to be achieved. If civil society is imbued with the ethic of freedom then neither civil society, nor citizenship, nor for that matter, modernity, can ever be viewed as finished projects. They are ongoing in their drives, constantly and relentlessly mining fresh ores of freedom. The manner in which universal franchise was achieved, or the way in which rights expanded from the civil to the political to the social (Marshall 1963: 76, 81), are examples of the development of freedom. As a citizen is a role player in civil society where the ethic of freedom is the governing principle, there is no other option than to be an active citizen. A passive citizen is as much of an anomaly as saying that a citizen is status without role. The distinction that Walzer (1987: 216) and Turner (1990: 207) draw between active and passive citizenship appears somewhat redundant in this respect.

It is in tradition that roles are passively reproduced. One of the significant diacritics of modernity is the constant rearticulation of roles to keep up with changing circumstances. In this kind of activism, roles are transformed to such an extent that they can now only survive in non-places. For example, the apprentice that could only live under the master's shadow in the medieval guild and the apprentice of today are completely different in terms of the roles they perform. Today an apprentice in many of the modern industrial enterprises functions as if in non-space, a state of affairs incompatible with the medieval guild.

The freedom that the civil society sets up is of a kind that does not allow for a passive role player. In medieval times too there was freedom for the worker, but this medieval freedom is totally different and unrecognizable from the freedom of the worker today. This medieval oath should make clear the distance between what was considered free then and what is considered free now. The oath reads as follows:

> By the Lord before whom this holy thing is holy, I will to N. be faithful and true, loving all that he loves, and shunning all that he shuns, according to the law of God and the custom of the world, and never by will or by force, in word or in deed, will I do anything that is hateful to him; *on condition that he will hold me as I deserve and furnish all that was agreed between us when I bowed myself before him and submitted to his will* (quoted in Sachse 1967: 11).

The freedom depicted in this medieval oath is a freedom to bond oneself. The right to one's judgement of things too is suspended so long as the lord takes care of his clients. This denial of one's self is in stark contrast to any modern contract, which is why it is not enough to say that one is free to contract. Instead it is important to appreciate the conditions under which contracts are arrived at. It is here that the civil society becomes an essential aspect of modern liberal democratic nation-states. Without civil society the conditions for inaugurating structures that ensure and deepen fraternity will be absent. Only legal statutes of formal equality will prevail, slowly eroding the basis for the realization of fraternity (see for an interesting discussion with reference to South Africa, Comaroff and Comaroff 1991: 367 ff.).

This is why it is so important to launch a concerted full blown critique against the modern Indian state for allowing citizenship to languish as little more than a legal title. But instead of pressuring the state to deliver to its citizens, the tension of the moment tempts one to promote an alienated and reactive mood. This leads one to either protecting institutional well-being, or, what is infinitely more dangerous, to valourizing tradition.

When civil society is seen as intrinsically related to citizenship, then it is easier to appreciate where modernization has gone wrong, or the distance it has yet to traverse in countries like India. This is a sounder way of examining the weaknesses of post-colonial societies than by opposing modernization against tradition, or by simply exalting the modern. When democracy no longer encourages the well-being of citizens along the lines of civil society it is largely because the ethics of freedom are being subverted by technological rationality, or by market principles, or by the majority principle, or by the pure and dogmatic assertions of communal or group equality (as in caste-based politics). None of these are compatible with the ethic of civil society, with the cultivation of citizenship.

It is true that most post-colonial democracies find themselves in a situation which is far from being anywhere near perfect when it comes to realizing citizenship. Cultural critics such as Kothari, Nandy, and even Chatterji, respond to this by recommending a return to traditional and customary ties. In doing so communities are revived uncritically with all their anti-individualistic, and, often, hierarchic assumptions. As the state has already been condemned as a ruthless modernizer there is no pressure on the state to deliver. The search for deliverance is on elsewhere, in other 'natural' realms.

Louis Farrakhan's strategy, as evidenced in the Million Man March in Washington, was based on the assumption that American Blacks, particularly the men, should look within them if they wanted to improve their lot. This is yet another example of letting the state off the hook. Farrakhan too finds the routes to Black assertion and pride within a constructed tradition where men play a significant leadership role. In expressing this sentiment Farrakhan is not alone. The Southern Baptist Convention came out with a proclamation in 1998 that spiritual leadership rests on the men in the family. Though Farrakhan and supporters of the Southern Baptists like Jerry Falwell, have been criticized by gender activists, the genesis of this male oriented position arises from the belief that if a community, such as of the Blacks or the Southern Baptists, is to improve its lot, spiritually and materially, it is 'tradition' that it must look up to. Considerations of civil society and pressuring the state to enhance freedoms are distal to such formulations.

Beginning from an entirely different position Béteille too lets the state off the hook by placing primary emphasis on institutional well-being. The state is only requested to stay clear of such institutions and let them function autonomously without hindrance. Quite unwittingly perhaps, Béteille's de Tocquevillean grounding of civil society leads him to uphold the drives of experts and not the aspirations of citizens.

The only real alternative is to force the state to respond to its citizens and not let it off the hook. Bourdieu once made a similar point while warning the new social movement activists that a cultural re-writing of meaning will be an effete exercise without challenging the state and forcing it to deliver (Bourdieu 1985a: 723–44). After all, as Hegel clarified, the state is not 'a mere mechanical scaffolding' (Hegel 1945: 170), but a vital source for realizing the ethics of freedom. Michael Walzer puts this across well when he writes that the state is not a mere framework for civil society. It is also the instrument of the struggle, and it gives 'a particular shape to the common life. Hence citizenship has a certain practical pre-eminence—among all our actual and possible memberships' (Walzer 1992: 105). Therefore, if the project of civil society is to be saved, and along with it the freedom accorded to citizenship, it can only be done through the constitutional democratic state and not by intermediate institutions outside it, or through traditional forums 'before' it.

The Construction of Fraternity Against Fraternity as a Given

The communitarian cultural critics however quite consciously steer clear of any substantive commitment to the notion of citizenship. For them the fraternity that is embedded in traditional and customary ties within a community forms the basis of a moral and authentic social order. Fraternity is thus a given and not something that has to be worked upon and arrived at. They ignore the many instances of tyranny and intolerance in the pre-modern period. Richard Burghart has vividly illustrated the persistent antagonisms between rival sects and communities in pre-modern India. For instance, in the Nashik Kumbh Mela festival of 1813, hostilities between Hindu Saivites and Vaishnavites led to the deaths of many sadhus belonging to rival sects (Burghart 1996: 127). Indeed, one can safely go on to say that such sectarian conflagrations were quite common in pre-modern times, particularly during festivals (see also Subrahmanyam 1996). The cultural critics, with their strong communitarian bias, overlook such details and see only a seamless fraternity in tradition.

A true liberal follower of constitutional democracy believes, however, that fraternity is not a primordial given, but something that has to be attained by deliberate policies (for example, Rawls' 'difference principle'; see Rawls 1971: 105–6). The fraternity thus constituted by constitutional democracies is not of blood brothers but of citizens. It is one that is *based on individual rights and not on birth rights*. Even Marx was very dismissive of the idea that the proletariat could of its own accord create a socialist revolution. In his view all such attempts would degenerate to petty-bourgeois revolts and no more. Working class solidarity does not grow spontaneously but requires a close and deliberate study of history and society.

It is necessary to ask why fraternity is never taken as a given by liberal philosophers. Traditional societies were governed by fixed, hierarchical principles which were generally in consonance with a closed natural economy. A person's status was known in advance and there was little one could do but obey the rules of the estate, or the community, that one was born into. The question of choosing one's profession, estate, or cultural lifestyle was largely non-existent. The cultural and economic status that people were born into locked them in fixed structural locations from which there was little scope for escape.

When peace reigned in such societies it was a peace between these entrenched differences which were largely insurmountable. The most benign condition in such a situation was one of peace between diverse and grossly different groups. The possibilities of such a peace were however dependent on the extent to which people adhered to their station in society and led their lives incognito. Diversity of social ambitions between groups were settled by wars. Once the war was over, and the distinction between the victor and the vanquished clearly established, communities and classes fell into place and observed the rules of living in multiple solitudes.

A modern society is completely different. Now, choice is the essence of life as citizens are imbued with the ethic of freedom.

This makes both horizontal and vertical mobility most commonplace. Public spheres are created where people of hitherto diverse cultural backgrounds are thrown together under conditions of anonymity. Quite naturally, rules of interaction have to be re-negotiated. This time these rules cannot take the fixed hierarchical estate model as its standard, but must begin with individuals. Fraternity must be constructed afresh and on principles entirely different from those based in tradition. The past is not at all a reliable guide in such a situation. In fact, all the pre-existing fraternities are extremely suspect and need to be dissolved if true citizenship is to emerge.

Even if one were to overlook the various inegalitarian elements in tradition it still does not make the revival of it a viable proposition. The secularization of society, the creation of public spaces, the development of the structures of the nation-state, all make such projections appear largely wistful, if not plainly utopian, in character. If we do not want to succumb to the naivete that Marx mentioned in the *Grundrisse* then it is best to heed the specifics of an epoch and realize the inevitability of the constitutional democratic state. It is also important to note that after one has tasted citizenship, however fleetingly, it is impossible to return to the past.

Civil Society as an Alternative Ideal

A final word on the contemporary relevance of the term 'civil society'. The importance that civil society is receiving from academics the world over is largely, as we said, because of the general disillusionment with the state. There is however a further reason for the revival of this term from its earlier classroom obscurity. The disillusionment with the state is not simply a kind of frustration with the apparatuses and structures of governance, but also with ideals that have sustained democracies for over several decades. The failure of capitalism and socialism as pure ideals must also be factored in to properly appreciate the return of civil society.

For about seven decades, democracy was ideologically charged not so much with notions of pure liberalism as with the differences between capitalism and socialism. Both sides claimed democracy to be their own. But neither socialism, nor pure market-driven capitalism were able to establish fraternity on an enduring and self-generating basis. In this sense, both capitalism and socialism have lost much of their shine, though it is only overtly acknowledged that socialism has lost out.

Civil society has moved in to fill the space that has thus been vacated. Civil society, no matter in which rendition, promises an ideal that can provide a way for the future. This is why it is necessary to seriously acknowledge and examine the many contributions on this subject in recent years, and not sneer at them as instances of academic hype. In our view, the aperture that civil society opens allows us to see more clearly the problems of our times. It also helps us to seek ways to overcome them.

Chapter VII

Fraternity, Citizenship and Affirmative Action: Recasting Reservation in the Language of Rights

Liberty, Equality and Fraternity: Divergent Logics

Civil society only sets the conditions for attaining fraternity, but the structures and policies of the nation-state that will actually bring it about have yet to be carefully deliberated. Fraternity, after all, is not a spontaneous thing, but has to be nurtured as a continuous long term project. It is therefore important to take cognizance of the obstructions that exist in the realization of fraternity. Some of the most persistent problems in this regard have to do with alleviating poverty, correcting historic injustices against certain communities, and in tackling the issue of minority rights. This chapter will discuss the various approaches in this regard and hopefully point towards a resolution.

Liberty, equality and fraternity have often been separated from each other in terms of their divergent logics. Thus, proceeding on the basis of market principles, F.A. Hayek argues in *The Constitution of Liberty* that in a truly free society an individual should be rewarded on the basis of value rather than moral merit. His objection is 'against all attempts to impress upon society a deliberately chosen pattern of distribution, whether it be an order of equality or inequality' (Hayek 1960: 87). Echoing Hayek, Nozick has more recently re-stated the view that the most fundamental right, the right to liberty, cannot be compromised at the door of equality

(Nozick 1976: 168). As equality does not flow naturally from the pursuit of individual liberty it must necessarily be brought by deliberate policies of redistribution. For Nozick, 'redistribution is a serious matter indeed, involving as it does, the violation of people's rights' (ibid.).

The contradictions between liberty and equality have also been highlighted by Béteille (1986) on a variety of occasions, more specifically in his critique of Louis Dumont. According to Béteille, Louis Dumont's *Homo Hierarchicus* (1980) mistakenly equates liberty, or individualism, with equality. The free pursuit of individual goals according to liberty principles would bring about inequality rather than equality. For, as enunciated by Hayek, a truly free and liberal society should reward people according to the 'value' of a person's actions or services (Hayek 1960). Therefore, as society prioritizes different kinds of services, the rewards for services rendered will be differentially valued by society.

It is not always, however, that liberty and equality are positioned in such a contradictory fashion. Even the most die hard and extreme follower of the market principle will unhesitatingly accept the fact that unless there is equality before law, and unless individuals are 'equal' as citizens, the context for liberal pursuits along market principles is impossible. It is this legal equality, or equality of citizenship status (see Marshall 1977), that makes a society free— free to operate on market principles unconstrained by the trappings of a closed hierarchical order. Equality in this case would mean formal equality before the law, where competition for jobs and education is open to all.

While this is undeniably a great historical advance, it can nevertheless be maintained that this notion of equality is blind to the divergent initial positions of individuals in society. In which case, those who have a headstart will continue to prosper at the expense of those who are not quite as well off, or fortunate. Without demanding an equality of results, there must still be ways by which those who are less fortunate can have a *fair* chance of competing against the better placed. Without such provisions, liberalism will only perpetuate initial differences and exaggerate them exponentially.

The differences in individual endowments of worthwhile attributes become all the more significant in the face of persistent historic inequalities. These inequalities emerge not because some individuals are deficient in terms of worthy qualities, but rather because as members of groups which have been historically subjugated these individuals function at a real initial disadvantage with respect to the rest. Claims of being historically disadvantaged can be, and are, made on the grounds that a particular race, religion, language or caste, or a combination of these, were subject to persecution, and/or denied opportunities to develop skills in areas which are deemed to be worthy in contemporary society.

The historical narrative of our time impresses upon us the importance of redressing community-based grievances within a democratic framework. This is also what makes democracy's notions of justice so historically specific. While all liberals would agree that it is essential 'to nullify the accidents of birth' (Rawls 1971: 15), the dispute is about how this can be done. As mentioned earlier, one option is to depend on the market mechanism to sort things out in the long run. This runs contrary to democratic urges as everybody wishes to realize some good in a finite space of time. Further, as democracy is premised on participation, interventions are often called for to hasten the process of negating accidents of birth without undermining the liberal framework. Will Kymlicka poses the question squarely when he says: 'Finding a way to liberalize a cultural community without destroying it is a task that liberals face in every country' (Kymlicka 1989: 170). If certain communities are recognized to be at an initial disadvantage because of circumstances of history, then the circumstances of democracy seem to insist that this be righted so that democratic potential may be fully realized.

It is with liberalism that rights came centre stage displacing the many medieval and absolutist renditions of duty. If duty, or notions of social good, are to have any purchase in contemporary societies they must not be antagonistic to individual rights. Yet, on the face of it the two seem to be so contradictory.

There is the additional question that one must necessarily ask in this connection. Why is it at all important to consider issues that relate to the social good? Why not just let individual liberties determine social outcome? Though the market mechanism would perhaps devise ways in the long run to sort out the constraints within which individual liberties will have to function (see Nozick 1976: 30–31, especially 105–10), it still does not squarely face the issue of citizenship.

A little while back it was argued that divergent versions of what is desired become contentious because now individual rights and formal equality before the law have been affirmed. It needs also to be added that a contemporary democratic state derives its rationale from the fact that it is based on legitimate, rational-legal, consensual authority, and not on force or cowardice. As Rousseau said in the *Social Contract:* 'Force made the first slaves, and their cowardice perpetuated the condition.'

Deontology and the Principle of Fraternity: Rawls vs. His Critics

It is in this fashion that liberty, equality and fraternity come together. It is this alchemy that has energized the democratic process, and it would be incorrect to separate them simply because they do not naturally reinforce each other. The perpetuation of initial disadvantages along pure market principles would undermine the true content of democracy. But so would 'perfectionist' valuations of certain end results, whether they be with regard to economic redistribution, moral values, art or aesthetics. Rawls quite correctly points out that unbridled perfectionism can devastate liberal principles as the former is not grounded in the individual or in democratic practice (Rawls 1971: 325–27). The only way one can round off the circle is by creating 'overlapping consensus' (ibid.: 476; see also Rawls 1985: 225) and encouraging fraternity in a democratic society (Rawls 1971: 106).

The principles of fraternity have not been theorized upon with the same degree of rigour as liberty and equality have. Most often fraternity is seen as a moral doctrine that one must believe in to be correct. John Rawls who is known largely for his work on the principles of justice in liberal democratic constitutions, was one of the few who also contributed extensively towards a fuller understanding of fraternity among citizens. In fact, much of the debate on the issue of establishing justice in an unequal but democratic society is largely because of Rawls' contributors in this field. This paper too is largely indebted to Rawls.

Rawls' formulations in *A Theory of Justice* (1971) are too well-known to bear repetition. A few points may however be recalled as they are of central significance to my argument. Rawls believes that it is possible to hypothetically imagine a situation where rational people can devise principles of justice behind a 'veil of ignorance' (ibid.: 142–45). This veil precludes them from knowing how exactly they will be positioned in society. It is likely that they could be the most under-privileged. It is therefore rational that they devise a system from the vantage point of the least well off. Consequently, attention is placed on the priority of rights and this supersedes any conception of what ends individuals might have once they know their social location. Without the veil of ignorance, individuals could rationally demand only that which advantages them, given their specific location in society. This would mean the privileging of certain end states and pre-determined goals which would thwart the democratic process as it would not necessarily nullify the accidents of birth.

The veil of ignorance, on the other hand, would ensure 'justice as fairness' (ibid.: 11–17), for it would insist on following the two principles of justice. The first of which is that 'each person is to have an equal right to the most extensive total system of equal basic liberties compatible with a similar system of liberty for all' (ibid.: 302). The second principle states that '(s)ocial and economic inequalities are to be so arranged that they are both: (a) to the greatest benefit of the least advantaged..., and (b) attached to offices and positions open to all under conditions of fair equality of opportunity' (ibid.).

As is evident, Rawls is prioritizing principles over any final end. This is the advantage of the 'veil of ignorance'. In this original position then there are no clashes over rival conception of the good, but an agreement instead on how to pursue individual interests. Nevertheless, Rawls has been frequently criticized because his original position can only work with deontological beings and not with live sociological persons, 'thick with traits' and with particularistic conceptions of the private good (see for instance Sandel 1982: 94, 100).

The Communitarian Perspective: Ontological Indentity as a Given

The other criticism frequently made against Rawls is that the emphasis on principles rather than the good assumes a homogeneous political community which just does not exist anywhere. Where cultural boundaries mark out discrete entities there are not only rival conceptions of the good, but a hierarchy of cultural communities, many of which suffer from historic disprivileges. It is contended, therefore, that Rawls' understanding of justice as fairness places far too much emphasis on principles without taking into account the fact that in society there are communities and groups which are unequally placed. As the political community in most cases does not coincide with the cultural community, a pure statement of principles based on a deontological original position is far from workable.

The issues then are as follows. Justice as fairness assumes to know the interests of the 'worst off', but it can never know this, for the real political community is usually internally fragmented along cultural lines. Moreover, as Charles Taylor would argue, it is incorrect to imagine that cultural horizons will not act as 'authoritative zones' that set goals and standards (Taylor 1979: 157–59). Or as MacIntyre writes in *After Virtue*: '(T)he story of my life is always embedded in the story of those communities from which I derive my identity' (1981: 205).

In place of deontological beings we now have ontological sociological persona, for whom notions of community and shared values within a community constitute the limits of justice. In other words, there is a basic incompatibility between the deontological positions of Rawls and the ontological ones of Taylor, Rorty or MacIntyre. While Rawls, I think, would argue for a neutral politics, those on the other side, and Taylor most stridently, would opt for a moral politics. Only moral politics of this kind can ensure participation in any relevant way. Meaningful political participation results when ontological beings are aware of the sources and content of their identities, and not otherwise.

This ontological, or communitarian, critique attacks the very heart of liberal theory. The fact that there are different conceptions of the good based on community identities has a direct effect on political participation. Liberal democratic politics of the constitutional kind, which Rawls talks about, is nothing if it cannot ensure political participation. Yet, the communitarians argue, political participation can be meaningful only when it springs from communitarian concerns.

For the communitarians fraternity is a finished product (recall our critique of this in the previous chapter). It is not as if individuals come together to work out principles that nullify the accidents of birth, they depend instead precisely on the conditions determined by ascription. As fraternity here is based on shared meanings within the community, it is not feasible to contemplate one which transgresses these boundaries. This is why communitarians generally endorse movements which valourize political separation on cultural lines. This can take a variety of forms from supporting the cause of Quebec separatists, to justifying the demands for autonomy for aborigines and tribals.

The distance between the communitarians and Rawls can also be seen in terms of the differences over what is meant by fraternity. Though the communitarians rarely use the term, if they were to do so it would only include those natural bonds that arise out of cultural identity. In this scheme of things fraternity is a cultural given, and not one that is to be striven for and attained. All 'moral' politics, therefore, ought to function well within these set limits. For Rawls, on the other hand, fraternity is to be achieved, step by step, but only by the enunciation of principles. Any doctrinal assertion of a particular good would jeopardize the careful cultivation of fraternity.

Rawls is quite clear that liberty and formal equality before the law do not ensure fraternity. This is why he believes that only justice as fairness can ensure this, not as a final good, but as a consequence of the original position. In the original position, where there is a veil of ignorance, it is rational to devise policies along the 'difference principle' keeping in mind the 'worst off'. This would naturally bring about fraternity, but not as a good that should have priority over justice, but rather as a result of the principles of justice (Rawls 1971: 105–6).

It is in this sense that Rawls comes through not just as an advocate of cold principles of justice but as a passionate advocate of fraternity as well. Even so, as one reads on there is a certain ambiguity in Rawls' text. Beginning as he does with the deontological original position, he goes on to write about the community rather than about citizens. Perhaps he is talking of the ultimate political community that the difference principle will establish, but the manner in which he equivocates between what is common and what is collective leaves room for some doubt (see Sandel 1982: 151).

While it is possible to fault Rawls on this score, it is still not quite fair. Rawls unequivocally states his opposition to pure moral postulates such as those of benevolence, or those that enjoin that one must love humankind. In this view benevolence is lost 'when the many objects of its love oppose one another' (Rawls 1971: 478; see also Sen 1982: 93). As for the love of humankind, it is Rawls' firm opinion that this can only arise from a sense of justice (ibid.). If this was not to be the case then both benevolence and the love of humankind would be superogatory, and as sentiments would reside only in exceptional people (ibid.: 479). The fact that Rawls still believes these sentiments are worthy is because they result from the difference principle. It is this difference principle that ultimately brings about a higher degree of shared final ends.

The differences between Rawls and his communitarian critics get difficult to disentangle because they seem to share some views, but disagree on many others. Both talk about shared final ends, both value political participation. The principle differences lie in the manner in which these positions are expressed in the total structure of their respective arguments. Participation and fraternity are givens for the communitarians. One calls out to the other. Individual differences and choice do not play a significant role in this framework. Unanimity is a natural product in such community solidarities. Participation is full-throated because it has the moral sanction of the community.

Rawls has a completely different perspective and agenda. His entire work is constructed in a situation where the circumstances of justice prevail. In these circumstances one must assume a conflict of interests and a situation of moderate scarcity (Rawls 1971: 126–27). If such a situation does not prevail, then, issues relating to justice become redundant. If the whole society is endowed with plenty, and if it is characterized by the absence of a conflict of interests (much like a family), then the compulsions for working out the principles of justice become non-existent.

This makes clear that Rawls and his communitarian critics are not talking about the same world at all. In the Rawlsian world fraternity has to be established in a situation where there are conflicting interests. His critics, like Taylor, Rorty or MacIntyre, believe that fraternity already exists within culturally bound communities, and the job of meaningful politics is to allow these groups free play and encourage their autonomous functioning.

As Rawls is averse to any particular moral conception of the good, he does not talk in terms of cultural communities, but rather in terms of political communities. In such political communities members are bonded by ties that are political and civic, and not ascriptive or moral. In which case, it is citizens rather than blood brothers who constitute the fraternity.

The blind spot in the communitarian position is that it does not take into account the possibility of breakdowns or dissensions within a historically constructed cultural community. The communitarians proceed as if cultural boundaries are firm and unchanging throughout history. They are seen to rise above contexts and the spirit that binds their members remains undiminished and unchanged over time. That cultural alliances are labile, and that loyalties based on community identities keep changing with time, are issues that are never seriously entertained. The communitarian theory of identity is, therefore, more naturalistic than sociological in character.

The communitarians can however argue back and say that morally authentic politics does not need to worry about historical fluctuations. Cultural communities should be accepted as they are and be taken as given. Reasonable as this may sound, it still does not solve the problem as to how newer identities can break away from older ones *sans* hostility, and without charges of persecution being hurled around. Thus, while at one point of time, and in certain contexts, a general aboriginal identity may be the sole point of reference, at another time and place it may be a named aboriginal community, or a cluster of such communities, that may assume salience. Likewise, it is often the case that while ex-untouchable castes in India may come together on a single platform against caste Hindus, they quite as often also fractionate from within to form antagonistic alliances.

Fraternity and the Difference Principle: A Non-communitarian View

The strong point of Rawls' difference principle is that the category of being the least advantaged is not pinned to any cultural group or community *a priori*. All that matters is that the persons concerned should be the worst off. Instead of sympathy, the original position encourages empathy, for the veil of ignorance conceals what kind of hand one will *actually* be dealt. This is why it is important that one should be sensitive to the perspectives of others and should be able to visualize the 'us in them'. In this sense it can be claimed that Rawls' difference principle favours a phenomenological empathy, at least of the kind proposed by Maurice Merleau-Ponty (1978).

While the communitarians may point out the heartlessness behind liberal enterprises in modern nation-states, they themselves have no answer when it comes to protecting the interests of those who dissent within communities. In addition, many communitarians, such as the proponents of the Meech Lake Accord in Canada (drafted in 1992), which sought to give greater autonomy to native Indians, dodge the issue by arguing that those who would like to opt out of the community have the liberty to do so. But the price of dissent was heavy as it might mean losing residential rights and the privileges that come with being 'status Indian'. This is indeed the way proponents of the Meech Lake Accord in Canada answered some of their critics. The Meech Lake Accord was fashioned by the Conservative government of Canada and sought to win over the native Indians by promising them greater autonomy. The Accord was rejected nationally, but what is more significant, it was rejected by native Indians as well. Many native people felt that this Accord gives too much power to the self-styled community spokespersons who would then wield unchecked power over them.

Local self-government as envisaged in the Accord would convert reservations into something akin to autonomous municipalities which would compete against other municipalities for resources. The overwhelming number of natives who opposed the Accord did so because they felt that this would give too much power to the local chiefs. Additionally, this would undermine the pan-Canadian bond among the natives which would make it difficult, particularly for the women, to assert their views against the local bands. The Quebec Native Women's Association (QNWA) came out strongly in public hearings against the male-dominated native band rule. According to QNWA: 'To speak truth...means to denounce violence in all its forms.... It means combating the lies suggested that collective rights are important and reducing individual rights—to an infectious illness transmitted by Whites of European origin' (Royal Commission on Aboriginal People 1993: 10). This statement gains further salience in the light of the prevalent aboriginal tendency of non-interference in instances of family violence (ibid.: 11).

In many cases women are left to be the upholders of tradition while the men go out and participate in the 'modern' world. This factor too depresses the conditions under which women can exercise their freedoms. Of course, women's segregation is often couched in very romantic terms. There are several instances of this particularly in late 19th century and early 20th century India (see Sarkar 1993: 1869–78). In South Africa too, as the Comaroffs document, the males went to work while women stayed home to 'embody rural tradition' (Comaroff and Comaroff 1997: 248) and be 'guardians of domestic virtue' (ibid.: 266).

This should make us pause for a while. Essentially it is being argued that individuals should have the freedom to decide whether communities should govern them, or whether they should abide by the liberal laws of a constitutional democracy. This strengthens the point made in the beginning of this essay that communitarian demands can be realistically realized only if they can be translated into the language of rights. Rights constitute the enduring substratum which alone provides the option of whether or not one wants to live by community rules.

In many ways Kymlicka's position is close to the official Meech Lake view, without being identical. After painstakingly stating the difficulties with the communitarian stances the only solution Kymlicka offers at the end is that of 'encouraging consensus' (Kymlicka 1989: 197). There is no mention as to who will encourage this consensus, and why. Obviously, it is to be from the outside by the agency of a liberal democratic regime which respects individual rights. As Kymlicka does not squarely recognize this aspect, his critique of communitarianism ends on a rather feeble note.

The problem is that a liberal government cannot overlook violations of its basic code if minority communities within it should happen to violate them. This may be with reference to freedom of movement, equality of sexes, freedom of conscience, and so forth. Political autonomy along communitarian lines does not answer the question raised earlier, namely, when and at what point can we say that no further sub-divisions and realignments of identities will take place? Communitarianism does not have a built-in logic, as Rawls arguments do, that will allow them to think of principles along which problems of identity formation, fragmentation and re-alignments can be envisaged and tolerated.

This is all the more reason why *community rights, as rights, can only be meaningfully addressed within a liberal perspective*. As there is logically, and empirically, no end to where community divisions and re-alignments can lead us, it is only the liberal guarantee of individual rights that one can ultimately take recourse to in a democratic society. Communities, in other words, do not create citizens. They create primordial solidarities redolent with passion, but as these solidarities are notoriously fickle, one can only appeal to the more enduring principles of liberalism. This is, as we said earlier, the sign of the times, and communitarians can either insist on going back in history, which is impossible, or be malcontents within liberal democracy, which is injurious to all. This is why, realistically, they are constantly forced to make concessions against the grain of their logic (such as with reference to the Meech Lake Accord in Canada).

Rawls believes that his difference principle can lead to greater fraternity for it is community and culture blind. Rawls' interest in this enlargement of fraternity neither presupposes 'extensive ties of natural sentiment' (Rawls 1971: 128), nor moral imperatives (see also Rawls 1985). Love of mankind should be factored within the conspectus of rights and justice (Rawls 1971: 478). This is why he can go on to say that 'one who lacks a sense of justice lacks certain fundamental attitudes and capabilities included under the notion of humanity' (ibid.: 488). It is possible to secure fraternity only after it is grounded in justice first. Only '(i)n justice as fairness men agree to share one another's fate' (ibid.: 102). Fraternity comes about in trying to work out a solution in a deontological original position when the circumstances of justice are prevalent. Sequentially, fraternity is a by-product of the difference principle. It can be consolidated over time to bind the principles of justice till they become second nature through inter-generational socialization (ibid.: 462, 470).

Such an understanding of fraternity is important because it gives depth to our understanding of citizenship. Citizenship, like justice, is not a question of balancing 'altruism and the claims of self' (ibid.: 502). It derives its rationale from the fact that 'persons need one another since it is only in active cooperation with others that one's powers reach fruition. Only in a social union is the individual complete' (ibid.: 525). This Rousseauian statement is not surprising to anyone who has read Rawls closely. Far from being an advocate of dispassionate principles of justice, Rawls, like Rousseau in the *Social Contract*, seeks a durable basis for humanity and fraternity (Rousseau 1913, especially Book I, Chapter VI and Book II, Chapter III). It is this quest that leads Rawls to formulate his liberal theory of justice.

Liberalism as Choice: Bringing the Communitarians Back in

Much of this seems quite clear. It is true that Rawls' theory of justice is more compatible with modern constitutional democracies than communitarianism is. Even so, we must seriously consider the persistent complaint from permanent minorities in a multi-cultural state (which most states are), that differences in ability are not distributed according to accidents of birth, but arise out of deep seated historical reasons. How can the theory of justice take care of such a situation when it manifests itself on the ground?

Rawls would certainly not want permanent minorities to be disadvantaged, but it appears that he has no clear answer to the problem. He argues that majority rule in some form or the other is the best guarantor of justice, even though we might have to occasionally put up with unjust policies. He nevertheless recognizes that if the burden of injustice is not evenly distributed in society then the 'duty to comply is problematic for permanent minorities that have suffered from injustice for many years' (Rawls 1971: 355). In situations where permanent minorities exist Rawls' only advice is that we should 'not invoke the faults of social arrangements as a too ready excuse for not complying with them, nor to exploit inevitable loopholes in the rules to advance our interests' (ibid.). Surely this is a very weak argument from a person who is so careful about logical correctness. If there are loopholes in the system then they are bound to be exploited. Obviously the deontological original position cannot guard against all loopholes.

It is not as if the classical Rawlsian position has no defence against such attacks. The problem seems to be one of reconciling principles to facts. As the ground rules for justice as fairness were laid out in a deontological position, how does one go ahead and apply these principles in the real social world of ontological beings? Is it still possible to secure fraternity even after the veil of ignorance is discarded?

Will Kymlicka's tackling of this problem is of great significance. According to Kymlicka all liberals, most of all Rawls, cherish the existence of difference. It may be recalled that plurality is an important aspect of Rawls' circumstances of justice. Accordingly, Kymlicka argues that liberals would prefer a greater to a lesser range of choices. In his view the protection of minority cultures and minority rights (inclusive of protective discrimination) enlarges the choice available to individuals. The range of options available is much greater if such policies with regard to minorities and the historically disprivileged are entertained (Kymlicka 1989: 165–67). Kymlicka's obvious support for a wider menu of choices is clearly for the sake of enriching cultural life and lending it greater timbre and vibrancy. If viewed thus, it is quite at variance with the Rawlsian position where no social good should be privileged *a priori*.

Kymlicka can, however, respond to this criticism by saying that he is not an uncritical follower of Rawls. He merely wants to integrate the liberal theory of individual choice with community rights of minority cultures. Even so, his support of minority rights can be viewed as an extension of the difference principle as there is every likelihood that if the cultures of the minorities are not supported they would come to both economic and social ruin. This means that it is essential to support the land claims of native Indians in North America, for without this land their culture would die (ibid.: 151). The native Indians are thus the worst off.

Even if we entertain this explanation, it is not clear how Kymlicka can account for the problems of dissenters within communities. In addition, the difference principle hardly recommends that those who are well off should choose lifestyles of the worst off just because the choice exists. What is most damaging is that the difference principle does not justify either why the worst off should cling to those very economic and cultural practices that made them the least advantaged in the first place. The difference principle is supposed to liberate the worst off and not fix them in that position in perpetuity.

On the question of enhancing the range of choices, it is not quite as straightforward as it seems. Much as I, a non-native aborigine, might want to be an aborigine and lead a lifestyle of an aboriginal Indian in North America, I simply do not have free and unimpeded ingress into that community. In fact, till 1951, native Indian women who married outside their community in Canada lost their status within the community (ibid.: 149). In the United States it is even tougher. Non-Indian spouses almost never acquire membership in the community (ibid.: 149). This clause has since been changed to a double mother rule. A person would lose status as a native Indian if both the mother and grandmother married non-Indians. When Bill C-31 was introduced in the eighties in Canada, which allowed those who had lost status as Indians in the past to reclaim it, there was opposition from many reserves. The resources of these reserves were already over-stretched and they could not accommodate any more. In some instances the membership in the reserves increased by as much as 50 per cent which gave cause to a lot of status Indians to oppose Bill C-31. If by freely exercising the choice of marriage one can lose one's membership in a community, imagine how hard it is for a rank outsider to be able to adopt the lifestyle of another community because of its intrinsic appeal.

It has also been recorded that the desire to be considered as a native Indian in America is often for reasons that are not purely cultural. If one can establish some kind of Indian connection then that gives an access to profits from gambling and cigarette sales (as Indian reserves are exempt from certain legal provisions). This surely cannot be the kind of choice that Kymlicka is advocating. Nevertheless, though blood lines are running thin among Indians, it is lucrative to be considered a member of the community for obvious economic considerations. It is reported that 383 members of the Mashantucket Pequot tribe in Massachusetts clear $ 1 million a day from slot machines alone. Predictably the tribe gets calls round the year from people eager to become members of that community 'even if they cannot pronounce the name of the tribe' (Foster 1997). This accounts, to a large extent, for the threefold rise since 1970 in the number of people who identify themselves as native Indians in America (ibid.).

It is true that liberals value choice, but the choices that Kymlicka mentions are of the kind that can never be realistically exercised, or when exercised it is for the wrong reasons. In India too one cannot choose to be a member of a tribe or a member of an ex-untouchable community simply because one wants to. To carry the matter of choice further, is it possible to opt out of a certain community's membership even if one somehow manages to get in in the first place? Opting out of one community for another would arouse intense hostilities, especially on the part of the community that is being rejected. The pressures that will be brought to bear on the individual will be quite considerable. The case of the Bohra community in India comes readily to mind.

To recall Albert Hirschman, a citizen should always be able to choose 'exit' over 'voice' (see Walzer 1983: 218). This takes us back once again to the fact that both theoretically and practically communitarians find it extremely difficult to handle dissenters within their ranks. Kymlicka's solution to this, as we noted earlier, is to encourage consensus. This presupposes a background of liberal conditions, but as it is coupled with straightforward communitarianism, it does not take us very far. The question of choice is really not workable. In the first place is it really possible to choose one's community? Besides being a practical difficulty, would it not also damage one's understanding of what a community is supposed to mean if one can jump in and out of them so easily? Second, why should anyone want to choose the culture of the worst off? Third, why should the worst off cling to those practices that have made them the worst off? Would this not be a restatement of Oscar Lewis' 'culture of poverty' that ran into so much trouble decades ago? Finally, when choice is actually exercised it is often for economic gain and not for relishing a pure cultural alternative.

The route that Kymlicka proposes to reconcile liberalism with communitarianism is therefore not workable. The position that Dworkin advocates also ends up in fracturing fraternity though he, in no sense is a votary of the communitarian perspective. Dworkin's reliance on Rawls is pronounced and yet he argues that a certain colour of skin or membership of a particular community becomes a socially useful asset which others cannot aspire to possess under any circumstance. He says this to justify the American affirmative action programme. However, unlike other assets, skin colour or caste membership cannot be pooled at the social level to benefit everybody. The issue then boils down to how positive discrimination in favour of minorities, ex-untouchables and backward castes can benefit everyone.

The fact that individuals are 'thick with particular traits' (Nozick 1976: 228), does not by itself discredit the original position. The original position is after all only an Archimedean point (Rawls 1971: 260–63) from which rational individuals can issue the rules of justice as fairness. Moreover, the very fact that Rawls believes that his theory of justice can only work in a constitutional democratic regime clarifies that he is not being ahistorical in his assumptions. It is not so much that we are thick with particular traits that the affirmative action solution proposed by Dworkin along Rawlsian lines runs into difficulties, but rather because the principle of fraternity has only the difference principle to stand on. It is not complemented by a fully worked out body of moral principles adequate for *citizenship* in democratic constitutional societies.

The difference principle makes us receptive to fraternity as a consequence. It would well be the case that some of us are trapped in the fraternity business quite against our inclinations. This is what lends credibility to Nozick's query as to why those who have legitimately acquired attributes cannot derive individualized benefits from them (Nozick 1976: 225–26). Obviously it would be impractical, if not impossible, to ask everyone to nurture their assets only for the social good. This is an extremely end result oriented postulate and it is indeed surprising that Rawls should be so emphatic about it.

The historic condition (or 'narrative', to use Rorty's term, Rorty 1985: 208) of constitutional democracy necessitates the foregrounding of the condition of citizenship. Citizenship in turn implies a set of morals which are like Durkheim's 'molds' (Durkheim 1961: 24). Our behaviour must conform to these historically conditioned moral postulates. In fact it is possible to revise the Rawlsian principles of justice as fairness and assert that if I have attributes which have been legitimately acquired I can exploit them so long as others marginally benefit. This would allow initial differences to be perpetuated through the agency of the family. By all counts such a situation can be reconciled without too much difficulty with the difference principle. It would, however, clearly fall short when we consider the issues of deepening citizenship, and of altering the historically disadvantaged position that 'permanent minorities' occupy.

This is where we differ again with Kymlicka. For Kymlicka, preservation of minority cultures is an end in itself (Kymlicka 1989:

165–67). But if these cultures block the development of citizenship and fraternity; if they impede the realization of the equality of opportunity that a liberal regime promises, then on what grounds can they be supported by constitutional democracies? Supporting minority cultures, no matter what, is quite different, as is easily apparent, from a positive discrimination programme (such as of affirmative action or reservations) which helps to release citizens from the iniquities of history as it consciously sets out to increase the set of resemblances which are basic for true citizenship to emerge. A reading of Durkheim, especially an awareness of the fact that organic solidarity needs mechanical solidarity as its basis, is a very helpful inspiration in this regard. We shall consider this aspect in the next chapter.

Chapter VIII

Positive Discrimination and the Question of Fraternity: Connecting Durkheim to Rawls

Ambedkar and Mandal: Divergent Logics

The ability to share one another's fate is what positive discrimination hopes to bring about in the long run. When certain ascriptive attributes are considered to be good in their own right whether or not they enhance fraternity, then, that breaks down intersubjectivity. When ascriptive attributes are converted into socially desirable traits for political and economic leverage then they block the development of socially desirable talents at the collective level. In such a situation skin colour or caste membership act as perpetual reserves of social hostility. Public policy gets mired in negotiating between claims of rival ascriptive groups, thwarting and delaying the development of citizenship. Consequently, historic differences and deprivations are constantly enlivened making it difficult to establish the conditions of civil society.

This chapter will examine the reservation policy in India in the context of the development of citizenship and the emergence of a larger common pool of talents. A useful entry point into this question is by contrasting Ambedkar's reservation policy that was enshrined in the Constitution, with the recommendations of the Mandal Commission that were implemented in 1990.

The divergences between Ambedkar's reservation policy and that of the Mandal Commission are quite remarkable. To begin with, Ambedkar's policy of reservations, or protective discrimination, was designed primarily to remove the scourge of untouchability from Indian society, and with it the role of caste in public life. The situation with the Mandal recommendations which came into effect in 1990 appears to be quite different. Instead of looking at caste as an institution to be undermined, the advocates of Mandal see it instead as an important political resource. This is why the agenda of Mandal and Ambedkar are quite different in principle. In the case of Mandal the driving logic is that caste identity is a permanent asset to be exploited for political and economic ends.

At this point it is also necessary to admit that the policy of reservations for Scheduled Castes and Tribes has deviated significantly from what was proposed by Ambedkar and his fellow constitutionalists. Instead of gradually modifying and adjusting the reservations programme, keeping in mind the changes in the course of India's post-Independence history, it became rigid and unyielding. For all practical purposes, therefore, caste was being used here too as a permanent political resource. This is why Mandal faced little opposition when his recommendations were introduced. The groundwork, so to say, had already been done by the inheritors of Ambedkar.

In spite of this empirical overlap, it is important to separate the divergent logics of Ambedkar and Mandal. Ambedkar had a larger social programme, viz., that of enhancing *fraternity* among citizens in a free, sovereign, republic. According to this vision, caste would gradually cease to make any difference in public life. This is why Ambedkar urged that the reservations policy be periodically reviewed. He was all too aware of the fact that reservations could either become a crutch or a permanent political resource. In both cases the end result would be to fractionate citizens.

Mandal's thrust was really much more limited. What mattered most to him was to ensure that members of certain designated backward castes got jobs and seats in educational institutions. There the matter ended. To a certain extent he cannot be faulted for the Ambedkar programme had already deviated from its earlier course. This is what has led to the formation of two camps, both among intellectuals and activists. On one side are those who believe that reservations are inherently unworkable as they perpetuate caste distinctions in public life. For this reason they advocate an open market approach instead. Opposing them are the many activists and 'committed' scholars who espouse quite a different view. In their opinion reservations are necessary as they right a historical wrong and bring about greater parity, albeit along caste lines.

Given the extreme poverty and backwardness among certain sections in Indian society, it would indeed be quite undemocratic not to devise special ways to uplift the lot of the poor and the socially disprivileged. Reservations, or positive discriminations, seem to be the right thing to do under the circumstances. On the other hand, reservations have quite clearly failed to diminish, if they have not actually increased, the level of caste-based politics in India. This is surely not a good thing. In such a situation it is important to take a more analytical view of the matter so that the policy of reservations can be recast keeping in mind the need for establishing fraternity and consolidating citizenship. In other words, reservations need not be against the establishment of fraternity, which was after all in the original vision of Ambedkar.

Fraternity and Reservations: Realizing Equality of Opportunity

While the market principle insists that in the long run initial differences in birth will become negligible, social interventionists are not quite so sure. Moreover, with the inauguration of the notion of equal and participatory citizenship, there is a greater sense of urgency in meeting certain valued ends in one's lifetime. This is what propels social interventionists to devise programmes that will allow greater scope, socially and economically, to the historically dispossessed communities.

The programme that is most relevant in this connection is that of reservation or affirmative action. Though the two are not the same, they resemble each other in that they both strive to accommodate members of historically disadvantaged communities by a deliberate relaxation of standard norms. This may take the form of reducing the required number of marks for admission into educational institutions, or by lowering the qualification bar for getting jobs. It may also be accomplished by creating special positions, or seats, for members of such historically disadvantaged groups and categories.

On the face of it this seems to be a laudable move, but a closer examination reveals a host of problems which must be taken into account. Critics of reservation, or affirmative action, complain that such policies create permanent schisms in society besides directly harming the case of the meritorious. In their view such provisions go against the essence and spirit of liberalism and of the free individual, creating instead reverse discrimination.

There are many who would probably argue that it is precisely a kind of reverse discrimination that they would like to institute to compensate for centuries, or millennia, of historic injustice suffered by particular communities. Such a justification of reservations, or positive discrimination, is not based on the spirit of contemporary citizenship. While revenge cannot be adequately justified, there have been attempts, particularly in America, to rationalize affirmative action on the principle of compensation. In India this line of argument has not found much favour. Instead of holding the current generation responsible for what their ancestors and forebears did, the Indian Constitution advocates positive discrimination and reservations in the spirit of 'fraternity'. In his famous speech on 26 November 1949, introducing the motion to adopt the Indian Constitution, B.R. Ambedkar said that India was wanting in its 'recognition of the principle of fraternity. What does fraternity mean? Fraternity means a sense of common brotherhood of all Indians—of India being one people' (see Shiva Rao 1968a; 1968b: 945).

It is not as if the policy of positive discrimination is designed to bring about the total elimination of inequality. While inequalities will persist in spite of such policies, they will largely be the result of individual differences and variations of family background. Yet these will be uncomplicated and unburdened by historical handicaps. It is in this sense that positive discrimination and affirmative action will lead to a truly liberal society. This also implies that the measures instituted in favour of deprived communities are time bound in character. This is the way the Indian Constitution devised reservations for the ex-untouchable castes and for the tribal population. Pierre Trudeau too steered a similar policy in his colour blind proclamation for a 'Just Society' in Canada. Here again the special privileges given to the native aboriginal peoples were limited by a specific time frame (see Kymlicka 1989: 142). Once community differences, on account of historic injustices, cease to matter in the participation of individuals along the market principle, there will be no need for reservations or for affirmative action.

This being the case, proponents of reservations must attend to two urgent tasks. (i) First, they must be able to distinguish their position from that of those who would like reservations to be a permanent measure comprehensively separating populations on an enduring basis. (ii) Second, they must also meet the objections of the advocates of the market principle and demonstrate that the role and scope of liberalism is enhanced and not diminished by measures of positive discrimination. They must be able to demonstrate that reservations and other similar measures will allow liberalism, and with it the market principle, to operate more freely and fully than they would otherwise. *It is for this reason that reservations and protective discrimination have to find their justification in the language of rights*. Therefore, even if there are those who justify reverse discrimination as a rejoinder to historic injustice, the fact is that we can no longer return to the past. One way or the other we know too much, and have won too much, to turn the clock back. It is for this reason that there seems to be no other way but to recognize the problem of historically deprived communities in the language of rights. As we cannot go back, the only option is to look ahead. This is why it is important to recognize Richard Rorty's significant observation that liberalism, and its accompanying considerations on justice, are not philosophical metanarratives, but 'mostly a matter of historical narratives' (Rorty 1985: 208).

Collective Assets and Natural Lottery: Rawls and Dworkin

At this point it is necessary to introduce John Rawls (1971) into the discussion once again. Rawls' work on the question of justice in a constitutional democracy has altered much of the thinking on this subject. Rawls' differences with the exponents of natural liberty, including in this case F.A. Hayek (1960) and Robert Nozick (1976), arise because he believes that talents and attributes may be housed in persons, but they are social attributes to be harvested for society as a whole. It is just a matter of chance, or a 'natural lottery' (Rawls 1971: 74), that these talents and traits are so randomly distributed in individuals. In which case individuals do not have a prior right to use these talents to their own advantage. As society has decided that certain attributes are important, the fortunate individuals who have these talents cannot claim them all for themselves (ibid.: 72–74).

In Rawls' view when distribution takes place on the basis of a 'natural lottery' of talents the 'outcome is arbitrary from a moral perspective' (ibid.: 74). Furthermore, the principle of fair opportunity can only be 'imperfectly carried out at least as long as the family exists' (ibid.). Individual differences are not to be negated but should be utilized for maximizing social advantages. Neither is Nozick correct to imply that adopting the Rawlsian position will justify taking the eyes out from a sighted person and giving them to the blind (Nozick 1976: 206). This is tantamount to a redistribution theory which Rawls is not in favour of. Rawls would like to maximize social advantages and not redistribute them as ruthlessly as Nozick's parody would suggest. Redistribution of this sort would contradict Rawls' principle of justice where an added benefit accruing to someone should not be at the expense of another.

This brings us directly to the issue that representatives of permanent minorities have been raising, and as we can see above, Rawls too anticipates. Using the Rawlsian notion of natural lottery, Roland Dworkin argues that it is possible to justify positive discrimination, or affirmative action, along the principles of liberty without giving in to either the communitarians, and, more particularly, to the advocates of natural liberty.

Like Rawls, Dworkin (1977a) too believes that what counts for merit cannot be decided in the abstract but in terms of what society values and considers relevant. In other words it all depends upon what society thinks should be cherished and the kind of institutions that it would like to uphold. Therefore, nobody has a prior right to go to medical college, or become a lawyer. Society will decide which mix of attributes it considers suitable for admission into medicine and law. Admission may not be only on the basis of marks scored, but on the additional basis of, say, colour of skin or caste background. As one's attributes do not belong to the individual but to society, it is up to society to decide which attribute, or bundle of attributes, it considers relevant. At a certain point in time society could decide that being Black or belonging to an ex-untouchable caste is a 'socially useful colour'. In which case then, academic merit alone will not count (Dworkin 1977a, 1977b).

Dworkin's support of positive discrimination on the basis of the notion of 'natural lottery' is a very surefooted demonstration of the strength of the Rawlsian position. There is however a loophole which both Rawls and more specifically Dworkin overlook. If black is deemed to be a socially useful colour, or attribute, then what happens to those who are Black but possess economic and cultural assets and in that sense do not require affirmative action? Would this not create resentment among those who are not Black but are poor and socially depressed? Fraternity and its corollary, intersubjectivity, that Rawls works so hard to protect and retain through the difference principle, appears to be the first casualty here. If the population is to be divided on the basis of colour and caste then fraternity will surely be problematic. How can we then 'share in one another's fate?' (Rawls 1971: 102). Further, and, this is most important, how do we decide when black is no longer a useful trait in individual cases? In other words, is the colour black, or one's membership in a certain caste background, equally important, from a social point of view, to all members of these communities?

To share one another's fate can justify the establishment of positive discrimination, or affirmative action (as in Dworkin), but as we saw above, when certain *ascriptive* attributes are converted into socially valuable traits then that breaks down intersubjectivity. While some traits such as those based on academic excellence or professional competence belong to society and should be harnessed through a collective pool, other socially valuable traits, such as skin colour and caste membership, remain the preserve of certain ascribed categories of the population. Thus, while Rawls' difference principle sets out to establish intersubjectivity, where social differences are allowed only if they result from choice, Dworkin's defence of affirmative action seems to create barriers to such an intersubjectivity.

Rawls' work on justice as fairness, however, has the vast potential of unleashing fraternity and consolidating democratic citizenship when to the circumstances of justice (which presumes 'moderate scarcity' and competition, Rawls 1971: 126–27) we add on the imperatives of constitutional democracy. After all, justice as fairness, by Rawls' own account, is only valid in the specific conditions of a 'constitutional democratic regime' (ibid.: 74). It is only when one keeps in mind the imperatives of democracy that a true reflective equilibrium (ibid.: 48–49) can be achieved. Without this reflective equilibrium there is every chance of becoming, what Amartya Sen calls, 'rational fools' (Sen 1982). The conditions of democracy enjoin certain moral principles which must coincide with the principles of justice as fairness. This does not mean that one must be thick with particularistic traits. All it does imply is that imperatives of democracy insist that citizenship be founded on a moral principle—the sentiment behind the nation-state. The judgements evolving from this moral imperative of citizenship should not be at variance with the principles of greatest equal liberty in terms of speech, assembly, thought, etc., and vice versa.

Moral Imperatives and the Principles of Justice: Against Lexical Ordering

This is in consonance with the Rawlsian position, though it is often not recognized as such. A major reason for this is because Rawls gives priority to the principle of freedom of speech, assembly, opinion, property, etc., over the principle of equality of opportunity, which he correctly subjects to the 'difference principle' (Rawls 1971: 124). As is well known, Rawls' 'difference principle' enjoins that policies should be formulated keeping in mind the interests of the 'worst off'. This should not be read as a redistribution manifesto for whatever benefits accrue to the 'worst off' on account of the difference principle should not be at somebody else's expense. In Rawls' view, the difference principle enhances fraternity as it takes into account the 'long term expectations of the least advantaged under conditions of fair equal opportunity' (ibid.: 199).

Equality of opportunity, therefore, cannot remain as a straight constitutional provision without substantiating it with legislative policies which are informed by the difference principle (ibid.). Only in this way can the equality of opportunity provision be saved from usurpation by those who have an initial advantage over others by virtue of birth and social station (ibid.: 75). To lexically order the difference principle below the first principle of equal liberty for all (ibid.: 124) conveys the impression that to realize the first without the second is not quite as 'unfair' as it would be if it were the other way around.

It is important to place the circumstances of constitutional democracy at par with Rawls' circumstances of justice, or else the issue of fraternity could well be left behind. As we know Rawls gave priority to the principle of equality of opportunities and basic liberties over the second principle in which social and economic inequalities should be to the greatest benefit of the least advantaged, and offices and positions must be open to all (see Rawls 1971: 60, 302). If the two are prioritized, or 'lexically arranged' in this fashion, then it covertly favours individualism over citizenship. Even advocates of natural liberty might employ it to justify their criticism of the difference principle. They could argue that it is most important to ensure equal rights and basic liberties in law, which in the long run would nullify the accidents of birth. Rawls probably realizes this problem but he can do no better in this case than to equivocate. Under certain conditions, he admits, lexical ordering may have to be altered. He does not press the matter preferring to leave it aside and 'not pursue these complications further' (ibid.: 301, 506–7).

Instead of insisting on prioritizing (Rawls' 'lexical ordering') one over the other, the two should be seen conjointly. After all, Rawls himself says that a constitutional government cannot be based on pure procedural justice bereft of a long-term goal or intent (ibid.: 197). The goal of all constitutional democracies is, by definition, to strengthen democracy. This is why it is often misleading to talk in terms of lexical ordering. A constitutional government that insists only on procedures regardless of the outcome of such procedures would certainly not satisfy the moral imperatives of citizenship. Indeed, in such cases, those with a headstart on account of their privileged birth will be at a permanent advantage over the rest.

Rawls' endeavour to put principles before morals is understandable as he distrusts perfectionist arguments. We have also seen how such perfectionist arguments, as witnessed in the Soviet Union and even China, can be completely oblivious of human rights and dignity. But it is quite a different matter when a moral vision, such as that of a constitutional democracy, is accompanied by the granting of the greatest basic liberty to all citizens. As Rawls does not see it quite this way he bases the difference principle, not in the fact that it would ultimately enrich society as a whole, but because it is a rational thing to do in the initial hypothetical condition when the policy makers function from behind a 'veil of ignorance'. This veil prevents them from knowing what their actual station in society will be. In such a case, of course, the difference principle makes sound sense because it is possible that once the veil is lifted the policy makers might find themselves to be in the position of the least advantaged.

For Rawls then, fraternity emerges, quite unwittingly, because of self-interests, and not because constitutional democracy is a moral project. In which case one must also ask what prevents the decision makers to abide by the difference principle in a pure token form once they are assured that they are not in least advantaged positions. As the dangers of such tokenisms cannot be discounted, it is important to stress the imperative of constitutional democracy in tandem with the principle of the greatest liberty for all.

In addition, there is also the live possibility that the policies endorsed under the difference principle can be later subverted for sectional interests. Of course, this could be seen as another variant of tokenism, but it is one that needs to be specially addressed. Indeed, as this paper will argue, this is precisely what happened when the Mandal recommendations were implemented by Prime Minister V.P. Singh in 1990.

Durkheim and Fraternity: Theorizing on the Minimum Set of Resemblances

It is at this point that Durkheim should be read into Rawls. Like Rawls, Durkheim too believed that individualism by itself can turn pathological. In a pre-existing situation of inequality, contracts often allow the strong to exploit the weak. He made this point first in *The Division of Labour in Society* (1933) and later again in *Professional Ethics and Civic Morals* (1957). It is not as if he was part of the romantic reaction against the establishment of individualism. Rather, he believed that while individual liberty and contract were necessary there was still so much left to be done to regulate the activity of the state (Durkheim 1957: 31; see also Durkheim 1961).

For Rawls as we well know by now, preconceptions of morality cannot be allowed in the original situation. If they do enter the original situation then, he believes, that they would perjure the formulation of the rules of justice as fairness. The difference principle in justice as fairness, for instance, does not begin with morality, but ends with it. It might be argued, as Nozick (1976) seems to imply, that Rawls has a moral position to begin with and then looks for ways by which this position can be justified a *posteriori*. In any case, the original position finds a secure emplacement from which fraternity can be established with the help of the difference principle: 'we agree to share one another's fate' (Rawls 1971: 102).

To understand the moral imperatives of citizenship it is necessary to recall Durkheim's *Division of Labour in Society* (1933). As is well known, Durkheim contrasted societies which are mechanically solidaire from those that are characterized by organic solidarity. In mechanical solidarity, people cohere on account of their sameness, but in organic societies solidarity is achieved by a division of labour. This is why in mechanical societies there is an overwhelming preponderance of penal law. As there is only similarity, a crime against one is a crime against all. In organic solidarity, civil law enjoys greater presence as the arenas in which individuals operate are functionally specific.

While all this is fairly well known, what is often overlooked is that Durkheim's contrast between mechanical and organic solidarities is a conceptual device and does not represent a pure dichotomy. In other words, for Durkheim, while there can be societies that are based solely on mechanical solidarity (early or 'primitive' tribal societies), there can be no society which is characterized by organic solidarity alone. For organic division of labour to establish itself it needs the substrate of mechanical solidarity (ibid.: 398, 405; see also 290, 360). Mechanical solidarity provides the basis on which organic solidarity can grow. The fundamental principle of mechanical solidarity is resemblance. It is because we resemble one another that crime against any one is a crime against society. If organic societies were not to be established on mechanical solidarity then society would cease to be a collective enterprise. It is this collective enterprise that makes society a moral order (ibid.: 298). Therefore the foundation of organic solidarity in a society also demands social resemblance. After all, even in organic societies, there are certain crimes that offend the entire society. This is why Durkheim pointedly asserts that 'one's first duty is to resemble everybody else' (ibid.).

It is not at all clear how the first duty to resemble everybody else can be worked out in hierarchical caste societies or in feudal estates. It is in democratic societies, however, that one can fully experience what Durkheim meant about resembling one another. Citizenship can only exist when there is a common core of civic values which everybody adheres to. This common core of values is not just legally stipulated, nor is it held unconsciously. Like Durkheim's collective representations these values too hold for the collectivity. The difference is that these 'representations are distinguished from other collective representations by their higher degree of consciousness and reflection' (1957: 49–50). In other words, citizenship is built around common values but these are consciously worked at and established by reflection (Rawls' 'reflective equilibrium'?). In this sense there is a similarity with Rawls' notion of fraternity. For Rawls too fraternity is not a natural condition (like it is with most communitarians), but must be arrived at by consciously and deliberately relying on the difference principle.

This is why it is important to bear in mind that the circumstances of justice and the circumstances of constitutional democracy go together. A conjoint reading of Rawls and Durkheim would certainly favour such an interpretation.

Operationalizing Minimum Resemblances through Practices: Realizing Substantive Citizenship

Fraternity can only come about through a basic set of resemblances. Resemblances in this case are not to be understood in terms of actual goods and lifestyles all the way down. Resemblances should ensure that certain practices are common to all such that the equality of opportunity can be effectively realized. Rawls' principles of justice as fairness only says that offices should be open to all. But what if people do not qualify for these offices? Does it mean that through positive discrimination and reservations they should be in them anyway regardless of the welfare of institutions?

It is because advocates of reservations and affirmative action have often presented their case in this way that the principle of positive discrimination in favour of historically disadvantaged groups has met with resistance from liberal thinkers. Béteille's warning that the reservation policy should be sensitive to institutional well being may once again be recalled (Béteille 1991).

A minimum set of resemblances can then be understood as a set of practices that are open to all individuals so that they can acquire socially valuable skills and talents. This would mean that access to education, knowledge, and skills should be operationally and realistically open to all regardless of the accidents of birth. As equality before the law cannot guarantee this on its own, it has to be buttressed by provisions that bring about a minimum set of resemblances in practice. People should have effective entry into skills and offices regardless of their initial situation at birth. As Dworkin and Rawls have both pointed out, the talents in society should be for the greater advantage of the society as a whole. But how is one to know what talents exist if some sections of the society cannot realistically be aware that they have them in the first place? Rawls does not consider this possibility seriously enough. What interests him most is to justify, through the difference principle, that those who are better off should help the worst off (Rawls 1967: 68). Rawls does not take into account that the worst off can also help themselves and not just be helped. The fact that those who are worst off can improve their lot on their own if circumstances allow them to exploit their dormant and unexcavated, but potentially valuable, assets does not seem to concern Rawls too much.

At this point we should recall with profit the classic debate between the two giants of Black assertion in America—Booker T. Washington and W.E.B. DuBois. Washington advocated training in skills that were practical in character and in keeping with the niches Blacks occupied in society. Blacks would then become self-reliant but would not compete against the Whites for their respective areas of expertise were widely divergent. Against this DuBois argued that Blacks should get education in areas that were socially valued and comparable to what college-going Whites received. DuBois was thus advocating equality in terms of setting up a minimum set of resemblances, rather than undermining fraternity on the principles of separation that the communitarians seem to favour (see Parikh 1997: 67). DuBois' point in this matter was further affirmed in the landmark judgement against segregation delivered by the United States Supreme Court in 1954 in the *Brown vs. Board of Education* case (see also Freeman 1995: 31).

If the core of citizenship is consolidated by a minimum set of resemblances made up of practices that allow people to acquire socially useful skills and talents, then differences between individuals is a matter of choice or an outcome of natural abilities, and not dependent on birth. This should also undermine to some extent the role the institution of the family plays in perpetuating sectional advantages. This provides a more durable basis for justifying equality of opportunity over equality of results. Citizenship is not about equality of lifestyles or income. Marshall's notion of citizenship as a status that tends towards equality (Marshall 1977) should be interpreted differently. Citizenship implies an equality of status insomuch as it encourages a minimum set of resemblances made up of certain baseline practices that are common to all. By virtue of having access to these practices citizens can later choose to be different in the ways they want to be. Let us recall Lord Marshall once again when he said that the 'uniform status of citizenship...provided the foundation of equality on which the structure of inequality could be built' (quoted in Marshall 1963: 91). To argue instead that substantive citizenship can only be achieved once there is equality in lifestyles and incomes (see Lockwood's discussion on this in Lockwood 1992: 260–62) is to impoverish the meaning of citizenship by introducing perfectionist and end result arguments.

That Blacks, like the Scheduled Castes, should be given the benefit of positive discrimination is undeniable. As Blacks are generally unable to realize the equal entry law it should be made realistically available to them by first ensuring that Blacks too participate in practices that make for the minimum set of resemblances. The problem with Dworkin is when he calls black a socially useful colour, or asset. Arguments along these lines can be quite misleading. In fact, the colour black is not a socially useful asset. Like one's low caste membership, the colour black is only a *ready reckoner* in some societies that great disprivileges of birth continue to exist in fact and in everyday practice, if not in law. So neither is the colour black, nor caste membership a badge of honour or shame, but a ready reckoner that helps policy makers to target groups for upliftment through positive discrimination. This would enlarge the numbers of those with the minimum set of resemblances socially necessary to realize substantive citizenship.

There is undeniably an intrinsic problem if one were to prioritize equality of individuals over fraternity (Rawls' 'laxical ordering'), instead of coupling the two together. What needs to be acknowledged is that individual equality must necessarily be accompanied by the moral imperatives of citizenship if equality of opportunity is to be substantively, and not just legally, realized. It must be remembered that individualism can truly flourish where citizenship exists. Without this, individualism would be a doctrine limited to exceptional individuals and heroes: to the virtuous and not to the ethical (Hegel 1945). Individualism is a social product coeval with citizenship and cannot exist without it.

In spite of the fact that Rawls at several points emphasizes that human beings are social individuals and can recognize their nature in society, he still retains the primacy of the individual above all else. His individualistic assumptions often come to the fore. At one point Rawls explicitly states (in a very anti-Durkheimian manner) that society is not 'an organic whole with a life of its own distinct from and superior to that of all its members in their relation to one another' (Rawls 1971: 264). It is this residue of fierce individualism that forces Rawls to favour a lexical ordering.

A Durkheimian position, on the contrary, would consistently assert that the whole is greater than the sum total of its parts. It would recommend, as we have just done, that the two principles of justice as fairness come together in one fell swoop. As a Durkheimian reading of Rawls would couple the circumstances of justice with the conditions of constitutional democracy and citizenship, concerns of fraternity would necessarily be at par with those of equality of opportunity and individual rights. Once the two are together it is clear that unless substantial equality exists in terms of minimum resemblances of practices, justice as fairness will never be fully realized. This is especially so when there are communities in society that have been historically disadvantaged.

In order to increase the basic sum of resemblances so that occupational differentiation and other forms of individualism can flower it is necessary to recommend positive discrimination.

Discrimination of this kind finds its justification in the circumstances of democracy and citizenship. Looked at closely, there is no need for any lexical ordering either. The imperatives of democracy and citizenship imply Rawls' two principles of justice conjointly. The unconscious urge to order two or more things in a hierarchy must sometimes be resisted. The nation-state, like Durkheim's society, is not a sum of parts arranged in order of precedence. The whole is always greater than an aggregation of its constituents. This is what makes society a reality *sui generis*.

Ascriptive Identities as Ready Reckoners: Resisting Reservations in Perpetuity

Under these circumstances it is important to realize the equality of status that citizenship endorses by enforcing a minimum set of resemblances. If being Black, or belonging to a particular caste, is a socially useful asset, as Dworkin claims, then these assets cannot be shared by others in society. This is contrary to the earlier Rawlsian position on the pooling of assets. If, however, the colour black, or caste membership, are only ready reckoners for enhancing fraternity, then as and when those who belong to this category acquire socially useful talents and attributes they should contribute them to the society as a whole and not employ them only for sectional advantages.

This should be the first duty of those who are beneficiaries of affirmative action. If society believes that the historically disprivileged have a just entitlement so that they can contribute more meaningfully to society, then it follows that those who benefit from affirmative action owe it to society to put their newly acquired social talents back into the collective social pool. This would mean that they would automatically fall outside the scope of affirmative action programmes in the future. The net would no longer cover them as they already have socially useful assets. Indeed the society will be richer and better endowed. Consequently it will progressively acquire a higher strike rate with the policy of affirmative action and protective discrimination. As members of hitherto disprivileged communities begin to fall outside the net of protective discrimination, they release, and at the same time contribute, resources for the extension of the affirmative action programme. In this process the society gains as a whole.

By increasing the numbers of those who possess the minimum set of resemblances, the society has now a larger component of talents in a variety of fields and specialities than it had before. This is how affirmative action which is aimed at the historically most disadvantaged sections, ultimately improves the lot of everybody in society. It is therefore better to begin by considering ways of enhancing the conception of citizenship in terms of a minimum set of resemblances for that encourages fraternity society-wide. If, on the other hand, one were to begin by considering that the colour black is a socially useful colour, or belonging to a certain caste a socially useful membership, then that would inhibit fraternity and sow the seeds of permanent divisions in society.

In Dworkin's opinion if the society thinks, for whatever reason, that Blacks, or the aborigines should be given special privileges, then others should not complain about it. Unfortunately, individuals will complain because Dworkin's proposals fractionate society on the plea that those who are Blacks or aborigines have these ascriptive attributes as social assets. Those who can never have these assets feel cheated in a liberal democratic society.

If, however, Blacks, aborigines, depressed castes, and members of minority religions are helped by positive discrimination to enlarge the pool of socially valued talents and skills (or assets) then, that helps the entire society. This also means that if one is Black or from a depressed caste background that alone should not be a qualifying factor in *perpetuity*. The most important point is the extent to which an individual has the opportunities to effectively utilize the equality of conditions available under liberal democracy.

Further, in contrast to what I think Kymlicka (1989) is arguing, liberal democracy should not be taken to mean that sectional privileges be upheld if they run counter to increasing the minimum set of resemblances. If certain community practices come in the way of enlarging the minimum set of resemblances necessary for realizing the freedoms of liberal democracy then there is no justification whatsoever for supporting those community practices. Diversities, as we discussed earlier (Chapter IV), can by themselves confine people into encysted cultural spaces. Consequently, diversities operate on a principle counter to those of fraternity. The only way diversities can be accommodated is if they are cleansed of their root metaphors and appear primarily as artifacts, or aesthetic alternatives.

It is possible now to justify affirmative action and positive discrimination on the grounds that it is not just good for certain individuals, but, properly applied, it is good for the society as a whole. If it is good only for certain individuals then it encourages the doctrine of equality of results. Instead, when positive discrimination policies emphasize that the base of minimum resemblances be increased the attention is on how to develop opportunities for acquiring socially valuable skills and not so much on the equality of results.

Equality of results is a stunted mutant of the liberal democratic process. It is born out of guilt and a lack of empathy. Instead of equality of results whose spirit is contrary to the principles of fraternity, the need is to pursue policies that will enhance the minimum set of resemblances which will help in the cultivation of a true citizenry. Only when positive discrimination policies free the beneficiaries from their past, can they be truly colour blind. When beneficiaries contribute to society then the society can be colour blind. It is only under these circumstances that affirmative action and reservation can also be mindful of institutional wellbeing (Béteille 1991). Equality of results, as we have just argued is tone deaf to such social obligations, and is therefore not a worthy doctrine to emulate under the guise of positive discrimination. After all the principles of justice should not just be fair, but should also be seen to be fair.

This clarifies what is meant here by a minimum set of resemblances. When Durkheim said that our first duty is to resemble one another he was drawing attention to the fact that only after certain fundamental aspects of life are collectively manifest is it possible to diversify in occupations and skills. The minimum set of resemblances in a liberal democratic market oriented society would *constitute of practices wherein opportunities to obtain socially useful assets are accessible to all.*

Rawls and Dworkin are right when they say that such assets belong to the society and are not simply those of the individual. But there is a significant oversight in the way they express their position. While these assets may be randomly located, it is also true that certain communities are effectively denied the opportunity to cultivate these assets. Intelligence by itself is not a socially useful asset unless it can be trained in ways which are socially valuable. In this sense the distribution of assets is not truly random. In order to make it properly random the opportunities to acquire socially useful assets should be accessible to all. Evidence is quite convincing that in most democratic societies there are certain sections of the population that just do not have the opportunities to realize these assets. Positive discrimination helps these deprived sections to gain socially useful assets by first targeting their economic vulnerability.

Poverty and Citizenship: The Scope of Democracy in Conditions of Scarcity

At this point it is necessary to recall that Rawls had categorically stated that the principles of justice as fairness only work in the 'condition of moderate scarcity' (Rawls 1971: 127, 256). This condition is important but does not have the same status as the circumstances of justice or citizenship. After all, if the condition of moderate scarcity does not prevail this does not mean that no effort should be made towards establishing a liberal democratic regime. In which case developing countries should resign themselves to dictatorships and worse. Regardless of what Rawls might think about this, it is a fact that countries like India have shown that democratic regimes are possible in poorer countries as well. Having said this, it also needs to be acknowledged that countries like India have not been able to broad base the minimum set of resemblances necessary for a substantive realization of citizenship.

The situation is not uniformly conducive to the establishment of justice as fairness in developed western democracies either. In most of these advanced societies there are pockets of misery and extreme penury. It is often stated that the poor in the United States have a life expectancy and infant mortality rate not much better than that of the average Bangladesh national. Surely the principles of justice as fairness cannot be abandoned when we come to the poorer quarters. What then will be the fate of the principle of fraternity and citizenship?

Citizenship and Scarcity: Poverty as the Key Variable

This brings us to the crux of the issue regarding what the minimum set of resemblances should be premised on. It was mentioned earlier that the minimum set of resemblances should be at the level of social practices which allow everyone to cultivate skills essential for acquiring socially valuable assets. It does not mean that people get these assets readymade, but the conditions for acquiring them are equalized as in a level playing field. This also allows for a greater play of individualism, for now individual differences (leaving aside the variations in natural aptitude) are essentially a matter of choice.

Obviously, therefore, positive discrimination should help in providing a foundation of economic well-being on the basis of which individuals can gain institutional access from where they can cultivate socially useful traits. Being poor is neither an asset nor a badge of honour. Policies with regard to reservations or affirmative action must help in rescuing those in abject poverty, and give them enough room and scope for developing socially useful skills. They accomplish this by relaxing the standard requirements for jobs, or for education and training, or for financial loans, when it comes to members of historically disprivileged communities.

There is nothing more pressing than the need for upliftment of the economically deprived. Being economically the 'worst off' is a kind of deprivation that cannot be matched. All other kinds of complaints about one's lot seem irrelevant and redundant when compared with poverty. The one factor that stands resolutely in the way of attaining the minimum set of resemblances in society is economic want. This is the key issue that needs to be addressed. When economic backwardness is sanctioned by historical prejudices of the dominant community then one's community membership provides a handy reckoner in devising the target group whose social skills have to be developed.

This is necessary for poverty exacerbates the low social status accorded to historically persecuted communities. There is hardly an instance when prejudice can be effective when it is aimed at the well-to-do, no matter which community they may come from. Such individuals have alternate sources of social prestige, arising from their economic security, to be able to defend themselves. In this process they adroitly take recourse to the process of law and often manage redressals very effectively. This is evident even in a hierarchical society like India. Once members of ex-untouchable castes achieve economic security, they not only claim higher caste status successfully, but are also able to defend themselves by taking recourse to the established laws of the land.

Positive discrimination is therefore aimed at giving the broadest possible base to citizenship and fraternity by making it possible for everyone to acquire those skills that a liberal democratic society values. For accomplishing this, as was just argued, it is necessary to remove conditions of abject scarcity so that these skills could be acquired by the entire society. Those who have a certain kind of socially useful asset, but mobilize to take advantage of affirmative action to convert it into another kind of socially useful asset have no claim to protective discrimination or reservations. As one kind of socially useful asset can be used to gain another, there is no justification for providing reservations for such sections or communities.

If the economically strong South Asian or East Asian migrants in North America demand reservations because they are visible minorities then the claim cannot be justified on the principles of justice as fairness. These people should not draw resources from the collective social pool, but should instead be contributing to it. As they are economically well positioned, and possess other valuable skills as well, that should disqualify them from taking advantage of affirmative action. Being brown or black by itself does not qualify. They are only ready reckoners when there is a strong statistical relationship between being black or brown and being economically backward, and therefore with little opportunity to develop the minimum set of resemblances necessary for substantive citizenship.

The 'Worst Off' or the Socially Backward: Creating Assets versus Converting Assets

Against this background the demand in India that the so-called 'Other Backward Castes' (OBCs) be given reservations in jobs and educational institutions lacks justification. Reservations for the ex-untouchables and tribes were instituted because they lacked those assets which a market oriented liberal society values. They had neither wealth, land, nor education. To romanticize the labours of hereditary cobblers, scavengers, agrestic serfs, and other menials is certainly a view taken safely from the outside. Why else is it that it is nobody's ambition to be a scavenger or an agrestic serf? Regardless of the intrinsic worth or dignity of such labours the moot point is that such skills that the historically disprivileged possess are not acknowledged as social assets worth acquiring. Only an apologist of the caste system and of the estates order can argue otherwise.

Unlike the Scheduled Castes and Tribes the OBCs are not without socially valuable assets as their initial point of departure. Large sections of the OBCs are made up of castes and caste clusters of the rural rich. The Yadavas, Ahirs and Kurmis are dominant agrarian castes in many parts of north and east India. Soon the powerful Jat caste may also be included among the OBCs. These castes demand reservations because they claim to be socially backward but not economically backward. Social backwardness is measured primarily in terms of educational attainment, and, to some extent, by urban jobs. This is clearly evident in the way the Mandal Commission put forward the demand of reservations for the OBCs. In order to justify the claim that OBCs are indeed backward, the Mandal Commission devised a weighted set of criteria. In this formulation it gave the lowest weightage to economic backwardness and the most to educational and social backwardness.

The demands of the OBCs are not fair because these OBCs are not without assets. They have land and money which are prized in market oriented liberal democracies. It is true that they do not have the assets that they now want, which is education and urban jobs. These assets can however be easily attained by them as one kind of social asset can be easily converted into another kind. Large sections of the OBCs are economically powerful as they are substantial landowners and cultivators. By using this all important asset they can get to others without reservations or affirmative action.

It must be emphasized that the reservation policy can be justified only when it expends resources from the collective pool for those who have no socially valuable asset whatsoever. Or else, it has the danger of degenerating into a kind of patronage politics which vitiates the quest for fraternity and gives affirmative action a bad odour.

The claims of the OBCs cannot therefore be upheld in the same way as reservations for ex-untouchable castes and tribes can. In the latter case they have no social assets. These communities were specifically identified by the Indian Constitution not only because they were despised for so many centuries, but because they were also the poorest in the country. It is correct to argue in this case that unless the members of these ex-untouchable and tribal communities are not made economically viable their degraded social status will continue. Economic viability, very simply, provides them with the capacity to acquire the minimum set of resemblances essential for acquiring socially valuable assets. It is in this manner that the indigent historically disprivileged communities can realize the liberties and egalitarian principles of constitutional democracies.

Prejudices of one sort or the other against communities of all kinds have always existed and will continue to exist. This is an anthropological truism that cannot be easily shaken off. What really matters is when such prejudices restrict the economic development of certain communities. This is where the historically disprivileged are not quite the same as the poor though they share many characteristics in common. A poor person has to fight poverty, but does not have to take on the additional burden of combating the prejudices of an entire society against them. Prejudices against the historically disprivileged are not disaggregated and scattered as other prejudices are, but exist in a concentrated and generalized form. This is where prejudices come in the way of those among the historically disprivileged who seek a better life for themselves. The need for affirmative action is pertinent in this case, for only by securing economic strength can they then combat prejudices and take on the bigots on their own.

Positive discrimination helps to economically succour members of these communities. Social prejudices against them gradually fall by the wayside or become ineffective. In any case, straightforward laws exist in all democratic societies that protect individuals against discrimination on grounds of race, religion, language, etc. These laws can always be invoked when gross injustices are committed against anybody because of accidents of birth. But these laws by themselves are useless when it comes to directly producing social assets among those who hitherto have had none. Moreover, as experience shows, going to court is not quite the same for the rich as it is for the poor. Again we return to poverty as the key variable.

If native Indians of America, or ex-untouchable communities in India, do not have those attributes that qualify as socially useful assets in liberal market oriented democracies, it is not because the potential does not exist among them, but because they lacked the economic wherewithal to cultivate them. The cultivation of these requires that a minimum set of resemblances be established among the citizens. This is in accordance with our earlier argument that when recipients of positive discrimination acquire assets they should be taken out of that category and placed in the common pool like the rest. This is an acknowledgement of the addition now to the numbers of those who possess a minimum set of resemblances. To that extent fraternity too is enlarged. Only under these conditions the quality of intersubjectivity in which, as Rawls said, people 'participate in one another's nature' can be nourished.

In this fashion liberty, equality and fraternity form a triumvirate. They are not discordant notes but fall in place when the circumstances of democracy co-exist with the circumstances of justice. In order to protect liberty it is necessary to be equal before the law. Yet these principles can only be upheld in a nation-state where citizenship is a crucial feature. If this were not so then liberty and freedom would be, as Hegel argued, only for kings and heroes (Hegel 1945). As citizenship is based on fraternity, it demands, in turn, a minimum set of resemblances. This vital feature was brought to our notice most vividly by Durkheim, but, in retrospect, we realize that it was also emphasized by Rousseau (1913) and Hegel (1945). Seen thus, positive discrimination is not just compatible with liberalism, but is often enough a necessary condition for its survival and consolidation.

Conclusion: Ambedkar and Mandal Revisited

The divergences between Ambedkar and Mandal on their respective reservation policies are now quite clear. It is not just that Ambedkar's programme envisions the removal of untouchability and with it the undermining of the caste system in public life, but it is also about creating assets among those who have none. This is what brings the moral imperatives of fraternity to the forefront.

The assets of the better off are put in the collective pool so that socially valuable assets may be created in sites where there were none. This measure has a moral resonance for out of this collective pooling new assets are being created.

The creation of such new assets is possible because the collective pooling of assets allows the nation-state to underwrite the expenses incurred for the establishment of certain baseline similarities in practices for all. As the most important feature in this case is not one's ascriptive badge, but the creation of socially valuable assets, it is expected that those who have been the beneficiaries of the scheme will gradually slip out of the net. They will cease receiving from the collective pool and instead will begin to contribute to it. Over time this will exponentially enlarge the collective pool of assets and the society as a whole will benefit from this outcome. This general social welfare will not emerge because of an unwitting consequence of the difference theory, but rather because of a conscious moral choice based on the principles of fraternity that underpin the sentiments behind a nation-state. The beneficiaries of reservations now have assets of their own which can be harnessed for social purposes. As far as public policy is concerned they cease to be members of certain designated castes or communities, and are now counted as individuals. It is in this sense that reservations and protective discrimination can be recast and justified in the language of rights. Ambedkar's reservation scheme has this potentiality. It is both time bound and aimed at removing from public life historical disprivileges on account of the accidents of birth.

Reservations in the Mandal scheme lack this moral quality. The targeted beneficiaries of Mandal, that is, those who are being aided from the collective pool, are quite plainly not without socially valuable assets. Further, they are unwilling to merge their existing tangible assets into the collective pool as their express purpose is to add one kind of asset onto another. In this case the advantages are purely sectional in character, which is why reservations for the OBCs cannot be seen as a simple extension of the Ambedkar programme. Consequently, quite unlike the Ambedkar model, the Mandal recommendations cannot logically demand the undermining of caste distinctions either. Caste in the case of the Mandal Commission is a socially useful attribute and an important political resource to be plumbed in perpetuity. The Mandal programme, therefore, is not in the spirit of enlarging fraternity, as the Ambedkar proposals are. In Mandal the ambitions are far too limited, and the goal too nearsighted, for the moral imperatives of citizenship and fraternity to have any room for manoeuvre.

Chapter IX

Minoritization and the Public Sphere

Liberal Democracy, Minorities and the Public Sphere

The demand for minority protection should be seen in conjunction with the public sphere and the growth of non-spaces. Together they frame the minorities issue and give it a contemporary character. Minority protection did not exist in pre-modern times. In the first place, minorities were in many cases the actual rulers. Second, the cultural minorities and subjugated population were allowed to practice their religion or culture only to the extent that the ruling community allowed them to. It was *noblesse oblige* all the way (Gupta 1996: 158–61).

If other cultures were allowed to practice their customs and rituals then it was because of the magnanimity of the ruling community. The hierarchies established in such societies were non-negotiable (ibid.), and the root metaphors of the governing hierarchy were embedded in large areas of social life, thus restricting the growth and development of non-spaces. In some cases, the ruling hierarchy only emphasized its cultural style and preferences at the upper levels of the imperial court, and its bureaucracies. It let the local worlds exist with their root metaphors so long as these did not conflict with the root metaphors of the ruling community.

The question of minority protection takes a different form in liberal democratic nation-states. The right to cultural practice is no longer up to the magnanimity of the rulers. It is now an established feature of citizenship. If this provision does not exist then that would make for a theoretic nation-state and not a liberal democratic one. However, the mere acceptance of the right to cultural practice does not mean that the minority problem has been resolved, only that a very important principle has been won on the basis of which minorities can present themselves in the public sphere.

The opening of the public sphere is a very important development of liberal democratic nation-states. The public sphere is essentially an arena for contestation. It allows representatives of different cultural spaces to make a pitch for influencing public opinion. It does not disallow the entry of root metaphors into its terrain, like non-spaces ideally do. The proponents of different root metaphors must however abide by certain ground rules. The most basic liberties of citizenship cannot be compromised, nor the root metaphors of the nation-state and issues such as sovereignty and territory. This constraint is a very severe one for it tempers all kinds of metaphors including those of the nation-state.

When the metaphors of the nation-state are excessively loaded by religious metaphors they are immediately suspect in the public sphere. If a nation-state has just one religious group then the matter is never seriously considered, as it was for long time in Lutheran Sweden. Today, however, it is practically impossible to find a nation-state with a homogeneous religious character. In such conditions, if a nation-state's metaphors are overwhelmingly religious then they would automatically exclude others in the nation-state who belong to different religions. This would immediately fracture citizenship well before the project could even begin. The French insistence on *laicite* can be understood most accurately as a disavowal of all religious connotations from the metaphors of the nation-state. Metaphors after all are not empty slogans but are enacted around a regnant set of meanings.

If the public sphere allows religious overtones to a nation-state's metaphors, it would cease to be a public sphere and become merely a vehicle for propaganda. What distinguishes one public sphere from another should ideally be only the dominance of the respective nation-state's metaphors in them. The fact that a public sphere openly allows the metaphor of its nation-state to have a presence in it distinguishes it from what would otherwise be a non-space. But to allow a religion (even if it be a dominant one) to mark this sphere would convert it into a closed 'space' and create exclusions at the sub-national level.

In India as well as in other parts of the world there are various nation-state metaphors which are either overtly religious or have a religious meaning attached to them. To declare a religion as the official religion is surely a great impediment to the development of the public sphere. While this prevails in both England and Pakistan, among other countries, it compromises to that extent the quality of their public spheres. In England the official religion aspect is gradually becoming an empty ritual devoid of practical content. It nevertheless provokes strong reactions from many quarters and probably hinders a solution to the Irish problem.

In India too many of the nation-state metaphors have a strong religious bias in them. This is not surprising given the fact of the Partition and the creation of Islamic Pakistan. But anti-Pakistan sentiments can also be kept alive without relying on religion, at least not directly. The fact that India is a democratic state and Pakistan was not for a long time is something that Indians often rely on to distance themselves from Pakistan. The emergence of secularism as an ideological credo that also includes within its ambit, anti-casteism, is yet another nation-state metaphor. Anti-colonialism, particularly the specifics of the Indian variety, is probably the strongest metaphor of them all. This anti-colonialism is an outcome of collective practice and engagement which has many unique attributes. These attributes are what make for India's 'original combination'.

In most cases the fact that there exists a majority religion in every nation-state puts the public sphere under considerable pressure. If the majority religion's metaphors do not actually intervene in the state structure of a nation-state then these metaphors are not actively of any consideration for the public sphere. While this has been achieved to some extent in countries like the United States, France, England, Germany and perhaps even India, there is always the danger of religious nationalism coming to the fore in these countries. Religious nationalism if it actually triumphs, will of course signal the closure of the public sphere, and will also mean the termination of liberal democracy.

Under perfect conditions one could hypothesize a public sphere where even the root metaphors of the nation-state can be questioned along with their territorial implications. Such a public sphere would approach Habermas' ideal of universal reason. This is still a long way from happening and there is little reason to believe that such an outcome is imminent. This implies that as long as nation-states exist public spheres will always be inflected by a certain amount of what Habermas would call 'strategic and instrumental reason'. A public sphere true to Habermas' canons of universal reason can only emerge in a post nation-state scenario. Speculations on this front are outside the scope of this work.

Even so, the presence of nation-state metaphors does not necessarily mean that the public sphere has been jeopardized by systematically distorted communication. The sentiments of the nation and the structures of the state are inclusive enough to include within their ambit other cultural spaces and non-spaces that lie within a given territory. As the nation is the most inclusive cultural membership, the public sphere can live with root metaphors at that level of generality.

A good test case for demonstrating this is the co-existence of linguistic loyalties with nation-state loyalty in India. When the demand surfaced in the early fifties that further provincial demarcation be done on linguistic grounds there was a general feeling of unease in the higher political quarters. Many feared that the clamour for linguistic provinces could well escalate to a full-throated advocacy of secession and national self-determination. This is why the Congress and the Constituent Assembly that was set up to frame the structures and laws of the India after Independence did not favour such a demand (Gupta 1996: 59).

Nevertheless, this urge could not be stifled. In this connection there are two significant issues that ought not to be sublated. In the first place, the demand for unilingual administrative provinces in India was being made on 'patriotic' grounds. The proponents of this movement did not ask for linguistic provinces to diminish the aura of the nation-state, but as good Indians (Nayar 1966: 33). It was argued that India would be better governed as a democracy, if democracy functioned in the languages of its people.

Second, the creation of linguistic provinces did not hurt other linguistic groups. If for the Marathi-speaking people, the bilingual province of Mumbai was made to yield a Maharashtra, then the same process gave the remainder to the Gujaratis as their Gujarat. Likewise, if Punjabi-speaking people got Punjab, the Hindi-speaking people in the erstwhile larger Punjab got Haryana.

Indeed, the Punjabi activists encouraged agitation for the formation of Haryana for that was a sure way of getting Punjab.

Even though linguistic demands were conceded over time to all the major linguistic groups in the country, nowhere has such a movement become a secessionist one. If anything, providing for linguistic provinces helped the nation-state stay together and not face a deep constitutional impasse as in neighbouring Sri Lanka. Once this deep-seated democratic demand for linguistic provinces was met there was no palpable hostility thereafter towards maintaining English and Hindi as official languages for inter-provincial communications. There have been occasional uprisings against Hindi or English, but they have been by and large controlled. To a large extent it has also been an awareness of the advantages of keeping alive a public sphere that has contained linguistic loyalties from becoming divisive in their expressions.

The ability to negotiate between non-spaces in the cultural space of the nation-state's territory has also played a significant role in limiting linguistic loyalties to the provincial level. A fanatic and one-sided devotion to language would have denied many the advantages of moving in and out of non-spaces scattered over the territory of India. The multitude of actual practices that thus helped reconcile linguistic demands with the need for maintaining nation-state fraternity has enhanced the conception of citizenship. This however took courage, statesmanship, and a disregard for western textbook notions of the ideal nation-state. Sri Lanka failed on all these counts as its bloody contemporary politics demonstrates.

Majorities, Minorities and Liberal Democracy

Maintaining liberal democracy within a nation-state is not an easy task. But without it a nation-state would renege on those with whom a common cause was made in the making of the nation's sentiment. There were a large number of Muslims in the Congress party who opposed Pakistan. Many Muslims in India suffered extreme hardships for the sake of Independence. To now turn around and say that India is a land of the Hindus would be tantamount to treachery and deceit. Likewise there were Blacks and Whites; Quakers, Catholics and Jews, who together contributed to the making of America. To exclude them by making America a land of the

White Anglo-Saxon Protestants would be equally unfair. It is after the moment of fusion that a cool, deliberate working out of the modalities of keeping fraternity alive becomes imperative.

It is probably inescapable that the majority communities in all nation-states believe that they are the most authentic patriots. The existence of such a sentiment and the root metaphors that accompany it, does not mean that considerations arising from such root metaphors should not be entertained in the public sphere. There can be nation-states where this happens but these would not be liberal democratic nation-states, as we have already mentioned. For example, if a nation-state does not allow the practice of other religions, or decrees that only the dress and deportment recommended by the majority religion should dominate, then the public sphere in such nation-states has already been perjured.

The public sphere can however entertain issues arising out of root metaphors provided they do not injure the basic liberties that are foundational and which cannot be compromised. The demand to wear a turban, or a certain kind of head dress, or to be allowed to build a temple or a mosque along culturally preferred aesthetic styles, does not take away from the foundational rights, and can therefore be entertained in the public sphere. The fact that these demands originate from a defined cultural space does not automatically disqualify them from being debated in the public sphere. The important point is that none of these demands take away from the foundational rights of, and basic liberties granted to, individuals.

The public sphere is a zone where representations from cultural spaces and non-spaces are debated and deliberated upon. Non-spaces might represent themselves in terms of the viability of alternative enterprise associations. This may be of the kind that proposes a hike in export duties, or the establishment of computer and software facilities, or the introduction of different kinds of labour legislations.

Likewise, non-spaces too should not allow those practices and individual preferences to exist which diminish the performance of non-spaces and fundamentally disarticulate its functioning. Contrarily, if there are certain individual variations of aesthetics and culturally informed preferences which do not militate against the functioning of non-spaces, and will not prejudice its future order, then they should be allowed to exist.

The fact that the public sphere entertains demands that may originate in space and non-space makes it a very critical institutional pre-requisite for liberal democracy. This institutional requirement of the public sphere can be met through a variety of structures, such as trade unions, political parties and elections, consumers' associations, voluntary agencies and groups. It is not as if these organizations have only debating as their express purpose, but it is in, and through, the accomplishment of their stated goals and overt activities that the demands of the public sphere are met.

Whether demands originate in space or non-space, once they enter the public sphere for deliberations the representatives of these demands must function like enterprise associations. This is certainly a more preferable alternative to multiple and counter public spheres as suggested by Nancy Fraser (Fraser 1994: 84). Such multiplicity of public spheres makes nonsense of the term 'public' and to the development of citizenship in a civil society. Enterprise associations, on the other hand, abide by the decisions of the public sphere and reserve the right to return and represent themselves repeatedly. Unfortunately, many community-based demands that emerge from root metaphors of cultural spaces have problems in adhering to this principle.

This problem takes on a rather acute form in the sphere of minority demands. Intellectually too it is a challenge as to how a liberal democratic state should respond to minority demands keeping the interests of fraternity alive at the same time. The minority communities often threaten that the lifestyle they wish to pursue, or the good that they wish to subscribe to, will be implemented regardless of the decisions arrived at in the public sphere. Typically, these have to do with women's education, right to polygamy, religious holidays, and language rights.

Before we enter into this issue it needs to be clarified that the public sphere is not a zone that is dismissive of aesthetic commitments and considerations which may have their initial provenance in cultural root metaphors. All that it insists upon is that the root metaphors do not force themselves on to the public sphere and convert it into an occasion for creating divisiveness. As we argued earlier, the divisiveness that untempered root metaphors create are not of the kind that promote open alternatives but closed diversities. This is why the public sphere is naturally suspicious of pre-given, and traditional fraternities based on caste, custom or religion. These bonds are not, in themselves, conducive for creating the ties of citizenship that the public sphere promotes. The public sphere then is an important aspect of the state structure that constantly revamps and revitalizes practices that enliven the membership of belonging to the nation. This membership, that was initiated at the high point of fusion, must be constantly stoked, and the public sphere is the best place to do it.

This does not mean that root metaphors cannot enter the domain of the public sphere. The constraint however is that they must be tempered enough so that they do not violate the basic rights of the individual that allows for the public to emerge in the first place. A public sphere is a sphere of fairness in which questions of justice are deliberated. Justice is after all a reflexive enterprise and cannot be presumed as a condition. Only fairness, which implies the Rawlsian conception of most extensive individual liberties, can be, and should be, a condition for the public sphere. There are various routes to justice, the 'veil of ignorance' is one such, and these routes should be open to discussion in the public sphere. The verdict that justice pronounces is always contextual. Is the society rich or poor? Are there historically disprivileged or only economically disprivileged? The condition of fairness is however non-contextual and not open to negotiations and cannot be compromised.

The decisions arrived at in the public sphere must observe the modalities of democracy. This is not to be confused with majoritarianism. Majoritarianism is a fixed and relentless position which is incapable of alteration. A majority opinion arrived at democratically allows for openness of information, freedom to change points of view, and is non-discriminatory in terms of individual differences of class and status. The decisions that are arrived at after these conditions are met need not always be rational decisions as Habermas would like it to be (Habermas 1985, vol. 2: 77; Habermas 1989), but they would represent the majority view.

A majority view that is nevertheless open to transformation and change in the ongoing debates and deliberations makes up the public sphere. Democratic decision making is not the same as an agreement that is rational, nor even a rational consensus (as in Habermas). A decision is democratically arrived at when the defeated party goes away disappointed but not because the rules of the decision making process were prejudiced in a certain direction which brought about the unfavourable outcome. If the complaint is of this order then there is either no real public sphere, or the representatives to the public sphere are not public spirited citizens.

The decisions taken at the public sphere are therefore political in character, and that is unavoidable. The fact that this political decision is democratically arrived at leaves open the option of further representations and the possibility of a reversal of the earlier decisions. This is after all how the Jews and other religious minorities got the right to vote in Europe, this is how South Asians won their political rights in Canada, this is how the suffragette movement made women full political participants. In a democratic process the decisions taken in the public sphere are not immutable but are open to the vagaries of opinion at different points of time. Care should however be taken, as John Stuart Mill would argue, that all that is necessary to make people change their minds, in terms of information and access, should be allowed, and indeed, encouraged.

Citizenship, Civil Society and Enlarging of Freedoms

After all, neither civil society nor citizenship are finished projects. The ethic of freedom is constantly being pressured to realize rights which at one point in history were not even perceived to exist. When the American Constitution was prepared the position of the Blacks was not even dimly recognized though the rights of 'men' were being extolled. When women were barred from voting it was not as if this right was being consciously taken away. It was rather because this right, this exercise of freedom, did not even strike the minds of those who participated in the public sphere. The list of rights is growing every day and today it also includes environmental rights, and, as in India, the right to public interest litigation. What is important to remember is that none of these victories of citizenship would have occurred if civil society and the public sphere were to be limited to majoritarianism. Needless to say, this kind of majoritarianism should be distinguished from majority opinion that is constantly under democratic pressure to change.

As the majority opinion keeps changing in the public sphere, what is majority view today could be minority view tomorrow. A minority community is however not a minority political opinion. A minority political opinion would abide by the decisions arrived at in the public sphere and reserve the right to contest again. The minority communities on the other hand, especially when they function along root metaphors, may not care what the public sphere decides. Irrespective of the opinion of the democratic majority they would like to pursue their alternative lifestyles. Thus, quite regardless of the public sphere minority communities may on different occasions keep their women from going to school, disallow inoculations or medical treatment, practice polygamy, and so on.

In this one important respect it would be incorrect to conflate minority political opinion with minority community demands. If, on the other hand, the representatives of minority communities put forward their proposals in the spirit of a political alternative then they should agree to abide by the outcome of the public sphere, without perjuring their chances of representing again. Perhaps in the future the decision of the public sphere may be to allow multiple languages to flourish as official languages, or perhaps the public sphere can accept that there should be a system of holidays which is neutral to all religions (for example Wednesday instead of Sunday). What the public sphere cannot accept is the denial of basic liberties to education, freedom of speech, freedom to opinions, and the equality of opportunity to enter non-spaces. If a minority community's demands infringe these, then it is not for negotiation in the public sphere for that would take away from the minimum set of resemblances that civil society and citizenship are premised upon.

Minority Rights, Space and Non-Space

The public sphere argument can be used to reformulate the pluralist argument of Parekh (1995: 207–9), and the equality argument put forward by Kymlicka (1995: 108–15). Parekh says that the operative public values which are cherished cannot be easily cast aside. On the basis of these public values one can decide whether certain minority demands should be entertained or not. For Parekh too the commitment to a position is not unchangeable, and a time may come when certain cherished beliefs could be over turned (Parekh 1995: 216–17).

For Kymlicka the equality argument is important because the minority cultures are at a disadvantage with respect to the majority cultures for they do not have the resources and numbers that the latter have. Thus while there is no danger of the majority culture disappearing the minority culture is always under threat. This is why it requires special privileges to undo the reality that minorities have smaller populations. Thus even if a relatively small number of people speak a certain language it might be advisable to give this language state protection or else it would die out. Majority languages face no such risks (Kymlicka 1995: 113). The problem is that Kymlicka does not clarify if protection of language is the same thing as allowing it equal play in the public domain. Neither does he make clear how the issue of holidays is to be sorted out.

It is possible to see oneself out of such tight corners if the reformulated public sphere argument were to be adopted. Parekh's argument that publicly cherished values, till such time as they are displaced by other publicly cherished values (Parekh 1995: 216), should be allowed to continue is a promising start. It needs to be recast to suggest that *those minority demands that do not obstruct the performance of non-spaces can be allowed to function, and even encouraged to do so.* Cultural rights that take away from the rights of citizenship which promote a basic set of resemblances in terms of education, health, and access to jobs should not be allowed to flourish. All other aspects of culture which do not extend logically to the public realm can be allowed to exist, even subsidized by the state. If there are certain features in these cultures that can be brought to the public sphere without damaging basic liberties, like the language issue, or the question of holidays, then they should be allowed to do so.

The fact that such cultures are allowed to exist and are state subsidized too, enables them to survive and repeatedly present themselves to the public sphere. So the equality argument of Kymlicka is taken care of as well, but only to the extent that minority demands are not contrary to the basic liberties and freedoms that encourage a minimum set of resemblances that qualify citizens to function in non-spaces. This is why Rawls argued that the rules of caste system (its root metaphors) are incompatible with the principles of justice (Rawls 1974). Minority cultures can be retained but subject to this constraint. Therefore unlike Kymlicka's position (Kymlicka 1995: 111), the public sphere argument would say that a government can decide which aspects of a minority culture, or even of a majority culture, should be supported. It cannot support those aspects that go against the grain of the ethic of freedom as realized in civil societies through citizenship.

The public sphere argument can also answer some of the issues that were left open by Parekh. Those cultural preferences which do not obstruct the functioning of non-spaces should be allowed to exist *even if they offend the majority*. This is where state legislations can be a useful weapon of changing public opinion that is based on bigotry. If the wearing of a turban, or a head dress, does not in any way take away from the functioning of the non-space then there is no reason to disallow them. In cases where the head dress or the turban means compromising with the efficacy of the non-space concerned there they should be kept out. There should be a case by case decision on these matters. In the case of the reluctance of the French to allow Muslim women to wear the head dress in school, it is quite clear that this was more an outcome of prejudice than an objective assessment. It must first be demonstrated how the head dress obstructs the functioning of a non-space which a secular French school is supposed to be. Failing this there is no reason why the head dress should not be allowed.

It is possible to objectively come to decisions regarding this. If the wearing of certain kinds of clothes inhibit free movement as is necessary in the army then apparels of that variety cannot be permitted. This is quite unlike the issue of education on which no quarter should be given in the public sphere with respect to the free and open availability of knowledge and of occupational positions. Seen in this light, minority communities would then function like cultural enterprise associations that abide by the norms of the public sphere.

The establishment of positive discrimination in favour of the historically disprivileged cannot be extended mechanically to cover communitarian demands as well. Positive discrimination, which includes affirmative action and the reservation of seats sometimes on a quota basis, is designed to enhance fraternity by creating a minimum set of resemblances among citizens. This also benefits the society as a whole as it increases the pool of assets that is available to a community.

Communitarian demands are often of a different order. They strive to impose root metaphors on non-spaces and thus fracture fraternity. If, because of majority swagger, root metaphors of the majority community exist in non-spaces then they should be excised. No root metaphor of any kind, other than those of the nation-state, can be compatible with the functioning of non-spaces. It is, therefore, necessary to replace a religious oath of taking office by a secular oath, or to replace signs of the majority community's regalia and emblems from non-spaces by neutral artifacts.

In spite of the differences between minority protection and positive discrimination it is possible to take a Rawlsian view on minorities as well. If one were to go back to the Rawlsian original condition behind the veil of ignorance and were to deliberate on the issues of minority protection then the following considerations would be uppermost. First, once the veil of ignorance is removed I may realize that I am a member of a minority culture. I would therefore like my culture and language to be retained. Second, since the veil of ignorance can be extended to include the situation that I may not like or feel comfortable in my ascriptive identity, there should be provisions that allow me to exit from it as well. In this way my foundational rights as an individual are protected. This enables me to function in the public sphere and in non-spaces. In other words, I know I belong to a certain community but I am not in agreement with the community's position on a variety of issues and would reserve the right to exit from it. I do not fully know how my community will react when faced with other communities, once the veil of ignorance is collectively lifted everywhere. Keeping at least these considerations conjointly in mind the following formulations can be arrived at. These formulations allow for cultural protection but within the framework of citizenship.

(1) A minority community should be allowed to practice its religion or language at the private realm so long as these practices allow members of the minority community to enter non-spaces without prejudice.

(2) Freedom to come to the public sphere to offer cultural alternatives as public alternatives without demanding that cultural root metaphors embed non-spaces.

(3) Those aspects of culture that do not endanger the functioning of non-spaces should be allowed to exist. The determination of this should be on an issue to issue basis.

A fractured fraternity may be the demand of a majority or minority group, or, these groups may be unconcerned about fraternity. Concerns of citizenship cannot be oblivious to the imperatives of fraternity. If it were to do so then the basis of realizing and keeping alive the sentiment of the nation-state would be perjured by the structures of governance. On the other hand, compliance with certain minority preferences when they do not militate against non-spaces, and the withdrawal of emblems that belong to a majority culture would reduce some of the anxieties that minorities face. Together these would gradually convert minority communities into cultural enterprise associations and perhaps even give them a voluntary character.

The public sphere is an important aspect of modern nation-states. This is the true intermediary zone that connects citizens to the state. Without the public sphere the process of secularization would be quite impossible. Understanding the process of secularization gives us another opportunity to dilate upon some other aspects of what we have called the public sphere. This also has repercussions on another kind of attitude towards minorities. This attitude is best seen among those who believe that the only way to be secular is to allow minority rights to continue unchallenged and in perpetuity. In India this tendency is seen among certain self-conscious 'secularists' who resolve the minority issue without paying heed to the importance of protecting and promoting fraternity. Unqualified minority protection becomes a good in its own right. This point of view is generally put forward under the rubric of secularism. This is why it is important to separate secularism of this sort from secularization which is the development of the public sphere.

Secularization and Secularism: Process and Ideology

In contemporary times secularism appears as an embattled ideology, no longer sanguine about its future. Though this note of despair is not entirely without foundation, it must also be said that it is not as if this is the first time that secularism is being questioned, nor will it be the last. As the fortunes of secularism are generally gauged from the success or failure of certain political parties, societies seem to go through their decennial crisis every now and again. In modern Indian history there were times when it seemed that the secular political option was over and done with. And yet, in spite of the worst prophecies, it has miraculously managed to survive in the Indian political firmament.

The Partition of 1947, which is still alive in many memories, was one such occasion when secularism seemed hopelessly doomed. Many activists of the Congress, and of various left organizations, felt completely betrayed at the way some of their trusted comrades and party faithfuls had succumbed to communal passions (Gupta 1994). Yet it is generally agreed that under Jawaharlal Nehru's stewardship, secularism successfully withstood this onslaught and went on to be the ruling credo for over two decades.

It may be objected that the terms secularism and communalism are being used here in a very loose sense, but that is simply because some concessions are being made to the ways in which these words are popularly employed. Secularism contains within it a host of alternative ideological possibilities, ranging from Maoism to liberal conservatism, and likewise communalism includes sectarianism, ascriptive loyalties, racism and other such ideological dispositions.

Even with an understanding as general as this it should be easily recognized that secularism as an ideology has its good days and bad, its triumphant moments as well as periods of decline. Since secularism is understood principally as an articulated political option, the emphasis is on the mercurial swings of public mood and not on the long duration of social process. As the heat of the ideological moment seems to overwhelm the observer, it is not at all surprising that it is this, and not the slow, prolonged grinding of social processes, that gets the main attention.

This is why the contemporary wave of sectarianism, communalism (and ethnicity) in India is often viewed, not as a phase, but rather as a permanent feature of our times. Naturally, despair seems to be legitimate under these circumstances. Contemporary secularists must nevertheless recognize that such a position objectively implies that they have little faith in the common people to question the communal agenda. Nor can they overlook the fact that both despair and complacency are products of ahistoricism, much as the contemporary secularists would like to refute such an allegation. Hence the secularist comes through as the last hero, tilting so gloriously at windmills.

While all this is good for the ego, there is little social science in it. It is perhaps for situations such as this that the Hungarian poet-philosopher Pettoffi was provoked to write that 'despair...is vanity'. For there is a lot of vainglory that abounds amongst some contemporary secularists as if they are privileged to be living in the worst of times. The truth however is that neither secularism nor communalism are permanent fixtures, but it is not easy to get this homily across for it takes the shine off what self-confessed secularists believe is their 'heroic thought'.

In order to overcome the limitations of heroic thought it would be well to heed the advice of sociologists who have always been very careful to distinguish between secularization and secularism (Béteille 1994: 560–61). For sociologists, secularization refers to an impersonal social process the effects of which are felt at the conscious level, no doubt, but whose working largely happens behind our backs. According to Luhmann (1982: 229; see also Béteille 1994: 561), secularization inaugurates a functional differentiation of the social order which frees individuals from the various kinds of stratified differentiation that prevailed in traditional societies. Consequently religion, and other forms of ascriptive ties, begin to lose their unquestioned status as systematic principles of organization. Secularism, the ideology, is not neglected by sociology, but seen as an aspect, or a feature of, the secularization process. As sociology sees the two as separate, though related, phenomena, it must conceptually distinguish one from the other. Even so it needs to be clarified at the outset that secularization allows for, and indeed even promotes, a variety of ideologies. Therefore, within the ambit of secularization, communalism can emerge as an option as much as secularism can. Demerath and Williams conceptualize this feature in terms of a dialectical tension between sacralizing and secularizing (1992: 190).

Likewise it is important to distinguish between secularization as a process and secularism as an ideology, and no matter how frequently the two may appear together in history, they need to be analytically separated. There is no denying the fact that the ideology of secularism did make its appearance before secularization had occurred, but it is also true that not every instance of secularization necessarily implies secularism.

From Toennies to Maine, and from Berger (1970) to Parsons (1974) to Luhmann (1982), there is little doubt that sociologists have seen secularization as a process that separates the modern world from the traditional. It is against this backdrop that the prospects and constraints of both secularism and communalism need to be examined. Sociologists have generally been able to resist giving in to the popular beliefs of their times. For example, while Parsons (1974) and Bellah (1967) following on from Maine and Durkheim (1957) detailed the unfolding of secularization in the western world, they were careful not to pronounce the demise of religion. In their view secularization changes religious institutions and makes them more voluntary, open and susceptible to pressures from the laity (which includes the political state). It is not as if religious ideologies have died, but they have lost their compelling character. They have to now compete against other ideologies in the secular political market place. Secularization, therefore, makes room for, and also promotes, a variety of ideologies. It even allows non-religious ideologies to gain a sacred, almost religious, character when they demand complete allegiance to some of their root metaphors and symbols. Among other things, Robert Bellah's thesis on contemporary 'civil religions' magnifies on this theme (Bellah 1967).

Civil Religion

At this juncture it is relevant to recall Bellah's seminal piece on civil religion (1967) in some detail. Perhaps it is best to began with a quote from Robert Bellah on what he means by civil religion. According to Bellah:

> What we have, then, from the earliest years of the republic is a collection of beliefs, symbols, and rituals with respect to sacred things and institutionalized in a collectivity. This religion—there seems to be no other word for it—while not antithetical to and indeed sharing much in common with Christianity, was neither sectarian nor in any specific sense Christian (ibid.: 175).

Bellah was obviously reflecting on Memorial Day and Fourth of July celebrations in America. In these national festivities, as well as in more routine political behaviour, there is a good degree of dependence on the symbols of Christianity, more specifically Protestantism. Bellah is quick to point out that, this does not mean that religious politics holds away in America. The substance of

American politics is premised on the role of the citizen even if its style draws a fair amount from religion.

Bellah goes further to say that civil religions of this sort arouse commitment among the citizens by sacralizing a core set of national symbols. As Demerath and Williams put it:

> Civil religious language has long enabled Americans to use religion in defining themselves politically. It was, and is, a language decidedly Christian in tone and assumption, but cleansed of references that are too specific or narrow.... Indeed, civil religious discourse produced a particularly American response to the religiopolitical problem: a culturally legitimate religion of the nation that transcended sectarian differences while justifying a social order at least partially based on those differences. The civil religion never became the civil church (Demerath and Williams 1985: 160–61).

The stark fact is that in the age of secularization politics is never free of religion. This does not make politics always religious. It is for this reason that this excursus into civil religion was necessary. But our understanding of civil religion should not stop here. Not only can secular citizens be moulded on the basis of civil religion, but secular ideologies can take on a religious mien by insisting on absolute adherence to its fundamentals.

Secularization, properly understood, neither implies the death of religion, nor does it mean that religion will be confined to the private sphere. In this context Luhmann's separation between 'religious function' which is private, and 'religious performance' which is public is particularly instructive (Luhmann 1982: 240–42; see also Williams and Demerath 1991: 418–19). Unlike the manichean ideologies of secularism that see only the tussle between good and evil, what secularization brings to our notice is the constant tension between diverse political and economic strategies that were simply not present in the pre-modern era.

Secularization and the Breakdown of Localism

Secularization implies a wide variety of phenomena, but the most important one is perhaps the development of institutions that are not bound by local customs and practices. This would, of course, have been impossible had not the industrial revolution occurred, which brought together large conglomerates in concentrated locations. In turn, this encouraged the science of statistics and population management. The Napoleonic wars gave evidence of this new form of social control and commissariat supervision, but it was also manifest in the emergence of hospitals and in the development of urban social engineering. Regardless of how authorities were casting about for more effective forms of legitimate control, the impetus to all this was the breakdown of the local order on an ever expanding basis. It is not as if large population concentrations happened only with the industrial revolution, but it cannot be gainsaid that the departure from local domination and interactional systems that the early 19th century witnessed was altogether new. The transition in Europe was from stable burghers and market towns (which were often political capitals), first to the development of mills, and then the emergence of factories, which created modern cities and urban sprawls. This happened in India too except that the process was much telescoped. This is probably one of the reasons why the tensions that secularization brings in its wake are particularly heightened in this country.

Nisbet (1970) argued that the emergence of sociology in the late 19th century was a reaction to too much individualism brought on by the industrial revolution. In such a situation the old moral order with its stable root metaphors could no longer embed and gird a variety of social practices. Non-spaces were slowly surfacing and there was no reliable guide in tradition. Intellectuals in the late 19th century perceived a crisis in the moral order and they believed that it was urban life and the indifference to established mores and customs that were creating social tensions and anomie. Sociology was spurred by the need to offer reliable scientific methods to first comprehend this new social development, and then to control it by creating new social values which would bind individuals into wholesome and healthy collectivities. One might, therefore, say that sociology from the beginning saw itself as performing a dual role: to examine the process of secularization, and to forward the credo of a civil religion. Parsons and Bellah were, therefore, not alone, nor without precedent in the discipline.

At this point the contributions of social anthropology can help in sorting out the importance of the distinction between secularization and secularism. In the Indian context, for instance, it has been repeatedly pointed out (among many others) by M.N. Srinivas, McKim Marriot, and by Milton Singer (see Marriot, 1959; Singer 1972), that tradition re-orients itself to keep up with the demands of urban life and the move to get away from localized existence. What needs to be added to this observation is that this malleability in tradition is possible because root metaphors are multivocal and carry with them regnant sets of meaning. It must also be remembered, however, that it is not as if a traditional root metaphor in tradition can cope with all kinds of transformations that modernization brings along. While root metaphors may be multi-vocal they are not equivocal in character. This sensitizes us to protect ourselves against two kinds of naivete, both extremist in nature. One argues that industrialization changes everything, and with time a new moral order emerges which separates itself unambiguously from past traditions and practices; the other believes that tradition, no matter what, will never yield ground to the process of secularization. The first variety is usually sponsored by sociologists in the west talking about their own society, and the latter by social anthropologists when they write about oriental or non-western civilizations. But both these versions are faulty, for nowhere does tradition remain unchanged, and in no corner of the globe is the past completely wiped out either.

It is not just large urban conglomerates but also the process of secularization, that objectively creates a 'society', perhaps for the first time. In this society hierarchical orders and rigid 'diversities' can no longer effectively block an awareness that other people also matter. Beyer puts this point across nicely when he writes: '(T)he person who used to be the unequivocal outsider is now often literally my neighbour. This is what Rushdie calls the metropolitan experience' (Beyer 1994: 91). This feature is nearly always accompanied by centralized forms of governance. These two are not independent characteristics but depend reciprocally on each other, and in this sense, give us a fuller understanding of the process of secularization.

Alexis de Tocqueville (1955) had noted long ago that the emergence of centralized authority was typical of post-revolutionary France, and that there was tremendous enthusiasm for it from the lower orders. The privileged classes, prior to the revolution, enjoyed status and power in a system of segmentary control. This segmentary system of governance was in consonance with localized juridical control on which all *ancien regimes* thrived. But obviously this was out of accord with the exigencies of the new era. Without centralization local juridical control can never be fully overwhelmed. Unless this happens aggregation of free people in towns and cities would be impeded, jamming the wheels of the secularization process itself. The lower classes are particularly keen to push ahead with this centralization as they are the least enamoured with either segmentary authority, or with localized juridical control. Contrary to Gandhi, Babasaheb Ambedkar consistently pressed for a strong Centre for only then, he believed, could depressed caste grievances be adequately redressed.

The development of centralized administration creates the minimum conditions for the emergence of a public sphere. The public sphere grows in strength in liberal democratic societies, but it also hovers like a threat over despotic and totalitarian regimes. The public sphere that emerges with centralization is also the arena where political contests are held, and no matter how despotic the winner, there can be no return to localism of the previous epochs. Thus, while this public sphere may not always meet Habermas' highly evolved criteria of a developed communication system, he is nevertheless correct in insisting that it is only in secularized societies that the minimal prerequisites of a communication system can be found (Habermas 1985: 77). What secularized societies share with Habermas' model is the recognition that mutual needs are in principle negotiable, and that these negotiations have a public character about them.

As secularization rides on the back of capitalism, it is characterized by a thermodynamic principle. The transition from mills to factories effectively depicts this transition. In closed pre-capitalist and pre-secularized societies, i.e., those that had not yet experienced the effects of heavy duty industrialization, it was physical coercion, more than anything else, which determined who would be the ruler. It is not as if this modality of conquering a throne was found objectionable in principle, for it was heartily engaged in by combatants on both sides. But after the war was over the vanquished resigned themselves to abiding by the rule of the victor. From then on it was primarily *noblesse oblige*, and the social order settled down to long periods of peace. Such long durations without obvious signs of protest have given the impression to contemporary observers, with their 20th century sensibilities, that in tradition diverse communities lived side by side in perfect amity. The absence of any demonstrable signs of tension is interpreted as no tension at all, and, indeed, the prevalence of inter-faith solidarity.

It is true that communal rivalry had no scope for routine social expression, but is not as if it did not exist. These tensions and suspicions became prominent in times of unrest and war. After the turbulence was over, if the Hindus had won then there would be no cow slaughter, and if the Muslims were the victors then the Hindu temples could never be taller than the Muslim *mazhar*. In modern parlance one might say that in a pre-secularized social formation there were fixed and stable diacritics that differentiated people along stratificatory lines (Luhmann 1982). History repeatedly testifies to the near exclusive use of ascriptive criteria to signify the distinction between the rulers and the ruled. The terminology of majority and minority makes little sense in these societies, as in most cases the rulers belonged to the minority group, and furthermore, political bargaining did not take place with currencies of that kind. But one could say this much with some certitude: if everyone behaved themselves and obeyed the prevailing rules then the structure and distribution of power would remain undisturbed. Such *ceteris paribus* postulates could be made about those times without appearing too idealistic. Individual volition was in any case greatly circumscribed, for the arena was a local one where status and face-to-face interactions provided an unchanging and stable backdrop.

Once secularization sets in, no such stability can be assured as the society is now thermodynamically powered. Capitalism forces money to search uninhibitedly for profits, and if enterprise is held back, as the guilds were in the past, then the whole edifice of modern society would collapse. In this search for profits there is every possibility of a near anarchy of production, for which reason it is hard to foresee where the cracks between different private interests will show up. There is a certain indeterminancy and unpredictability regarding the maintenance of social harmony because the natural economy no longer operates. When Marx distinguished between collective interests and private interests (as early as in *On the Jewish Question*), he also alerted us to the divisions between private interests of different kinds, and how alliances and class coalitions appear and disappear in somewhat unpredictable ways. Capitalism, therefore, is quite capable of throwing up in entrepreneurial churn newer fractions of the capitalist class as dominant groupings, or it may also warn the more established sections to take preemptive action against a rising competitor. The point is that all this upheaval, uncertainty, and conflict, does not bring about a breakdown of order, but is in fact a demonstration of a new kind of order—one in which secularization has taken place. In this new secularized order the stable scenario of yore, with its entrenched root metaphors is not only absent but becomes increasingly defunct.

Secularization and the Minorities Question

The relevance of keeping the process of secularization distinct from the ideology of secularism can be appreciated if we take up the concept of minorities. Minorities are often visualized as permanent entities with fixed and definite empirical manifestations. Nowhere is this tendency demonstrated as well as it is in India. To put in a piece of background information, from 1993 onwards the official and permanent minorities in India are the Muslims, Christians, Parsees, Buddhists and Sikhs (see Government of India, *Ministry of Welfare Notification* dated October 23, 1993).

In the contemporary context these minorities as listed by the Indian government may seem perfectly justified, even 'natural'. One nevertheless needs to be reminded of the fact that minority communities are not fixed and permanent entities but keep fluctuating like the sacral-secular dialectic of Demerath and Williams (1992: 190). Sample the following variations: In the *Report of Advisory Committee on Minorities* (May 11, 1949), Muslims, Scheduled Castes and Indian Christians were considered to be minorities (Shiva Rao 1968a, vol. 4: 604). Earlier, in the Constituent Assembly debates, K.M. Panikkar wanted Nambudris to be listed as minorities (ibid., vol. 2: 259). Recall that the 1932 Ramsay MacDonald Communal Award recommended that Marathas be protected in certain selected constituencies of Mumbai (Shiva Rao 1968b: 742). Frank Anthony strongly advocated in the Constituent Assembly that the category of Minority be enlarged to include all kinds of minorities, whether of language, community, or religion (Shiva

Rao 1968a, vol. 2: 280). In the course of these debates Sardar Hukam Singh argued that Sikhs and Parsees should be classified as minorities, but it was turned down as being unnecessary (Shiva Rao 1968b: 772–73). There was no public outcry either against it in those years. In fact, the Parsees made no specific claims towards minority status either. Today, more than 40 years later, the Parsees and the Sikhs have been given minority status by the Government of India. In the case of the Sikhs, after the killings of 1984, it seems perfectly justified, but this demand never resonated earlier. It should also be noted that what makes a minority is not just religion but also certain privileged and dominant ways of designating themselves. A Sanatani, or a member of the Budha Dal, or a Vaishnavite would not qualify here as a religious denomination no matter how strenuously the believers of these denominations may stake their claim.

But this is perhaps the least of the problem. Pushed to it, the proponents of secularism will merrily add to the list of official minorities. But in doing so it is never quite realized that with every passing year these categories rigidify and become impervious to the actualities that secularization generates on the ground. The most dangerous outcome of this tendency is that it is blind to the process of *minoritization* which often breaks protocol and targets those who are not official and permanent minorities. When secularism as an ideology estranges itself from the dynamics of secularization as a process, it immediately surrenders itself to a historicism and to the most backward forms of positivist posturing. In doing so it frequently leaves the door wide open for its stated enemies to function both legitimately and effectively in the political system. When that happens almost anybody can become the next minority, for the process of minoritization has no permanent or official favourites.

Though Sardar Patel would have liked minorities to be limited to the Scheduled Castes, and as for the rest they should 'trust the good sense and sense of fairness of the majority and place confidence in them' (Shiva Rao 1968a, vol. 4: 606), experience has shown that minority persecution has been a very common phenomenon in independent India. As even this quote from Patel shows, the framers of the Indian Constitution were quite clearly prisoners of the majority/minority paradigm. In fact, the sub-committee on fundamental rights held in February and April of 1947 was of the view that it 'is difficult to expect in a country like India where most persons are communally minded those in authority will give equal treatment to those who do not belong to their community' (Shiva Rao 1968a, vol. 2: 98). Sardar Patel's plea to trust the majority seems weak in this light.

The functionaries of the Constituent Assembly were the main believers in majority/minority distinctions. Shyama Prasad Mookherjee, who later founded the Hindu right wing party, the Jana Sangh, was also in favour of minority provisions. In many ways he was the forerunner to Mandal too. Not only did Mookherjee press for the reservation of seats for minorities (Shiva Rao 1968b: 756), but also recommended that only 50 per cent of seats be open to merit and the rest were to be proportionately distributed among the minorities (Shiva Rao 1968a, vol. 2: 339).

In all of this it is interesting to note that Ambedkar, who is known today as the father of reservations, issued a warning, while moving the draft Constitution on November 23, 1948, that it would be 'equally wrong for minorities to perpetuate themselves' (Shiva Rao 1968b: 766). In the midst of the clamour for protecting minorities it is easy to overlook how such provisions can create vested interests, and in the process go counter to some of the express intentions of the constitutionalists. Even so, except for a small group made up most significantly by Rajkumari Amrit Kaur, Alladi Krishnaswamy Ayyar, Hansa Mehta, and occasionally, B.N. Rau, the overwhelming mood of the Constituent Assembly was moulded by majority/minority consciousness. At one point when the discussion on fundamental rights was being overwhelmed by issues of minority discrimination, Alladi K. Ayyar was provoked to remark: 'Is this a chapter on fundamental rights or is it a chapter on discriminatory provisions?' (Shiva Rao 1968a, vol. 2: 221). Ayyar's pique is understandable, for the discussion on fundamental rights should insist first on the inalienable and fundamental rights of citizenship, and not let the exceptions eat up the rule.

Minoritization and Secularization: For a Dynamic Perspective

In addition, as noted earlier, the thermodynamic principles of secularization make it irrelevant to think in terms of stable minorities and majorities, for bigotry too refuses to be shackled along predetermined lines. In such situations it is difficult to predict who will be the new minority tomorrow. The Sikhs till 1984 never imagined that they would be hunted down and quartered the way they were after Mrs. Indira Gandhi's assassination. It is this fact that makes the inclusion of the Sikhs today eminently deserving of minority status, though such a claim was never entertained seriously earlier. The south Indians in Mumbai had no foreknowledge that they would be the victims of Shiv Sena's wrath prior to the mid-sixties.

It must be borne in mind that not all ideological emanations of capitalism and secularization fit in neatly with their original impulses. Though secularism, the ideology, is a product of contemporary times, as it thinks in terms of majorities and minorities, it nevertheless refuses to accept the inherent dynamic character of the social process of secularization. Consequently, it sees majorities and minorities as permanent distinctions which are fully fleshed out. This leads to the development of vested interests, as Ambedkar foresaw, and the tendency of minority spokespeople to emerge as permanent champions of designated communities.

To pursue our argument further, it will be quickly noticed that listings of minorities are of little consequence for they do not take into account the process of secularization which can easily nullify at one stroke the most elaborate categorizations of this kind. Instead of making a comprehensive inventory of minorities, greater attention should be paid to the question of minoritization and to examining the effects of that process. Rather than fixing in advance, or even adding to, minority lists, the aims of secularism can be served better if it pays attention to minoritization, for the truth is that nobody can tell who the next minority will be—it could be you.

There are then two major variants of secularism as an ideology. The first is of the 'progressive history' variety, and the second is governed by majority/minority considerations. The first believes that in an advanced democracy there is no scope left for bigotry to be active on a social scale, now that religion has been effectively privatized; and the latter is predisposed to see the world in terms of fixed expressions of bigotry which can only be overcome by upholding the sectional interests of these persecuted groups. The common feature that binds secularism of the first and of the second variety is that both see the world as a finished product. In one case there is the cheerful announcement of the end of prejudice, while in the other it is believed that minority persecution will, by and large, follow pre-determined trajectories. This then justifies the position that certain designated communities should be categorized as minorities on a permanent basis.

But, in fact, prejudice knows no limit, and the lengths it can go to are truly incalculable. Does this mean that in the face of relentless secularization there is no scope for secularism? Should the uncertainties of minoritization mean that we can only observe the process of secularization without any scope for intervention? While it is true that will power and good intentions by themselves are inadequate, it can nevertheless be maintained that when will power and humanism take cognizance and learn from objective social processes, then the chances of success are so much greater.

The making of minorities is quite different from the process of minoritization. Minority consciousness grows first from within the community, and later it is recognized as such by those outside it. Any particular constitution of minority consciousness may have several historical or sociological causes behind it. There is no common factor that informs the making of the different minority groups other than the issue of numbers. Of these, the most effective minorities are those with a sizeable population. But other than being smaller in numbers than the majority community, there is nothing that Parsees, Sikhs, Muslims, or Buddhists have in common.

The acceptance of such communities as minorities is premised on the existence of majority and minority consciousness. Sadly, therefore, democracy is often played out in such cases as a game of numbers, and community representatives on all sides are fairly comfortable with this. It may have been possible to stem this process during the days when the Constitution was being discussed, but there was a lost chance there. Rajkumari Amrit Kaur and B.N. Rau provided an opening when they advocated that 'religious worship' and not 'religious practice' be allowed as a fundamental right (Shiva Rao 1968b: 260). But this was opposed by the majority, from the Hindu sectarians like S.P. Mookerjee (quite predictably) to Congress leaders like C. Rajagopalachari (ibid.: 261). In contrast, according to Amrit Kaur, allowing for freedom of religious practice meant that the playing of music before mosques, or the institution of sati, will have to be allowed. To recast Amrit Kaur's position in

Luhmann's terms, she was allowing for the function of religion but not for the practice of it (Luhmann 1982: 240–42).

Once minority and majority consciousnesses are in place, then it would appear as if the job of secularism is done. The minority communities are kept passive by co-opting their leaders and spokespeople into organizations like the Minority Rights Commission, and even as Members of Parliament, and in other prestigious public positions. Mrs. Indira Gandhi's 15-point programme is a good illustration of a political strategy of this kind that seeks to cater specifically to majority/minority consciousness. Time and again her 15-point programme made elaborate allowances for minorities at all levels, including loans for housing and education. It appeared then that if Muslims got any education at all it was because of Mrs. Indira Gandhi's largesse, or because of the militancy of certain minority leaders, and not because as citizens Muslims have every right to be treated as equals. In a patronage scenario of this kind there is enough scope to play backroom politics and to grandstand as heroes of minority communities.

But all these calculations do not pay attention to the fact that secularization is a dynamic process and therefore new minorities may emerge without much warning. This process, by which minorities are created, quite unbeknownst to the community concerned (for example the Sikhs in 1984) is what has been termed as *minoritization*. When minoritization takes place the communities that are picked on for persecution are decided upon by the majority, or those 'others' who are on the outside. The constitution of minority identity in these cases takes place from without rather than from within. The latter process occurs only in the case of self-constituted and self-conscious minorities.

The point, however, is that nobody wants to be minoritized for that can happen swiftly and unpredictably. One never knows what combination will be brought to bear in the next round of minoritization, and nobody is, therefore, completely safe. But there is a vested interest in self-constituted minority awareness for that enables one to effectively play the minority card, and both majority and minority spokespeople are fully aware of this.

Minority classifications can also lead to tensions between minority communities. This process can be illustrated with the instance of the native communities in Canada. To begin with there are many categories of natives in Canada. 'Status Indians' (i.e., those who were registered in bands and were assigned individual numbers), 'Non-Status Indians', 'Metis' (of half-breeds), Innuits and Eskimos. As Noel Dyck points out these distinctions have had a 'divide and conquer effect' (Dyck 1992: 827). It has kept up a strong sense of distinction between various categories of natives who fight among one another to be the beneficiaries of Canadian state policy. The Saskatchewan Indians do not want to give up the category 'Native' and merge with the disadvantaged sectors of Canadian society (ibid.: 32–33). Of course, the process of categorizing the natives began very much along the minoritizing trajectory. The Indian status was a product of 'others', of the Canadian Parliament, 'rather than the handiwork of the "self"' (ibid.: 34). Consequently, as Dyck observes, 'after hundred years of reserved life, Indians in Saskatchewan see themselves as different from other people of aboriginal ancestry' (ibid.: 34; see also Sawchuk 1992: 73). Not only has Canadian policy on native Indians kept the natives dependent on the government, it has also raised other barricades—those between different categories of Indians. Metis and non-status Indians had once come together, but now they too have fallen out with each other and have different organizations.

Towards a Rawlsian Perspective

Minority categorizations which formed the basis of state policies in several countries can therefore have the very effect it demonstratively sets out to undermine. These categorizations foster divisions on ascriptive bases and fracture the commonalities of citizenship. In addition, such minority policies create a complacence that leaves the door wide open for minoritization to take place.

As the process of minoritization can be indiscriminate and disrespectful of previous consensus, then no matter how exhaustive the listing of minorities, the exercise will always be both incomplete and futile. Anyone could be the next victim, and, therefore, it is important to step outside this framework and see the issue of protecting cultural rights and communities on a different basis. After all the juggling with criteria for designating minorities is over and done with, minoritization still remains a threat. However, the one factor, that remains resolute and indissoluble through it all is that of 'citizenship'. It is only by protecting the dignity of the individual as a citizen that one can mitigate the harshness of minoritization when it takes place. Amrit Kaur, Hansa Mehta, Alladi Ayyar, emphasized this point time and again in the Constituent Assembly debates, but their views were not entertained in the end.

Nevertheless, it is time now to take a fresh look at this subject, for the situation regarding persecution has not improved with the majority/minority framework in operation. Since minoritization has unpredictable consequences, and the next minority could be anyone, it is best to proceed on the Rawlsian 'principle of difference' (Rawls 1971: 76–77), in which legislation is done keeping in mind that anyone, including the legislator, could, at some point of time, be the least fortunate. Rawls, of course, advocates that there be a hypothetical 'veil of ignorance' which prevents law makers from identifying their interests in advance and favouring themselves accordingly. But with the unpredictability of the process of secularization the veil of ignorance becomes a practical and real one, and no longer hypothetical. In fact, this is one place where one might be able to argue from a strong Rawlsian perspective. Regardless of the finer points of this exercise, the thrust of such a Rawlsian outlook towards secularism would undermine minority listings, and the formation of minority and majority interests, and will strengthen instead the idea of citizenship. As was mentioned earlier, only one's identity as a citizen remains steadfast in the maelstrom of the secularization process. It is by protecting this identity, and by not allowing it to be overwhelmed, or undermined, by minority and majority legislations, that the ideals of secularism can best be met. There is no guarantee, of course, that communalism and sectarianism will roll over and die, but the sides will be clearly distinguished, and it will be a glorious fight out in the open and not in the corridors of power.

References and Select Bibliography

Anderson, Benedict, 1983, *Imagined Communities*, London: Verso.
Anderson, David G., 1996, 'Bringing Civil Society in an Uncivilized Place', in Chris Hann and Elizabeth Dunn, eds., *Civil Society: Challenging Western Models*, London: Routledge.
Anderson, Perry, 1979, *Lineages of the Absolutist State*, London: Verso.
——, 1990, 'A Culture in Counterflow, (1)', *New Left Review*, no. 180, pp. 41–78.
Appadurai, Arjun, 1996, *Modernity at Large: Cultural Dimensions of Globalization*, Minneapolis: University of Minnesota Press.
Aran, Gideon, 1991, 'Jewish Zionist Fundamentalism: The Block of the Faithful in Israel', in Martin E. Marty and R. Scott Appleby, eds., *Fundamentalism Observed*, Chicago: University of Chicago Press.
Arato, Andrew and Jean Cohen, 1993, 'Civil Society and Social Theory', in Peter Beilhorz, G. Robinson and J. Rundell, eds., *Between Totalitarianism and Postmodernity: A Thesis Eleven Reader*, Boston: MIT Press.
Augé, Marc, 1995, *Non-Places: Introduction to an Anthropology of Supermodernity*, London: Verso.
Balibar, Etienne, 1991, 'The Nation Form: History and Ideology', in Etienne Balibar and I. Wallerstein, *Race, Nation, Class: Ambiguous Identities*, London: Verso.
Banfield, E.C., 1958, *The Moral Basis of a Backward Society*, Glencoe: Free Press.
Barth, Fredrik, 1981, *Process and Form in Social Life*, vol. 1, London: Routledge and Kegan Paul.
Barthes, Roland, 1983, *Selected Writings*, Oxford: Fontana.
Bayly, Chris, 1986, *Rulers, Townsmen and Bazaars: North Indian Society in the Age of British Expansion, 1770–1870*, Cambridge: Cambridge University Press.
Bellah, Robert, 1967, 'Civil Religion in America', *Daedalus*, vol. 96, pp. 1–21.
Bellah, Robert, Richard Madsen, William M. Sullivan and Steven M. Tipton, 1985, *Habits of the Heart: Individualism and Commitment in American Life*, New York: Harper and Row.
Benedict, Ruth, 1934, *Patterns of Culture*, Boston: Houghton Mifflin.
Berger, Peter L., 1970, *The Sacred Canopy: Elements of Sociological Theory of Religion*, Garden City: Doubleday.

Beyer, Peter L., 1994, *Religion and Globalization*, London: Sage.
Béteille, André, 1986, 'Individualism and Equality', *Current Anthropology*, vol. 27, pp. 121–34.
———, 1991, 'Distributive Justice and Institutional Well-Being', *Economic and Political Weekly*, Annual Number, vol. 26, pp. 591–600.
———, 1994, 'Secularism and the Intellectuals', *Economic and Political Weekly*, vol. 29, pp. 559–66.
———, 1996a, 'The Mismatch Between Class and Status', *British Journal of Sociology*, vol. 47, pp. 513–25.
———, 1996b, 'Civil Society and its Institutions', First Fulbright Memorial Lecture delivered in Calcutta on February 22, 1996. Reproduced in *The Telegraph* (Calcutta), March 12 and 13, 1996.
Bhabha, Homi, 1990, 'Introduction: Narrating the Nation', in Homi Bhabha, ed., *Nation and Narration*, London: Routledge.
———, 1991, '"Race" Time and Revision of Modernity', *Oxford Literary Review*, vol. 13, pp. 193–219.
Bidney, David, 1953, *Theoretical Anthropology*, New York: Columbia University Press.
Blaney, David L. and Mustapha Kamal Pasha, 1993, 'Civil Society and Democracy in the Third World: Ambiguities and Historical Possibilities', *Studies in Comparative International Development*, vol. 28, pp. 3–24.
Bonacich, E. and J. Modell, 1981, *The Economic Basis of Ethnic Solidarity: A Study of Japanese Americans*, Los Angeles: University of California Press.
Bourdieu, Pierre, 1977, *Outline of a Theory of Practice*, Cambridge: Cambridge University Press.
———, 1984, *Distinction: A Social Critique of the Judgement of Taste*, Cambridge: Harvard University Press.
———, 1985a, 'Social Space and the Genesis of Groups', *Theory and Society*, vol. 14, pp. 723–44.
———, 1985b, 'The Forms of Capital', in John G. Richardson, ed., *Handbook of Theory and Research of the Sociology of Education*, New York: Greenwood Press.
Brazeau, Jacques E., 1964, 'Language, Differences and Occupational Experience', in Marcel Rioux and Yves Martin, ed., *French Canadian Society, Vol. I*, Toronto: Mclelland and Steward.
Breman, Jan, 1974, *From Patronage to Exploitation: Changing Agrarian Relations in South Gujarat*, Berkeley: University of California Press.
Burghart, Richard, 1996, *The Conditions of Listening: Essays on Religion, History and Politics in South Asia*, Delhi: Oxford University Press.
Burnet, Jean R. and Howard Palmer, 1988, *'Coming Canadians': An Introduction to a History of Canada's Peoples*, Toronto: McCelland and Stewart in association with the Multiculturalism Program, Department of the Secretary of State and the Canadian Government Publishing Centre, Supply and Services, Canada.
Chandhoke, Neera, 1995, *State and Civil Society: Explorations in Political Theory*, New Delhi: Sage.
Chatterji, Partha, 1997, 'Beyond the Nation? Or Within?' *Economic and Political Weekly*, vol. 32, pp. 30–34.
Comaroff, John L. and Jean Comaroff, 1991, *Revelation and Revolution, vol. 2*, Chicago: University of Chicago Press.

Comaroff, John L. and Jean Comaroff, 1998, 'Occult Economies and the Violence of Abstraction', Max Gluckman Memorial Lecture, International Centre for Contemporary Cultural Research, University of Manchester.

Cox, Oliver Cromwell, 1970, *Caste, Class and Race: A Study in Social Dynamics*, New York: Monthly Review (Modern Reader Paperback).

Das, Veena, 1982, *Structure and Cognition: Aspects of Hindu Caste and Ritual*, Bombay: Oxford University Press.

Dawson, Michael C., 1994, *Behind the Mule: Race, Class and African American Politics*, Princeton: Princeton University Press.

———, 1995. 'Structure and Ideology: Shaping of Black Public Opinion', (Mimeo): University of Chicago.

de Tocqueville, Alexis, 1954, *Democracy in America*, vol. 1, New York: Alfred A. Knopff.

———, 1955, *The Old Regime and the French Revolution*, New York: Doubleday.

Demerath, N.J. and Rhys H. Williams, 1985, 'Civil Religion in an Uncivil Society', *Annals of the American Academy* (480), pp. 154–66.

———, 1992, 'Secularization in a Community Context', *Journal for the Scientific Study of Religion*, pp. 189–206.

Desai, I.P., 1976, *Untouchability in Rural Gujarat*, Bombay: Popular Prakashan.

Deutscher, Isaac, 1967, *The Unfinished Revolution*, Oxford: Oxford University Press.

Dirks, Nicholas B., 1994, 'Ritual and Resistance: Subversion as a Social Fact', in Dirks, Nicholas B. Geoff Eley and Sherry B. Ortner, eds., *Culture/Power/History: A Reader in Contemporary Social Theory*, Princeton: Princeton University Press.

Douglas, Mary, 1978, *Purity and Danger: An Analysis of the Concept of Pollution and Taboo*, London: Routledge and Kegan Paul.

———, 1995, 'Forgotten Knowledge', in Marilyn Strathern, ed., *Shifting Contexts: Transformations in Anthropological Knowledge*, London: Routledge.

Dumont, Louis, 1970, *Homo Hierarchicus: The Caste System and Its Implications*, London: Weidenfeld and Nicholson.

———, 1980, *Homo Hierarchicus: The Caste System and Its Implications*, Delhi: Oxford University Press.

Dunn, Elizabeth, 1996, 'Money, Morality and Modes of Civil Society Among American Mormons', in Chris Hann and Elizabeth Dunn, eds., *Civil Society: Challenging Western Models*, London: Routledge.

Durkheim, Emile, 1912, *The Elementary Forms of Religious Life*, New York: Free Press.

———, 1933, *The Division of Labour in Society*, Glencoe: The Free Press.

———, 1957, *Professional Ethics and Civic Morals*, London: Routledge and Kegan Paul.

———, 1961, *Moral Education*, Glencoe: The Free Press.

Durkheim, Emile and Marcel Mauss, 1963, *Primitive Classifications*, Chicago: Chicago University Press.

Dworkin, Roland, 1977a, 'Why Bakke Has No Case', *New York Review of Books*, November 10, pp. 141–50.

———, 1977b, *Taking Rights Seriously*, London: Duckworth.

Dyck, Noel, 1992, 'Metis, Natives: Some Implications of Special Status', in Joe Sawchuk, ed., *Readings in Aboriginal Studies, Vol. 2: Identities and State Structures*, Manitoba: Bearpaw Publication, Brandon University.

Eggan, Fred, 1968, 'Social Anthropology and the Method of Controlled Comparison', in Robert A. Manners and David Kaplan, eds., *Theory in Anthropology: A Source Book*, London: Routledge and Kegan Paul.

Embree, Ainslee T., 1988, *Sources of Indian Tradition*, vol. 1, New York: Columbia University Press.

Evans-Pritchard, E.E., 1969, *The Nuer: A Description of the Mode of Livelihood and Political Institutions of a Nilotic People*, Oxford: Oxford University Press.

Foster, David, 1997, 'Who's Real? American Indians Face Identity Crisis', *The Times of India*, February 1, p. 7.

Foucault, Michel, 1975, *Discipline and Punish*, New York: Vintage.

———, 1981, 'Omnes et Singulation: Towards a Criticism of Political Reason', *Tanner Lectures on Human Values*, Salt Lake City and Cambridge: University of Utah Press and Cambridge University Press.

———, 1986, 'Of Other Spaces', *Diacritics*, vol. 16, pp. 22–27.

Fraser, Nancy, 1994, 'Re-thinking the Public Sphere: A Contribution to the Critique of Actually Existing Democracies', in Henry A. Diroux and Peter McLaren, eds., *Between Borders: Pedagogy and the Politics of Cultural Studies*, New York: Routledge.

Freeman, Alan David, 1995, 'Legitimizing Racial Discrimination Through Anti-Discrimination Law: A Critical Review of Supreme Court Review', in Kimberley Crenshaw, Neil Gotanda, Gary Peller and Kendal Thomas, eds., *Critical Race Theory: The Key Writings that Formed the Movement*, New York: The New Press.

Geertz, Clifford, 1969, 'Religion in Java: Conflict and Integration', in Roland Robertson, ed., *Sociology of Religion*, Harmondsworth: Penguin.

———, 1984, *The Interpretation of Cultures*, London: Hutchinson.

Gellner, Ernest, 1994, *Conditions of Liberty: Civil Society and its Rivals*, London: Hamish Hamilton.

Gluckman, Max, 1963, *Order and Rebellion in Tribal Africa*, London: Cohen and West.

Goffman, Erving, 1961, *The Presentation of Self in Everyday Life*, Harmondsworth: Penguin.

Goodenough, Ward H., 1965, 'Rethinking "Status" and "Role": Towards a General Model of the Cultural Organization of Social Relationships', in Michael Banton, ed., *The Relevance of Models for Social Anthropology*, London: Tavistock.

Gramsci, Antonio, 1971, *Selections from Prison Notebooks*, New York: International Publishers.

Granovetter Mark, 1985, Economic Action and Social Structure: The Problem of Embeddedness', *American Journal of Sociology*, vol. 91, pp. 481–510.

Gray, John, 1988, 'The Politics of Cultural Diversity', *The Salisbury Review*, September 1988, pp. 38–45.

Groulx, Abbe Lionel, 1938, *L Naissance D'Un Race*, Montreal: Library Granger Freres.

Gupta, Akhil and James Ferguson, 1992, 'Beyond "Culture": Space, Identity and the Politics of Difference', *Cultural Anthropology*, vol. 7, pp. 6–23.

Gupta, C. Dwarkanath and S. Bhaskar, 1970, *Vyasas—A Sociological Study*, New Delhi: Ashish Publishing House.

Gupta, Dipankar, 1991, 'Continuous Hierarchies and Discrete Castes', in Dipankar Gupta, ed., *Social Stratification*, Delhi: Oxford University Press.
———, ed., 1992, *Social Stratification*, Delhi: Oxford University Press.
———, 1993, 'The Indian Diaspora of 1947', in Milton Israel and N. Wagle, eds., *Ethnicity and Migration: The South Asian Experience*, Toronto: University of Toronto Press.
———, 1996, *The Context of Ethnicity: Sikh Identity in a Comparative Perspective*, Delhi: Oxford University Press.
———, 1997, *Rivalry and Brotherhood: Politics in the Life of Farmers of Northern India*, Delhi: Oxford University press.
Habermas, Jurgen, 1985, *The Theory of Communicative Action (in two volumes). Vol. 1: Reason and Rationalization in Society; Vol. 2: Lifeworld and System—A Critique of Functionalist Reason*, Boston: Beacon Press.
———, 1989, *The Structural Transformation of the Public Sphere: An Inquiry into a Category of Bourgeois Society*, Cambridge, Massachusetts: MIT Press.
Habib, Irfan, 1963, *The Agrarian System of Mughal India*, Bombay: Asia Publishing House.
Hall, J.A., 1995, 'In Search of Civil Society', in J.A. Hall, ed., *Civil Society: Theory, History and Comparison*, Cambridge: Polity Press.
Hall, John A., 1993, 'Nationalism, Classified and Explained', *Deadalus*, vol. 122, pp. 1–28.
Hann, Chris and Elizabeth Dunn, eds., 1996, 'Introduction', in Chris Hann and Elizabeth Dunn, eds., *Civil Society: Challenging Western Models*, London: Routledge.
Harvey, David, 1990, *The Condition of Postmodernity: An Enquiry into the Origins of Cultural Change*, Oxford: Blackwell.
Hayek, F.A., 1960, *The Constitution of Liberty*, Chicago: University of Chicago Press.
Hegel, G.W.F., 1945, *Philosophy of Right*, Oxford: Clarendon Press.
Herskovits, M.J., 1965, *Cultural Anthropology*, New York: Alfred A. Knopff.
Hervieu-Leger, Daniele, 1998, 'The Past in the Present', in Peter Berger, ed., *The Limits of Social Cohesion: Conflict and Mediation in Plural Societies*, Boulder, Colorado: Westview.
Hocart, A.M., 1945, *Caste: A Comparative Study*, London: Methuen and Co.
James, Allison, 1996, 'Cooking the Books: Global or Local Identities in British Food Cultures', in David Howes, ed., *Cross Cultural Consumption: Global Markets, Local Realities*, London: Routledge.
Kawlra, Aarti A., 1997, 'Weaving as Praxis: The Case of the Padma Saliyars', Unpublished Ph.D. thesis submitted to the Department of Humanities and Social Sciences, Indian Institute of Technology, New Delhi.
Keane, John, 1988, *Democracy and Civil Society*, London: Verso.
Khare, R.S., 1992, 'The Untouchables' Version: Evaluating the Ideal Ascetic', in Dipankar Gupta, ed., *Social Stratification*, Delhi: Oxford University Press.
Kishwar, Madhu, 1994, 'Codified Hindu Law: Myth and Reality', *Economic and Political Weekly*, vol. 29, pp. 2145–161.
Kleinmann, Arthur and Joan, Kleinmann, 1991, 'Suffering and its Professional Transformation: Towards an Ethnography of Interpersonal Experiences', *Culture, Medicine and Psychiatry*, vol. 5, pp. 275–301.

Kluckhohn, Clyde, 1962, *Culture and Behaviour*, New York: The Free Press.
Kohn, Hans, 1946, *The Idea of Nationalism: A Study of its Origin and Background*, New York: The Macmillan Company.
Koontz, Theodore J., 1981, 'Religion and Political Cohesion: John Locke and Jean Jacques Rousseau', *Journal of Church and State*, vol. 23, pp. 96–115.
Kothari, Rajni, 1984, 'The Non-Party Political Process', *Economic and Political Weekly*, vol. 19, pp. 216–24.
———, 1988a, 'Integration and Exclusion in Indian Politics', *Economic and Political Weekly*, vol. 23, pp. 2223–2227.
———, 1988b, *State Against Democracy: In Search of Human Governance*, Delhi: Ajanta.
———, 1991, 'Human Rights: A Movement in Search of a Theory', in S. Kothari and H. Sethi, eds., *Human Rights: Challenges for Theory and Action*, New York: New Horizon Press.
Kroeber, A.L., 1967, *Anthropology*, Delhi: Oxford and IBH.
Kuper, Adam, 1983, *Anthropology and Anthropologist: The Modern British School*, London: Routledge and Kegan Paul.
Kymlicka, Will, 1989, *Liberalism, Community and Culture*, Oxford: Clarendon Press.
———, 1995, *Multicultural Citizenship: A Liberal Theory of Minority Rights*, Oxford: Clarendon Press.
Lan, David, 1985, *Guns and Rain: Guerillas and Spirit Mediums in Zimbabwe*, Berkeley and Los Angeles: London and Berkeley University of California Press.
Lash, S. and Urry J., 1987, *The End of Organized Capitalism*, Cambridge: Polity Press.
Leach, Edmund, 1964, *Political Systems of Highland Burma*, London: G. Bell and Sons.
———, 1982, *Social Anthropology*, New York: Oxford University Press.
Lebovics, Herman, 1992, *True France: Wars Over Cultural Identity, 1900–1945*, Ithaca: Cornell University Press.
Lemeille, Anthony J., 1995, *Black Male Deviance*, Westport, Connecticut: Praeger.
Lenin, V.I., 1960, *The Development of Capitalism in Russia*, in *Collected Works*, vol. 4, Moscow: Progress Publishers.
Levi-Strauss, Claude, 1985, *The View From Afar*, New York: Basic Books.
Lipson, E., 1953, *The Growth of English Society: A Short Economic History*, New York: Henry Holt and Company.
Locke, John, 1967, *Two Treatises of Government*, Cambridge: Cambridge University Press.
Lockwood, D., 1992, *Solidarity and Schism*, Oxford: Clarendon Press.
Lovejoy, A.O., 1960, *The Great Chain of Being: A Study of the History of an Idea*, New York: Harper Torchbooks.
Lucas, C.P., ed., 1912, *Lord Durham's Report on the Affairs of British North America* (in 3 volumes), vol. 2, Oxford: The Clarendon Press.
Luhmann, Niklas, 1982, *The Differentiation of Society*, New York: Columbia University Press.
MacIntyre, Alisdaire, 1981, *After Virtue: A Study in Moral Theory*, London: Duckworth.
Madan, T.N., 1987, *Non-Renunciation: Theories and Interpretations of Hindu Culture*, New Delhi: Oxford University Press.

Malinowski, Bronislaw, 1974, *A Scientific Theory of Culture*, University of North Carolina Press.

Mannheim, Karl, 1960, *Ideology and Utopia: An Introduction to the Sociology of Knowledge*, London: Routledge and Kegan Paul.

Mansergh, Nicholas and Penderal Moon, eds., 1976, *Transfer of Power*, vol. 6, New Delhi: UBS Publishers.

Marriot, McKim, 1959, 'Interactional and Attributional System of Caste Ranking', *Man In India*, vol. 39, pp. 92–107.

Marshall, T.H., 1963, *Sociology at the Crossroads and Other Essays*, London: Heinemann.

———, 1977, *Class, Citizenship and Social Development*, Chicago: University of Chicago Press.

Marx, Karl, 1973, *Grundrisse*, Harmondsworth: Penguin.

Marx, Karl and F. Engels, 1969a, 'Feuerbach, Opposition of the Materialistic and Idealistic Outlook', in Karl Marx and F. Engels, *Selected Works* (in 3 vols.), vol. 1, Moscow: Progress Publishers.

———, 1969b, 'Manifesto of the Communist Party', in Karl Marx and F. Engels, *Selected Works* (in 3 vols.), vol. 1, Moscow: Progress Publishers.

Merleau-Ponty, Maurice, 1978, 'The Philosopher and Sociology', in Thomas Luckmann, ed., *Phenomenology and Sociology*, Harmondsworth: Penguin.

Mingione, Enzo, 1991, *Fragmented Societies: A Sociology of Economic Life Beyond the Market Paradigm*, Oxford: Basil Blackwell.

Morris, D. Morris, 1965, *Emergence of an Industrial Labour Force in India: A Study of Bombay Cotton Mills 1854–1947*, Bombay: Oxford University Press.

Mouffe, Chantal, 1992, 'Democratic Citizenship and the Political Community', in Chantal Mouffe, ed., *Dimensions of Radical Democracy: Pluralism, Citizenship, Community*, London: Verso.

Nandy, Ashis, 1984, 'Culture, State and Rediscovery of Indian Politics', *Economic and Political Weekly*, vol. 19, pp. 2078–83.

———, 1989, 'The Political Culture of the Indian State', *Daedalus*, vol. 18, pp. 1–26.

Nayar, Baldev Raj, 1966, *Minority Politics in Punjab*, Princeton, New Jersey: Princeton University Press.

Nisbet, Robert, 1970, (1961), *The Sociological Tradition*, London: Heinemann.

Nozick, R., 1972, *Community and Power*, New York: Oxford University Press.

———, 1976, *Anarchy, State and Utopia*, Oxford: Basil Blackwell.

Oakeshott, Michael, 1975, *On Human Conduct*, Oxford: Clarendon Press.

Ouellet, Fernand, 1969, 'The Historical Background of Separatism in Quebec', in Ramsay Cook, ed., *French Canadian Nationalism: A Anthology*, Toronto: Macmillan of Canada.

Parekh, Bhikhu, 1995, 'Cultural Diversity and Liberal Democracy', in David Beetham, ed., *Defining and Measuring Democracy*, London: Sage.

Parikh, Sunita, 1997, *The Politics of Preference: Democratic Institutions and Affirmative Action in United States and India*, Ann Arbor: University of Michigan Press.

Parsons, Talcott, 1951, *The Social System*, Glencoe: The Free Press.

———, 1974, 'Religion in Post Industrial America: The Problem of Secularization', *Social Research*, vol. 41, pp. 193–225.

Pepper, Stephen, 1942, *World Hypotheses,* Berkeley and Los Angeles: University of California Press.
Peery, Nelson, 1994, *Black Fire: The Making of an American Revolutionary,* New York: The New Press.
Pirenne, Henri, 1937, *Economic and Social History of Medieval Europe,* New York: Harcourt, Brace and World, Inc.
Polanyi, Karl, 1944, *The Great Transformation,* New York: Rinehart Press.
Putnam, Robert, 1993, *Making Democracy: Civic Tradition in Modern Italy,* Princeton: Princeton University Press.
Ramanujam, A.K., 1990, 'Is There an Indian Way of Thinking: An Informal Essay', in McKim Marriot, eds., *India Through Hindu Categories,* New Delhi: Sage.
Rapaport, Roy A., 1979, *Ecology, Meaning and Religion,* Richmond, CA: North Atlantic Books.
Rawls, John, 1967, 'Distributive Justice', in Peter Laslett and W.G. Runciman, eds., *Philosophy, Politics and Society,* Oxford: Basil Blackwell.
———, 1971, *A Theory of Justice,* Cambridge, Mass: Harvard University Press.
———, 1974, 'Constitutional Liberty and the Concept of Justice', in C.J. Friedrich and J.W. Chapman, eds., *NOMOS, VI,* New York: Liberal Atherton Press.
———, 1985, 'Justice as Fairness: Political Not Metaphysical', *Philosophy and Public Affairs,* vol. 14, pp. 223–51.
Renan, Ernest, 1990, 'What is a Nation', in Homi K. Bhabha, ed., *Nation and Narration,* London: Routledge.
Richter, Melvin, 1963, 'Tocqueville on Africa', *Review of Politics,* vol. 25, pp. 362–98.
Ricoeur, Paul, 1974, *The Conflict of Interpretations,* Evanston: Northwestern University Press.
Rioux, Marcel, 1971, *Quebec in Question,* Toronto: James Lorimer and Co.
Rorty, R., 1985, 'Postmodern Bourgeois Liberalism', in B. Hollinger, ed., *Hermeneutics and Praxis,* Notre Dame, Indiana: University of Notre Dame Press.
Rousseau, Jean Jacques, 1913, *The Social Contract and Other Discourses,* London: E.P. Dutton and Co., J.M. Dent and Sons.
Royal Commission on Aboriginal People, 1993, *Public Hearing: Exploring the Options—Overview of the Third Round,* Ministry of Supply and Service, Canada: Ottawa.
Russel, Kathy, Midge Wilson and **Ronald Hall,** 1992, *The Colour Complex: The Politics of Skin Colour Among African Americans,* New York: Anchor Books, Doubleday.
Russell, Dick, 1998, *Black Genius and the American Experience,* New York: Carol and Graf Publishers.
Sabel, Charles F., 1989, 'Flexible Specialization and the Re-emergence of Regional Economies', in Paul Hirst and Jonathan Zeitlin, eds., *Reversing Industrial Decline? Industrial Structure and Policy in Britain and Her Competitors,* Oxford: Berg.
Sachse, William L., 1967, *English History in the Making: Readings from the Sources Upto 1689,* Waltham, Massachusetts: Blaisdell Publications.
Sacks, Karen Brodkin, 1994, 'How Did Jews Become White Folks', in Stephen Gregory and Roger Sanjek, eds., *Race,* New Brunswick: Rutgers University Press.

Sahlins, Marshall, 1985, *Islands of History*, Chicago: University of Chicago Press.
Said, Edward, 1978, *Orientalism*, New York: Pantheon.
———, 1994, *Culture and Imperialism*, New York: Vintage.
Sandel, M.J., 1982, *Liberalism and the Limits of Justice*, Cambridge: Cambridge University Press.
Sanjek, Roger, 1994, 'Intermarriage and the Future of Races in the United States', in Steven Gregory and Roger Sanjek, eds., *Race*, New Brunswick, New Jersey: Rutgers University Press.
Sarkar, Tanika, 1993, 'Rhetoric Against Age of Consent: Restricting Colonial Reason and Death of a Child Wife', *Economic and Political Weekly*, vol. 28, pp. 1869–78.
Sawchuk, Joe, 1992, 'Metis, Non-Status Indians and the New Aboriginality: Government's Influence on Native Political Alliance and Identity', in Joe Sawchuk, ed., *Readings in Aboriginal Studies, Vol. 2: Identities and State Structure*, Manitoba: Bearpaw Publication, Brandon University.
Schneider, David, 1976, 'Notes Towards a Theory of Culture', in Keith H. Basso and Henry A. Selby, eds., *Meaning in Anthropology*, Albuquerque, University of New Mexico.
Schnudson, Michael, 1997, 'Paper Tigers', *Lingua Franca*, pp. 49–56.
Schutz, Alfred, 1978, 'Phenomenology and the Social Sciences', in Thomas Luckmann, ed., *Phenomenology and Sociology: Selected Readings*, Harmondsworth: Penguin.
Scott, James C., 1985, *Weapons of the Weak: Everyday Forms of Peasant Resistance*, New Haven: Yale University Press.
Seligman, A., 1992, *The Idea of Civil Society*, New York: Free Press.
Sen, Amartya, 1982, *Choice, Welfare and Measurement*, Oxford: Oxford University Press.
Seton-Watson, Hugh, 1977, *Nations and States: An Enquiry into the Origins of Nations and the Politics of Nationalism*, London: Methuen.
Sheth, D.L., 1984, 'Grass Roots Initiatives in India', *Economic and Political Weekly*, vol. 19, pp. 259–62.
———, 1989, 'State, Nation and Ethnicity: Experience of Third World Countries', *Economic and Political Weekly*, vol. 24, pp. 615–26.
———, 1991, 'An Emerging Perspective on Human Rights in India', in S. Kothari and H. Sethi, eds., *Rethinking Human Rights*, New York: New Horizon Press.
Shiva Rao, B.D., 1968a, *The Framing of India's Constitution: Selected Documents*, (in 4 vols.), Delhi: Indian Institute of Public Administration.
———, 1968b, *The Framing of India's Constitution: A Study*, Delhi: Indian Institute of Public Administration.
Singer, Milton, 1972, *When a Great Tradition Modernizes: An Anthropological Approach to Indian Civilization*, New York: Praeger Press.
Silk, Marc, 1997, 'Something New Something Old: Changes and Continuities in American Religious History', Report on a Conference held at Harvard Divinity School, September 5–8 (Mimeo).
Smith, Anthony D.S., 1979, *Nationalism in the Twentieth Century*, Oxford: Martin Robertson.
———, 1981, *The Ethnic Revival*, Cambridge: Cambridge University Press.

Smith, Gavin A., 1991, 'Writing For Real: Capitalist Constructs and Constructions of Capitalism', *Critique of Anthropology*, vol. 11, pp. 213–32.
Sowell, Thomas, 1990, *Preferential Policies: An International Perspective*, New York: William Morrow and Company.
Spencer, Jonathen, 1997, 'Post-colonialism and the Political Imagination', *Man*, vol. 3, pp. 1–21.
Spulbeck, S., 1996, 'Anti-Semitism and Fear of the Public Sphere in Post-Totalitarian Society: East Germany', in Chris Dunn and Elizabeth Hann, eds., *Civil Society: Challenging Western Models*, London: Routledge.
Steinberg, Stephen, 1989, *The Ethnic Myth: Race, Ethnicity and Class in America*, Boston: Beacon Press.
Subrahmanyam, S., 1996, 'Before the Leviathan: Sectarian Violence and the State in Pre-Colonial India', in Kaushik Basu and Sanjay Subrahmanium, eds., *Unravelling the Nation: Sectarian Conflict and India's Secular Identity*, New Delhi: Penguin.
Tamir, Yael, 1993, *Liberal Nationalism*, Princeton, New Jersey: Princeton University Press.
Tarlo, Emma, 1996, *Clothing Matters: Dress and Identity in India*, New Delhi: Viking.
Taylor, Charles, 1979, *Hegel and Modern Society*, Cambridge: Cambridge University Press.
———, 1993, *Reconciling the Solitudes: Essays on Canadian Federation and Nationalism*, Montreal, Kingston: McGill-Queen University Press.
Thorner, Daniel, 1981, *The Shaping of Modern India*, Delhi: Oxford University Press.
Touraine, A., 1992, 'Beyond Social Movements', in Mike Featherstone, ed., *Cultural Theory and Cultural Change*, London: Sage.
Trudeau, Pierre, 1974, 'The Province of Quebec at the Time of the Asbestos Strike', in Pierre Trudeau, ed., *The Asbestos Strike*, Toronto, James Lewis and Samuel.
Turner, Bryan S., 1990, 'Outline of a Theory of Citizenship', *Sociology*, vol. 29(2), pp. 189–217.
Turner, Victor, 1964, 'Symbols in Ndembu Rituals', in Max Gluckman, ed., *Closed Systems and Open Minds: The Limits of Naivety in Social Anthropology*, Chicago: Aldine Publishing Co.
———, 1974, *Dramas, Fields and Metaphors: Symbolic Action in Human Society*, Ithaca: Cornell University Press.
Uberoi, J.P.S., 1969, 'Five Symbols of Sikhism', in Fauja Singh, et al., *Sikhism*, Patiala: University of Patiala Press.
Walzer, Michael, 1983, *Spheres of Justice: A Defence of Pluralism and Equality*, Oxford: Martin Robertson.
———, 1987, 'Citizenship' in Terence Ball, et al., eds., *Political Innovation and Conceptual Change*, Cambridge: Cambridge University Press.
———, 1992, 'The Civil Society Argument', in Chantal Mouffe, ed., *Dimensions of Radical Democracy: Pluralism, Citizenship, Community*, London: Verso.
Weber, Max, 1948, 'Politics as a Vocation', in Hans Gerth and C.W. Mills, eds., *From Max Weber*, London: Routledge.
———, 1968, *Economy and Society*, New York: Bedminister Press.
White, Leslie, 1967, 'On the Concept of Culture', in Robert. A. Manners and David Kaplan, eds., *Theory in Anthropology: A Source Book*, London: Routledge and Kegan Paul.

Wilke, T., 1993, *Perilious Knowledge: The Implications of the Human Genome Project*, London: Faber.
Williams, Raymond, 1973, *The Country and the City*, London: Chatto and Windus.
———, 1977, *Marxism and Literature*, Oxford: Oxford University Press.
———, 1989, *Resources of Hope*, London: Verso.
Williams, Rhys and **N.J. Demerath**, 1991, 'Religion and Political Process in an American City', *American Sociological Review*, vol. 56, pp. 417–31.

Index

affirmative action, 165, 170, 208, 209, 212, 213, 214, 215, 216, 221, 225, 226, 227, 229, 230, 231, 232, 247; programmes, 71, 75, 133, 225
Ambedkar, B.R., 210, 211, 212, 213, 233–35, 256, 260, 261
Amrit Kaur, Rajkumari, 260, 262, 265
Anderson, Ben, 111, 113
Anderson, Perry, 109, 111–12
Anthony, Frank, 258
anti-Bangladeshi uprisings, 125
anti-colonialism, 119–20, 121, 124, 238
Appadurai, A., 21, 150
artifacts, diversity as, 143, 226–27; as representing matter, 58; and space, 55, 57, 58, 62
Auge, M., 22
Ayodhya, as a cultural space, 42
Ayyar, Alladi K., 260, 265

Banfield, Edward C., 172, 173
Barth, Fredrik, 68
Bayly, Chris, 83
Bellah, R., 92, 116, 177, 252, 254
Benedict, R., 90, 91
Berger, P.L., 251
Béteille, A., 162, 165, 167, 171, 174–75, 176–78, 181, 183, 188, 193, 222
Beyer, P.L., 255
Bharatiya Janata Party, 124

Bidney, David, 55–56
bilingualism, 132
Bombay Plan, 121
Bourdieu, P., 52, 59, 60, 91, 188
Brazeeau, Jacques, 44–45
Breman, Jan, 86
Burghart, Richard, 188

capitalism, 127, 140–41, 142, 143, 190, 191, 256, 257, 258, 261
castes, ideology of, 76; origin tales of, 77; as a political resource, 211, 234–35; relative status of, 77, 78; as a root metaphor, 19, 26
chaebol system, 36
Chatterji, Partha, 165, 169, 170, 178, 181, 187
citizenship, 20, 21, 152–56, 163, 173, 177, 178, 181, 183–90, 193, 194, 203, 208, 209, 210, 212, 213, 216, 217, 218, 220, 221, 222, 224, 225, 226, 228, 230, 233, 235, 237, 240, 242, 243, 244, 245, 246, 247, 248, 260, 264, 265
civic values, collective, 221
civil religion, 116, 117, 252–53, 258
civil rights, 146
civil society, and the ethic of freedom, 175–76, 179–82, 244, 247; and the privileging of custom, 163, 165; and the return to model sentiments, 161–62; and the rural

sphere, 166; and the state, 159–91
collective rights, 201. *See also* community rights
colonialism, 119, 121
Comaroff, Jean, 29–30, 59, 202
Comaroff, John, 29–30, 59, 202
communalism, 250, 251, 265
communitarianism, 20, 169, 180, 181, 182, 188, 189, 196–200, 201, 202, 203, 204–09, 215, 222, 247–48
community rights, 203, 205. *See also* collective rights
Congress Party, 64, 122, 124, 240, 250
consumerism, 71, 160
Cripps, Sir Stafford, 122
cultural boundaries, 97, 102, 197
'cultural capital', 56, 59–60
cultural homogeneity, and industrialization, 26–27
cultural hybridization, 61, 62, 63
cultural identity, 21, 27, 139, 140, 198
cultural space, 36, 37–40, 41, 45–46, 48, 49, 53, 58, 63, 73, 75, 94, 95, 101–02, 103, 104, 105, 106, 107, 113, 115, 119, 121, 124, 128, 129, 130, 133, 134, 135, 139, 141, 142, 144, 145, 151, 152, 153, 154, 155, 156, 159, 226, 239, 240, 241, 242; and overlapping memberships, 96–98
culture, and artifact, 18, 56, 59, 61, 62, 96; change, 17; concept of, 17–19, 28–29, 31, 57, 60, 67; and membership, 44, 96, 97, 101, 103, 155; political element in, 70; as power, 70; as practice, 18; and religion, 92–93; unifying meaning of, 87, 88, 90

De Laval, Mgr., 40
de Tocqueville, A., 145, 171–75, 178, 181, 182, 188, 255–56
Demerath, N.J., 87, 251, 253, 258
deracination, cultural, 48, 49; fear of, 48
Desai, I.P., 77
diaspora, and membership, 149
diasporics, and minority rights, 147–50

'difference principle', 189, 198, 199, 200–204, 205, 208, 216, 217, 218, 219, 220, 221, 222, 234, 265
Dirks, Nicholas, 76
diversity, and the nation-state, 141–45, 155; and traditional societies, 141
Douglas, Mary, 51, 145
DuBois, W.E.B., 222–23
Dumont, Louis, 29, 193
Durkheim, Emile, 67, 106, 112, 208, 209, 219–21, 224, 225, 227, 233, 252
Dworkin, R., 179–80, 207, 208, 215, 216, 222, 223, 225, 226, 227
Dyck, Noel, 264

Eggan, F., 91
'elective affinity', 33, 34, 51
embeddedness, 81, 83, 84, 93
Enlightenment, the, 170
equality and participation, as metaphors, 121, 122, 125
equality, 192, 193, 195, 224, 233; formal, 193, 195, 198, 222, 233; of opportunity, 74, 212–14, 217, 221, 223, 224, 245; of results, 223, 227
ethnic pluralism, 149
'ethnie', 113
Evans-Pritchard, E.E., 95

Falwell, Jerry, 87, 187
family, and civil society, 181; and the ethic of freedom, 179, 180, 182
Farrakhan, Louis, 149, 187
feudalism, as a root metaphor, 126
Foucault, M., 106–7, 160
Franklin, Benjamin, 113, 114
Fraser, Nancy, 242
fraternity, 153, 154, 155, 159, 160, 163, 167, 169, 180, 184, 186, 188–91, 192, 195, 198, 199, 200, 203, 205, 207, 208, 210, 211, 212, 213, 216, 217, 218, 219, 220, 221, 222, 224, 225, 226, 227, 228, 230, 232, 233, 234, 235, 240, 241, 247, 248–49
French Revolution, 116, 118, 153, 172, 255–56

Gaddafi, M.A., 127
Gandhi, Indira, 261, 263
Gandhi, M.K., 256
Geertz, C., 31–32, 70, 90, 91
Gellner, E., 21, 161
geography, and the nation-state, 111–12, 116; and space, 20, 45–47, 60, 101–2, 104, 105, 106, 107, 108
Goffman, E., 25
Goodenough, W.H., 185
Gramsci, A., 116, 147, 175, 176
Granovetter, M., 130
Groulx, Abbe, 39–40

Habermas, Jurgen, 67, 68, 145, 163, 239, 243, 256
Habib, Irfan, 81
Hall, John, 113
Harvey, David, 105, 108
Hayek, F.A., 192, 193, 214
Hegel, G.W.F., 145, 162, 163, 169, 171, 173, 174, 175–76, 179, 180, 181, 182–83, 184, 188, 233
Heideggar, M., 47, 163
Herskovits, Melville, 32
Hirschman, Albert, 207
Hobhouse, L.T., 114
Howe, Irving, 147
Hukam Singh, Sardar, 259
Hussein, Saddam, 128
Hutchinson, Anne, 71

'imagined space', 105
individual rights, 201, 202, 203, 224
individualism, 64, 71–76, 86, 87, 118, 127, 132, 133, 193, 218, 219, 224, 229, 254; liberal, 154
inter-subjectivity, 145–47, 163, 216, 233

Jackson, Jesse, 87
James, Allison, 58
Jana Sangh, 260
Jewish nation-state, and Jewish identity, 148

Kant, Immanuel, 80, 104, 108
King Jr., Martin Luther, 87

Kluckhohn, Clyde, 56–57
Knox, T.M., 176
Kohn, Haus, 114–15
Kothari, R., 21, 160, 162, 165–66, 169, 170, 181, 183, 187
Kroeber A.L., 28, 87
Kymlicka, Will, 143, 194, 202, 205, 206, 207, 208, 226, 245, 246

laicite, 87, 117–18, 139, 237
Leach, Edmund, 29, 70
Lefebvre, Henri, 104, 105, 106, 107
legitimacy, 67–68
Lenin, V., 123, 140, 176
Levi-Strauss, C., 48
Lewis, Oscar, 207
lex, 33–37, 44, 45, 64, 80, 81, 85, 105, 110, 120, 127, 130, 133, 134, 135, 146–47, 151
liberalism, 118, 127, 153, 191, 194, 203, 207, 213, 214, 233; 'do-good', 177; economic, 120
liberty, 192, 193, 195, 198, 217, 218, 219, 233
linguistic membership, and root metaphors, 98–100
Locke, John, 120, 162, 169, 173, 174, 175
Luhmann, N., 251, 253, 263
Luxembourg, Rosa, 140

MacIntyre, Alasdair, 24, 88, 197, 199
majoritarianism, 154, 243, 244
majority consciousness, 262, 263
Malinowski, B., 87, 90
Mandal Commission, 53, 75, 210, 211, 231, 233–35
Marcuse, H., 27
Marriott, McKim, 30, 255
Marshall, Lord Alfred, 184, 233
Marshall, T.H., 26, 178, 223
Marx, Karl, 69, 170, 175, 180, 181, 189, 190, 214, 257–58
Mauss, M., 106
medicine, and root metaphors, 54–55
Meech Lake Accord, in Canada, 201, 202, 203
Mehta, Hansa, 260, 265

melting pot metaphor, 87, 139
Merleau-Ponty, Maurice, 201
Mill, J.S., 244
minoritization, 259, 261, 262, 263–65
minority classifications, 264
minority communities, and alternate lifestyles, 242, 245
minority consciousness, 262, 263
minority protection, as a metaphor, 124
modernity, 17, 44, 127, 130, 144, 164, 165, 169, 170, 180, 185
modernization, 21, 22, 47–50, 86, 115, 126–29, 150, 181, 187, 255
Mohammed, Prophet, 48
Mookherjee, Shyama Prasad, 260, 263
morality, 146, 220
Mouffe, Chantal, 146
multiculturalism, 132, 133

Nandy, Ashis, 165, 167, 169, 170, 187
nation-state, and communism, 38; creation of, 138; and diverse cultural identities, 21; and ideology, 112; and industrialization, 27; and membership, 109, 110, 123, 154–55; and morality, 146; sentiments, 110, 113, 114, 115, 116–17, 122–23, 125, 144, 155; sentiment and structure as twin aspects of, 19, 20, 22, 152–56; and territory, 20–21, 22, 111, 112, 116, 118–19, 120–21, 122, 125, 129, 139, 149, 150, 151, 156, 237, 240
nationalism, 111, 113, 114, 115, 116, 117, 137, 238
Nehru, Jawaharlal, 118, 119, 121, 122, 164, 250
Neruda, Pablo, 144
'new social movements', 164, 165, 188
Nisbet, R., 254
non-governmental organizations, 166–67
non-places, 21–22
non-spaces, 93, 94, 95, 96, 105, 108, 110, 115, 120, 126, 130–35, 141, 144, 185, 186, 236, 237, 239, 240, 241, 245, 246, 254; accommodative nature of, 27; and context, 44; and cultural space, 23–24, 30, 36, 37; and institutional norms, 89; and mobility, 48; and root metaphors, 23, 24–25, 30, 33, 80, 89, 90, 247–48; and traditional societies, 86
Nozick, Robert, 74, 177, 178, 192–93, 208, 214, 215, 220

Oakeshott, Michael, 33, 146
'otherness', 141

Packard, V., 27
Pakistan, metaphor of, 121, 124
Panikkar, K.M., 258
Parekh, Bhikhu, 118, 121, 245, 247
Parsons, T., 23, 251, 252, 254
Partition, 37–38, 98, 99, 101, 102–3, 118, 119, 122, 238, 250
Patel, Sardar Vallabhbhai, 259, 260
patriotism, 38, 115, 123, 127, 151, 152
Pepper, Stephen, 32
Petain, Marshall, 142
Pirenne, Henri, 83
Polanyi, Karl, 81, 83, 84, 93
political community, 197, 198, 200
popular sovereignty, 114, 116
positive discrimination, 205, 207, 209, 210, 211, 212, 213, 214, 215, 216, 221–22, 223, 224–25, 226, 227, 228, 229, 230, 232, 233, 234, 247, 248
postmodernity, 129
'public sphere', 145–47, 156, 236–49, 256
purity and pollution, as root metaphors, 19, 40, 52–53, 76, 77, 78, 79, 86, 88, 118, 121, 125, 130–31
Putnam, R., 173

Quebec Native Women's Association (QNWA), 201

Rajagopalachari, C., 263
Ramanujam, A.K., 44
Ramsay MacDonald Communal Award, 258–59
Rau, B.N., 260, 262–63

Rawls, John, 153, 179, 183, 189, 195–201, 202, 203, 204, 205, 207–8, 214–22, 224, 225, 227, 228, 233, 243, 246, 248, 265
redistribution, 193, 215, 217
religious identity, 136
Renan, Ernest, 113, 114, 118
reservation, 209, 212, 213, 214, 221, 222, 227, 229, 230, 231, 234, 247, 260
reservations, in India, 210, 211, 212, 230–35
respublica, 145–47
reverse discriminations, 213, 214
Ricoeur, Paul, 32
Rioux, Marcel, 39
root metaphors, 18–19; adjustments of, 82, 85, 109, 110, 124; and aesthetics, 79, 80; atrophy of, 85, 103, 104; and the caste system, 19, 26, 76–79, 82, 95, 109, 123; and conflict, 51–52, 53, 75, 76, 77, 78–79; as heterogeneous, 88, 89; and institutional practices, 130–31; as internally consistent, 88; as interwoven in different spheres, 84–85; as learned behaviour, 51; and *lex*, 33–35; and membership, 25, 32, 34, 68, 86, 89, 95, 96, 102, 107; and modernity, 44; multiplicity of, 32, 103; and the nation-state, 116, 120, 124–26, 128, 129, 130, 131, 133, 134, 135, 137, 139, 141–42, 143, 145, 146–47, 151, 152, 154, 156, 237, 238, 239; and political ideologies, 64, 65; and the preservation of a moral, social order, 18–19, 59, 66–67, 79, 81, 82, 83, 86, 87, 88, 92, 93, 94, 95, 99; regnant meanings of, 18, 32, 34, 39, 40, 42, 48–49, 51, 52, 53, 56, 61, 64, 66–95, 102, 103, 105, 107, 109, 116–17, 130, 141, 152; and religion, 92, 237, 238; as resistant to change, 85; and rituals, 93; rival, 42; and social hierarchies, 93, 94, 95 and social interaction, 80, 97, 103; and socialization, 34; and style, 74; switching of, 63; and time, 47; and tradition, 44; and traditional societies, 47–48; transplantation of, 61–62; as unifying, 67, 87
Rorty, R., 197, 199, 208, 214
Rousseau, Jean-Jacques, 116, 117, 162, 171, 173, 174, 195, 204, 233

Sabel, Charles, 134
Sahlins, Marshall D., 89
Said, Edward, 141, 144
Sartre, Jean-Paul, 153
Savarkar, Veer, 122
Schneider, David, 78, 86, 87, 88, 89, 90
Scott, James, 70
secularism, 118, 119, 124, 125, 127, 238, 249–51, 255, 258, 259, 261–62, 263, 265
secularization, 249, 251–65
Sen, Amartya, 217
Seton-Watson, H., 114
Shaw, Bernard, 38
Sheth, D.L., 165, 167, 170, 184–85
Shiv Sena, 125, 261
Singer, Milton, 85, 255
Singh, V.P., 219
slavery, as a root metaphor, 126
Smith, Adam, 173, 174, 175
Smith, Gavin, 131
social capital, 60, 173
socialism, 39, 190, 191
socialization, 203; and interpretation of metaphors, 34
space, bureaucratic, 35–36; and context, 43, 44; and culture, 19–20, 21, 22, 34, 35, 36, 39, 40, 45, 46, 47–50, 55, 56, 96, 107–108; homogenization of, 144; and the issue of control, 106–07; and membership, 107; and modernization, 47; and root metaphors, 41–42, 45–47, 51, 121; and site, 43, 44, 46, 61, 62, 63, 106; stability of, 44; and time, 47, 48, 49; traditional, 41; universalistic, 34–35

Srinivas, M.N., 255
state, as an alien construct, 166; and the autonomy of institutions, 162, 163, 164–65, 174, 175, 177, 179, 188; as divisive, 161; homogenization efforts of, 166, 167; and intermediate institutions, 162–63, 164, 171–79, rational-legal framework for the, 178, 195
supermodernity, 129
superpower metaphor, 132, 133
superstructure, root metaphors as belonging to, 80
symbolically integrating forces, 163
symbols, 21, 34, 68, 88
system integrating forces, 163

Tagore, Rabindranath, 144
Tamir, Yael, 117, 143
Taylor, Charles, 197, 199
technology, universalization of, 133
Thackeray, Bal, 125
tolerance, 167, 169
Toleration Act of 1689, 139, 140

tradition, 17, 21, 44, 47, 85, 142, 143, 153, 154, 162, 163, 164, 165, 167–70, 171, 172, 180, 181, 185, 187, 189, 190, 202, 254, 255, 257
traditionalism, 44
tribalism, as a root metaphor, 126
Trudeau, Pierre, 213
Turner, B.S., 185
Turner, Victor, 30–31, 70
Tylor, Edward, 28

vicarious space, 41, 43, 61, 63, 93, 94, 96, 104, 105, 130, 135, 147, 148, 149, 150, 152

Walzer, Michael, 95, 139, 176, 185, 188
Washington, Booker T., 222
Weber, Max, 64, 68, 151, 178, 181
Williams, Raymond, 39, 56, 63–64
Williams, Rhys H., 87, 251, 252, 258
Williams, Roger, 71
Wittgenstein, L., 31, 42, 51–52

Yeats, W.B., 144

About the Author

Dipankar Gupta is Professor at the Centre for the Study of Social Systems, School of Social Sciences, Jawaharlal Nehru University, New Delhi. He has earlier taught at the Department of Sociology, Delhi School of Economics, University of Delhi. Professor Gupta has also been Visiting Professor at the Department of Anthropology, University of Toronto, Canada. He is the co-editor of the journal *Contributions to Indian Sociology*. Among his recent publications are *The Context of Ethnicity: Sikh Identity in a Comparative Perspective; Rivalry and Brotherhood: Politics in the Life of Farmers of North India; Interrogating Caste: Understanding Hierarchy and Difference in Indian Society;* and *Mistaken Modernity: India Between Worlds.*